Semiotics of Religion

BLOOMSBURY ADVANCES IN SEMIOTICS

Semiotics has complemented linguistics by expanding its scope beyond the phoneme and the sentence to include texts and discourse, and their rhetorical, performative, and ideological functions. It has brought into focus the multimodality of human communication. *Bloomsbury Advances in Semiotics* publishes original works in the field demonstrating robust scholarship, intellectual creativity, and clarity of exposition. These works apply semiotic approaches to linguistics and nonverbal productions, social institutions and discourses, embodied cognition and communication, and the new virtual realities that have been ushered in by the Internet. It also is inclusive of publications in relevant domains such as socio-semiotics, evolutionary semiotics, game theory, cultural and literary studies, human–computer interactions, and the challenging new dimensions of human networking afforded by social websites.

Series Editor: Paul Bouissac is Professor Emeritus at the University of Toronto (Victoria College), Canada. He is a world renowned figure in semiotics and a pioneer of circus studies. He runs the SemiotiX Bulletin [www.semioticon.com/semiotix] which has a global readership.

Titles in the Series:

Buddhist Theory of Semiotics, Fabio Rambelli
Introduction to Peircean Visual Semiotics, Tony Jappy
Semiotics of Drink and Drinking, Paul Manning
The Structure of Visual Narrative, Neil Cohn

BLOOMSBURY ADVANCES IN SEMIOTICS

Semiotics of Religion

Signs of the Sacred in History

ROBERT A. YELLE

BLOOMSBURY

LONDON • NEW DELHI • NEW YORK • SYDNEY

Bloomsbury Academic
An imprint of Bloomsbury Publishing Plc

50 Bedford Square	175 Fifth Avenue
London	New York
WC1B 3DP	NY 10010
UK	USA

www.bloomsbury.com

First published 2013

British Library Cataloguing-in-Publication Data
A catalogue record for this book is available from the British Library.

ISBN: HB: 978-1-4411-4282-5
PB: 978-1-4411-0419-9

Library of Congress Cataloging-in-Publication Data
Yelle, Robert A.
Semiotics of religion : signs of the sacred in history / Robert A. Yelle.
p. cm.—(Advances in semiotics)
Includes bibliographical references and index.
ISBN 978-1-4411-4282-5—ISBN 978-1-4411-0419-9 (pbk.)—ISBN 978-1-4411-6765-1
(pdf)—ISBN 978-1-4411-7237-2 (epub)
1. Semiotics—History. 2. Religion—History. 3. Semiotics—Religious aspects. 4.
Structuralism (Literary analysis) 5. Representation (Philosophy) I. Title.
P99.Y45 2012
210.1'4—dc23
2012011980

Typeset by Newgen Imaging Systems Pvt Ltd, Chennai, India
Printed and bound in India

For my daughter, Maya Alexandria Yelle,
whose name means magic!

CONTENTS

ACKNOWLEDGMENTS

This book represents a summation of my work on the semiotics of religion over the past 15 years. I recall expressing an interest in the study of symbols in my application to the History of Religions program at the University of Chicago Divinity School, where I matriculated in 1994; but my attraction to the symbols of different religious traditions long predated that, and was a central occupation of mine while a student at Harvard College in the late-1980s. Graduate study at Chicago, however, was clearly the point at which I fully embraced the "linguistic turn." Studying Sanskrit made me keenly aware of cultural differences in theories and practices of language, and facilitated an emergence from semiotic naïveté. The faculty of the History of Religions program, particularly Wendy Doniger, continued to emphasize the importance of structuralist ideas. I have heard her tell, more than once, the story of how one ought to relate to Claude Lévi-Strauss: "It's like the man who asked directions from a stranger on the bus. The stranger replied: 'It's easy to get there; just follow me and get off one stop before I do.'" Wendy of course meant to say that one ought not to push the method beyond the point at which common sense bids us take our leave.

I never got off the bus, but found myself going beyond (and before) Lévi-Strauss, into Ferdinand de Saussure, Roman Jakobson, and less well-known structuralists and semioticians. Much of this study was self-guided. Another turning-point came when I was encouraged by some graduate school friends from Sanskrit class—Spencer Leonard, Aditya Sood, and Ananya Vajpeyi—to enroll in Michael Silverstein's class on "Language in Culture" in the Anthropology Department. Michael's scientific approach to the study of the form and function of language was inspirational. His approach, which developed his teacher Roman Jakobson's poetics into a theory of the pragmatic function of language, had important implications for the study of religious ritual that few scholars of religion, even in neighboring departments at the University of Chicago, had fully recognized. Michael served as one of the readers on my dissertation, which examined the poetic and rhetorical dimensions of the *mantras* or verbal formulas of Hindu *Tantra*. Some of the ideas I first learned from him—such as the concept of the "indexical icon," and of the importance of examining metricalization or repetitive structures in ritual texts—I credit with providing the solution to the puzzle of the structure and function of mantras.

Another fortunate step in my development as a semiotician came when I arrived at the University of Toronto, where I was Mellon Postdoctoral Fellow from 2003–05. Soon after arriving, I introduced myself to Paul Bouissac, whom I knew by reputation as one of the key figures in the international study of semiotics and a founder of the Toronto Semiotic Circle. Although that group was by then inactive, Paul was busy with numerous efforts to promote the public awareness and intellectual revitalization of semiotics. I contributed to some of these endeavors, including as a speaker at a symposium on gestures that was subsequently published in the journal *Gesture*.[1] Paul enthusiastically supported younger scholars such as myself. So when I returned to Toronto in August 2010 for the International Association for the History of Religions Congress, for which I organized a panel on the semiotics of religion, I naturally asked him to be the respondent. It was over dinner later that week that Paul first proposed that I contribute the volume on the semiotics of religion for a new series he was editing. I will take this opportunity to thank him publicly for his invitation, which, as you can see, was too intriguing to refuse.

When I arrived at Toronto in fall 2003, my dissertation on mantras had just been published as a book,[2] and I was beginning to broaden my study of semiotics to pose historical questions—such as what had happened to the mantras I studied in my dissertation—and to examine cultural differences, especially those between traditional Hindus and British Protestants, as revealed in the colonial encounter. The end result of this research was another book which is appearing in print around the same time as this one. *The Language of Disenchantment: Protestant Literalism and Colonial Discourse in British India* (New York: Oxford University Press, 2013) explores how Protestant ideas concerning language influenced British colonial attitudes toward Hinduism and proposals for the reform of that tradition. Similar to this book, *The Language of Disenchantment* attempts to combine semiotics with careful attention to the history of linguistic theories and practices, as an approach to describing both traditional religions and secular modernity.

Another influence reflected in both books, but particularly in this one, was my studies of the semiotics of law as this field intersected with religion. I had trained as a lawyer before becoming a historian of religions, and found myself drawing on my legal training to analyze rituals. Structuralist poetics helped me to appreciate the parallels in form and function between legal and religious rituals; while a study of the history of Protestant literalism, especially in Jeremy Bentham, helped me to understand the sources and motivations of the genre distinctions that segregate the language of modern law from that of poetry and ritual.[3] More recently, I have come to appreciate the influence of Christian typological interpretations of the Bible on secularization, including particularly the separation of law from religion.[4] These researches were encouraged also, in their initial phases, by the International Roundtables for the Semiotics of Law, which I attended as a spectator while presenting at the International Association for Semiotic Studies Congress in Lyon, France, in 2004, and as a presenter the following year at McGill University, Montréal. I remember fondly conversations with Sophie Cacciaguidi-Fahy, Richard Sherwin, Anne Wagner, and other participants at the Roundtables. I collaborated with Richard later at some semiotically themed panels at the meetings of the Association for the Study of Law, Culture and the Humanities in Austin, Texas in 2005 and the Law and Society Association in Berlin in 2007.

Over the course of the years, in addition to those interlocutors noted above, my studies of semiotics have benefited from conversations with many people, including especially Peter Jackson, Jens Kreinath, Christopher Lehrich, Frank Reynolds, and Winnifred Fallers Sullivan.

Parts of this book resulted from research conducted both while at Toronto and during a year at the Illinois Program for Research in the Humanities at the University of Illinois at Urbana-Champaign in 2005–06. My academic home since 2006 has been the Department of History at the University of Memphis. I would like to thank these institutions for their generous support. The academic life is a privilege, as well as an occupation, and I am grateful for the opportunity it has afforded me to pursue my research. Portions of the material herein were presented at these universities and also, in addition to the venues already mentioned, at the American Academy of Religion Annual Meetings, the Legal History Group at the University of Toronto Faculty of Law, Osgoode Hall Law School, and the Department of Anthropology at the University of Chicago.

Much of *The Semiotics of Religion*, including most of Chapters One and Five and all of Chapter Six, is new. Chapter One reproduces a few pages from "Law's Trouble with Images: Fetishism and Seduction from Athens and Jerusalem to Madison Avenue," in Anne Wagner and William Pencak, eds, *Images in Law* (Aldershot, UK: Ashgate, 2006), 267–79, reprinted by permission of Ashgate Publishing. Chapter Two incorporates portions of several previously published essays, including "Rhetorics of Law and Ritual: A Semiotic Comparison of the Law of Talion and Sympathetic Magic," *Journal of the American Academy of Religion* 69 (2001): 627–47, reprinted by permission of Oxford University Press; "Poetic Justice: Rhetoric in Hindu Ordeals and Legal Formulas," *Religion* 32 (2002): 259–72, reprinted by permission of Taylor & Francis Ltd. (http://tandf.co.uk/journals); "Hindu Law as Performance: Ritual and Poetic Elements in *Dharmaśāstra*," in Timothy Lubin, Donald R. Davis, Jr, and Jayanth K. Krishnan, eds, *Hinduism and Law: An Introduction* (Cambridge: Cambridge University Press, 2010), 183–92, for which I thank the press; and "Semiotics," in Michael Stausberg and Steven Engler, eds, *Handbook of Research Methods in Religious Studies* (London and New York: Routledge, 2011), 355–65, reprinted by permission of Taylor & Francis Books (UK). Chapter Three incorporates portions of "The Rhetoric of Gesture in Cross-Cultural Perspective," in Paul Bouissac, ed., "Gesture, Ritual and Memory," special issue of *Gesture* 6, no. 2 (2006): 223–40, reprinted with kind permission by John Benjamins Publishing Company, Amsterdam/Philadelphia (www. benjamins.com); and "Punishing Puns: Etymology as Linguistic Ideology in Hindu and British Traditions," in Steven E. Lindquist, ed., *Religion and Identity in South Asia and Beyond: Essays in Honor of Patrick Olivelle* (New York, London, Delhi: Anthem Press, 2010), 129–46, reprinted by permission of Anthem Press. Chapter Four incorporates, in revised form, portions of "Bentham's Fictions: Canon and Idolatry in the Genealogy of Law," *Yale Journal of Law & the Humanities* 17 (2005): 151–79, reprinted by permission of the journal. Chapter Five incorporates portions of "To Perform or Not to Perform?: A Theory of Ritual Performance versus Cognitive Theories of Religious Transmission," *Method & Theory in the Study of Religion* 18 (2006): 372–91, reprinted by permission of Koninklijke Brill NV.

CHAPTER ONE

Semiotics beyond structuralism

Why a semiotics of religion?

Why a semiotics of religion? Why now? What can we learn from semiotics about religion, and vice versa? Any book such as this must provide persuasive answers to these questions, in response to the not unjustified skepticism lingering from prior attempts. At this time when reconstruction is badly needed in the study of religion, I aim to show that semiotics has much to offer to our understanding of both the structural and historical dimensions of religion, beyond and, in some cases, in opposition to the lessons learned from structuralism and poststructuralism a generation or two ago. Equally important is the contribution that a focus on religious phenomena can bring to reinvigorating the field of semiotics.

Semiotics is the discipline devoted to the systematic study of signs, symbols, and communication; it overlaps in its method and subject most directly with linguistics and rhetoric. A semiotic approach can contribute to the elucidation of many religious phenomena, including: the belief in a magical language; the types of signs used in magic; the prevalence of poetic devices in spells, chants, and other forms of ritual language; the law of talion ("an eye for an eye") and other symbolic or ritualized punishments based on analogy; trials by ordeal, which often invoke the intervention of supernatural forces; the taxonomies or systems of classification deployed in the cosmologies of many religious traditions; ritual purity laws, including dietary prohibitions; not to mention myth. It is obvious that many of the phenomena traditionally grouped together under the category of religion have semiotic dimensions, even leaving aside the fact that they are forms of human expression, incorporating words, images, and symbolic actions. If communication requires, at minimum, an addresser and an addressee—one who sends the message and one who receives it—then many prototypical religious actions would appear to conform to, or rather to attempt to construct, such a relation. Both prayer and sacrifice are largely efforts to communicate with the gods, either through words and gestures or through the destruction and translation of some object to the heavenly realm.[1] In the repeated refrain of Leviticus (King James Version), the burnt offering becomes "a sweet savour unto the Lord" as the smoke is conveyed upward. Like magic, sacrifice may depend on a certain dissimulation: although the god may be the one to whom the sacrifice is nominally addressed, the fact that the benefit of the sacrifice is distributed to the priests or congregants shows that the circuit of communication is implicitly located elsewhere. The same could be said of the rhetorical devices in many prayers, which, even if they never reach the ears of the gods to whom they are addressed, reinforce their own efficacy in the ears of the speaker and other listeners.

The very distinction between ordinary and ritual behaviors has sometimes been founded on the distinction between technical and expressive actions.[2] Although every cultural performance is to some degree symbolic—meaning not reducible to the purely utilitarian—in ritual behaviors the symbolism arguably predominates, to the extent that such behaviors may appear to serve no pragmatic objective. Our inability to ascribe a practical purpose to some behavior or artifact may lead to the inference that it is "ritualistic," an epithet frequently invoked by archeologists in lieu of a better explanation. In this regard, religious objects or behaviors appear closer to the artistic or the aesthetic, with which domain they are often closely linked. Indeed, the point of some rituals—as Viktor Shklovsky claimed of literature—is to convey a sense of "estrangement," of awe and wonder, to give pause, and to provoke reflection.[3] However, unlike purely aesthetic performances, magical rituals do have a practical objective. The problem then becomes one of accounting for how magic promotes, from an insider's perspective, the belief in its own efficacy. This is why, in Chapter Two, I present an argument for the rhetorical function of repetition and other poetic devices in such rituals.

These examples reinforce the conviction that many religious phenomena are best viewed as a form of communication or rhetoric. Although many of these phenomena have been analyzed previously as modes of semiosis or signifying processes, a number of newer theoretical approaches promise to alter substantially our understanding of these phenomena, to integrate them under a more comprehensive explanatory framework, and, above all, to introduce dimensions of nuance in keeping with our recognition of cultural and historical differences in modes of semiosis. Indeed, perhaps the most promising new direction in the semiotics of religion bears on the question of the nature of the secular that has been recognized increasingly as crucial for religious studies and related disciplines.[4] Many religious phenomena, including myth, magic, and ritual, have arguably declined in a disenchanted modernity. Some of the greatest debates in the history of religions concerned precisely the communicative power of modes of ritual such as prayer and sacrifice. Broadly speaking, as detailed in later chapters of this book, secular modernity has rejected or severely qualified this communicative power by, among other things, devaluing the symbol, denying the efficacy of symbolic magic, and limiting poetic repetition in certain genres of discourse. Yet the prevailing structuralist approaches to such phenomena, inasmuch as they invoke ostensibly universal principles, have proved unable to account for or even, in some cases, to acknowledge such historical differences. Counterbalancing this neglect is a recent emphasis on the need to attend to the specificities of the "linguistic" or "semiotic ideologies" of different cultures—including our own—and the ways in which these ideologies mediate semiotic practices.[5] It is not possible to appreciate fully the communicative and rhetorical dimensions of the religious data of different cultures by applying a one-size-fits-all theory: it is necessary also to consider the philosophies and cosmologies of the sign that shape religious practices and narratives in their indigenous contexts of performance.

A quarter century ago, two distinguished scholars described the challenge confronting a prospective semiotics of religion:

> The ideal text on semiotics and religious studies would use a general and crossculturally valid theory of semiosis to compare systematically distinct religious traditions in terms of their respective perception of the nature of religious semiosis. But there is, as of this writing, no theory that would permit a group of scholars to compare widely diverse traditions against one another.[6]

This description of the goals of a semiotics of religion expresses a problematic that is endemic to any science of culture. On the one hand, there needs to be a common set of principles, in terms of which we may compare and contrast different traditions so as to illuminate what is universally human and what is culturally specific. On the other hand, there must be recognition also of the way in which the "perception" of semiosis or, as it is now more commonly termed, the "semiotic ideology" of a particular culture informs, mediates, and structures its practices of communication. It is impossible to account for semiotic systems without incorporating also the dimensions of consciousness and of *poiesis* or meaning-making. Given this fact, it is still the case that there is no single accepted semiotic theory that can "square the circle" and mediate between the particular and the general. In lieu of such a theory, and as a step toward establishing a more adequate typology of semiotic systems, the present work focuses on some basic distinctions between the modes of semiosis that characterize many traditional religions and those that characterize secular modernity.

A number of features of the semiotic ideology of modernity, at least in certain European cultures and other cultures affected by them, have been influenced by earlier Christian theologies, particularly as these were transformed during and after the Protestant Reformation. The Puritan critique of "vain repetitions" in prayer, efforts to explain pagan idolatry and polytheism as an error of language, and a deepened critique of the symbolic dimensions of the Jewish ceremonial laws were all associated with the movement that we standardly call Protestant literalism, which represented much more than an effort to read the Bible in a certain way. Protestants depicted the Crucifixion as a semiotic event that ushered in a mode of "plain speech"[7] that replaced the figurative ceremonies of the Mosaic law and silenced the pagan oracles and their obscure pronouncements. Such mythemes contributed to the modern idea of disenchantment, meaning the banishment of miracles, mystery, and magic from the world.[8] Disenchantment had linguistic dimensions. Poetic form was displaced in some cases, particularly but not only in prayer or liturgy, by more simplified, less ornamented forms, signaling a shift of emphasis from form to content; while the performative or magical function of discourse was subordinated in keeping with a privileging of semantics over pragmatics. These aspects of the Reformation influenced not merely those discourses we regard as religious, but also the ostensibly rational discourses of science and law, which were established in opposition to poetry, rhetoric, and myth.

Recent scholarship in religious studies and allied disciplines, much of it deeply influenced by poststructuralism, has called into question the validity of the categories of religion and the secular.[9] While appreciating the contribution that such arguments have made to deepening the interrogation of both of these categories, and remaining skeptical in particular of our ability to distinguish the secular from earlier theological modes of thought, I do not agree fully with such critiques. A semiotic approach can contribute to defining both many of the phenomena traditionally gathered under the rubric of religion, and the category of the secular itself, understood as a particular semiotic ideology.

For example, as detailed in Chapter Two below, many spells represent an extreme form of the poetic function involving such devices as extensive repetition, rhyme, alliteration, and palindromes.[10] Such performances announce themselves as acts of communication. To this extent, they depend on what we might call "semiotic recognition." The very same features also enable the second-order definition of such semiotic events as rituals. By the same token, the relative exclusion of poetic and figurative language from certain genres of discourse, under the influence of Protestant literalism, also serves to characterize the secular as a particular semiotic ideology and mode of praxis. Unfortunately, the argument that both "religion" and the "secular" are categories without content has too often been used as an excuse to avoid the difficult work of accounting for such regularities in the structure and history of religions.

Among the semiotic dimensions of the historical process known as secularization or disenchantment are the following:

● The decline or sequestration in particular genres of densely symbolic discourses such as myth, ritual, and magic.

- The decline of a symbolic, allegorical, or typological view of the world, and the gradual ascendancy of realism, literalism, or a prosaic view of the world.

- The shift away from a conviction in the natural or nonarbitrary status of signs, or from a "magical" theory of language, and the ascendancy of the idea that the sign is arbitrary and bears no essential connection to that which it represents.

- The rise of scientific projects for the purification of language from errors, and the substitution of a perfect, rational, or universal language, as associated in particular with the Baconian movement in seventeenth-century England and its descendants.

- The decline of many modes of oral performance and the rise of a culture of the printed book, especially after the development and widespread application of movable type in European culture beginning in the fifteenth century, and subsequently around the globe.

Although it would clearly be impossible to address all of the above developments in the present essay, an effort is made to address a number of them in different chapters, and to grasp them as part of an overall transformation in semiotic ideology. The burden of this book is to demonstrate that any adequate account of the structural and historical dimensions of both religion and the secular must confront the challenge of defining both of these categories in semiotic terms. The centrality of semiosis to the self-definition of religion and the secular is evidence of the preeminently cultural status of both of these categories. However, this fact has been obscured as a result of the secular bias against symbolism and poetic performance, which has hindered inquiry into the semiotics of religion.

There are additional reasons why such historical differences in semiosis have not been investigated sufficiently. First, the insistence on the arbitrary nature of the sign, which is basic to modern semiotics, marks a break with many earlier semiotic ideologies that affirmed the naturalness of certain signs, and that consequently have been categorized as naïve and as untrustworthy guides to a science of signs. The semiotic theories of earlier cultures have been ignored except as historical curiosities. Second, the typologies of signs developed within both structuralist semiology and Peircean semiotic themselves contain no reference to the historical dimensions of signification. Whether Roman Jakobson's dyad of "metaphor and metonymy" is in question,[11] or Charles Sanders Peirce's triad of "icon, index, and symbol,"[12] these categories of relation between signifier and signified are regarded not only as exhausting the logical range of possibilities, but as ever-present alternatives for communication. The representation of such typologies as the keys to an atemporal, one-size-fits-all science of semiotics obscures the fact that different modes of sign relation have been emphasized within different cultures, and that there have been, within this overall variety, some larger trends that allow us to characterize the semiotic ideology of modernity as distinct in some important respects from many of those that have obtained in earlier historical periods. Third, the otherwise valuable impulse of semiotics to establish itself on a scientific basis and thereby to secure recognition of its legitimacy as an independent academic discipline has led in many cases to a scientism or bias against historical and cultural approaches that has, instead of strengthening the discipline, limited its explanatory power and appeal.

The view of the semiotics of religion proposed in this book is quite different. It recognizes that any valid semiotics must attend to both the structural and historical dimensions of culture and, rather than perpetually reconfirming some predetermined theoretical model, it aims to develop a flexible theory capable of accounting for differences in semiosis. If this goal can be met, then in my view, semiotics offers the prospect of connecting the historical and anthropological sciences, while recognizing the prerogatives of each of these areas of enquiry.

A brief critical survey of some semiotic theories of religion

Over the past century and more, numerous schools of thought that embrace the label of "semiotics" or "semiology" have announced themselves, including structuralism, whether that of Ferdinand de Saussure (1857–1913), Roman Jakobson (1896–1982), Claude Lévi-Strauss (1908–2009), or others; poststructuralism, including that of Michel Foucault (1926–84) and Jacques Derrida (1930–2004); and the semiotics of Charles Sanders Peirce (1839–1914) and the American school of pragmatism that he helped to found. The late Thomas Sebeok (1920–2001) worked tirelessly to organize the various branches of semiotics under a single institutional rubric, and this work has been continued by others.

My own brand of semiotics draws on a number of different traditions: in particular, Jakobson's studies of the "poetic function" of language;[13] the synthesis between such approaches and Peircean semiotics developed by Jakobson's student, the linguistic anthropologist Michael Silverstein, who emphasizes the pragmatic function of poetic form;[14] and Webb Keane's recent studies of the semiotic ideology of secular modernity, as revealed in the colonial encounter between Dutch Protestants and native Indonesians.[15] Other influences on my approach are classical rhetoric and philosophy, and my studies of the semiotic ideologies of Hinduism and British Protestantism, in particular as these two traditions interacted in colonial India. Rather than endorsing any particular school of semiotics, I prefer an approach that draws on different schools and concepts as these prove useful. A description of each of the different semiotic schools is omitted as unnecessary and redundant; for such a description, the interested reader may turn to several valuable works already available.[16] My comments in this section do not present a comprehensive account of the different theories addressed, but are intended only to indicate some of the important differences between some well-known approaches and my own approach.

Although it may seem perverse to begin by pointing out the weaknesses of some earlier efforts toward a semiotics of religion, I believe it is necessary to clear the path before proceeding. It is always good practice to acknowledge flaws, vices, and defects so that these may be remedied effectively. Some atonement is necessary for the hubris of earlier semiotic approaches, and to respond to the not unjustified skepticism that many readers will have adopted regarding the potential of semiotics as a method.

Semiotics has promised more than it has delivered in the way of a science of culture. The truism that all culture is communicative or expressive behavior, mediated primarily though not exclusively by means of language, has been invoked in order to establish the claim of semiotics to a position of dominance among the human sciences, as a totalizing meta-discourse with universal application. Yet the more universal in pretension semiotics has become, the more detached it has become from facts on the ground. The point of much semiotic theorizing appears to be to reconfirm theoretical presuppositions, in a manner similar to medieval scholasticism, rather than to illuminate the specificities of data.[17] However, any theory is only as good as the account it provides of a body of data, and must be prepared to argue its superiority against other, competing theories.

It is ironic that so many semioticians, who might be expected to have gained from their study of communication a special expertise in the practice of that art, have presented their arguments before the public in an esoteric jargon that, when it is not guilty of the sin of hermeneutic narcissism, at the very least places unnecessary barriers to the uninitiated who might otherwise benefit from the insights a semiotic approach has to offer. The use of complicated concepts and special terminology can be justified by offsetting their costs against gains in precision and comprehensiveness. In the case of many semiotic theories, however, such gains are small or not to be observed.

It may therefore come as little surprise that the discipline of semiotics, with important exceptions (some of which have been noted already), appears to be in a state of stagnation or even outright decline. One measure of this is the paucity of new, truly seminal theories that have been advanced in recent decades. Much theorizing is concerned with defending a semiotic canon, and with policing the borders of the discipline, rather than with extending the application of semiotics to novel terrain. Semiotics is a discipline that has not yet and, one fears, may never attain the promise of its youth; it is either stillborn or past its prime.

A relative measure of this decline is the condition of semiotics within religious studies. While symbolism has been a concern in the history of religions since nineteenth-century Romanticism—and in theological traditions long before then—approaches to religion that draw on contemporary semiotic theory are a much more recent phenomenon. There was a surge of interest in semiotic methodologies within religious studies from the 1960s to the 1980s, coinciding with an efflorescence in other disciplines, particularly anthropology, where Claude Lévi-Strauss, Edmund Leach, Victor Turner, and Mary Douglas, among others, all applied structuralism to religious materials in innovative ways.[18] Semiotic analysis is still being pursued in other disciplines, for example by linguistic anthropologists.[19] However, following the poststructuralist critique of structuralism and a general shift of emphasis from the analysis of symbols to that of social processes, religious studies has largely moved away from explicit engagement with semiotic methodologies and questions. There are exceptions: for example, Wendy Doniger and Seth Kunin continue to use Lévi-Straussian analyses of myth,[20] and the emerging field of cognitive science of religion, as noted below, often addresses religious phenomena with explicitly semiotic dimensions. In addition to these applications of semiotics to the structural dimensions of religious phenomena, the past several decades have witnessed important work on the historical dimensions of the semiotics of religion, including accounts of particular semiotic traditions;[21] of earlier projects for a perfect or universal language, which often had religious dimensions;[22] of the religious aspects of the semiotic shift in early modernity and the Reformation;[23] and of the ways in which this shift informed the colonial encounter between European and non-European cultures.[24]

Certain scholars in the cognitive science of religion have addressed issues of semiotic importance, such as ritualization—meaning the use of expressive techniques to mark the boundaries of ritual events—and modes of religious transmission.[25] A number of fundamental semiotic categories, including the Peircean icon and index—which, as described in Chapter Two, are based on the association of ideas through similarity and contiguity, respectively—do appear cognitive in nature, and in principle it would be a good idea to study them using the methods of cognitive science, to learn why human beings are predisposed to recognize and construct such associations. However, this needs to be done in full awareness of the embeddedness of religious praxis within emic theories or the semiotic ideologies indigenous to different cultures. The path to an accommodation between scientific and cultural approaches lies through the deeper study of anthropological and historical systems.

Despite these new developments and lingering interest in older methodologies, it nevertheless appears that semiotics has made little progress in persuading the field of religious studies as a whole of the importance of its potential contribution. This is likely for various reasons. Religious studies as a discipline was never as productive in developing new theories and applications of semiotics as were several other disciplines, including not only anthropology but also literary studies. Much of the semiotic work done in religious studies has been derivative. Semiotics is viewed by many as an esoteric subdiscipline, now long past its prime, that has been discredited by poststructuralist and more broadly postmodern critiques.

When Alfred M. Johnson, Jr compiled *A Bibliography of Semiological and Structural Studies of Religion* in the library of the Pittsburgh Theological Seminary in 1979, his list extended to around 1,900 items, although it did not include many works in related disciplines.[26] There is nothing comparable to this output today. Scholars continue to produce works on the semiotic and especially the structuralist analysis of religion, some of which are of very high quality. However, the flowering of semiotic approaches to religion that occurred a few decades ago seems unlikely to return without some new impulse.

To a certain extent, this situation reflects the absorption of structuralism within religious studies.[27] Structuralist analyses of myth and ritual have been so widely disseminated within both anthropology and the study of religions that they are now commonplace. Such a development has been followed in turn by an equally broad dispersal and popularity of poststructuralist approaches, including Derridean deconstruction and Foucauldian discourse analysis.[28] It could therefore reasonably be argued from these developments that the semiotics of religion has been a success, rather than a failure.

In my view, such an argument would be mistaken. Although the lessons of structuralism and poststructuralism have indeed been learned, many of these lessons were either wrong in themselves or were misapplied, and the current state of the study of religion, no less than that of semiotics itself, reflects some of these inherent defects. Most debilitating, perhaps, has been the commonly held idea that all signs depend upon opposition or the construction of difference.[29] This idea has hampered investigation into the specificities of forms deployed in ritual—which often depend upon iconicity or resemblance, rather than opposition[30]—and, at the same time, has encouraged the false view that all semiotic systems depend equally upon the same principles. The propensity to elaborate totalizing methodologies that focus on the unveiling of universal structures that are sometimes trivial or so vague as to be unfalsifiable, while also effacing cultural and historical differences, has led to certain contradictions or aporias within semiotic theory itself. If all semiotic systems are the same, then how do we account for the position of superiority of the semiotic analyst, who stands outside of, and hierarchically above, discourse?

It is now presumed, following Saussure and Lévi-Strauss, that the recognition of the arbitrariness of the sign is a scientific achievement that enabled the understanding of the ways in which human communication works around this basic condition of the lack of relation or fit between sign and referent by, primarily, imposing binary distinctions on the network of signs and, through this, on the world. The fact that many magical traditions assert the opposite of this doctrine, by maintaining a natural or divine fitness of certain signs, is on the other hand seen as a confirmation of the difference between these naïve and more modern, scientific approaches. Yet the fact of the arbitrariness of the sign is assumed to be universal and, as such, its own historicity and genealogy rarely examined.

Lévi-Strauss's great achievement was to demonstrate that myth constitutes a specialized language in which binary structures of opposition are deployed in different registers and repeated in such a way that they convey a message that is transmitted unconsciously or subliminally. Given the ostensibly objective nature of these structures—which is what allows them, like language, to communicate across the divide separating individuals within a particular culture in the first instance—they can, in principle, also be decoded and interpreted by an analyst outside of those cultures. Lévi-Strauss's premise is that language is the model for all other semiotic systems; consequently, myth, which is already a form of language, should reflect the same techniques that language uses: the imposition of distinctions in order to produce meaning out of arbitrariness. The primary distinction is that between nature and culture, which underlies the arbitrariness of verbal and other signs as man-made products. Not only the technique but the message of myth is consistent: it articulates the irresolvable contradiction between nature and culture, which is variously policed, repressed, and acknowledged (at least implicitly) in the language of myth. The message of myth is located not in its meaning, but in its form; or rather, the distinction between form and content is obliterated from a semiotic perspective. This enabled an entirely new methodological approach to the interpretation of myth.

However, as fruitful as this approach was, it led to new problems. Not only, as has often been pointed out, is there the empirical challenge of distinguishing between structures that are truly there in the mythic narrative and structures that are merely imposed by the interpreter. The gap implied by the existence of an interpretive standpoint "outside" of myth also leads to intractable philosophical and historical difficulties. If both the technique and the message of myth are absolutely general, then how do we define the boundaries of myth to begin with, as distinguished from other modes of discourse or semiosis? If myths exemplify universal, and irresolvable, problems of the human condition, then what is the source of privilege of the scholar of myth, whose own discourse is, by implication, necessary to reconstruct the message of a myth that is not in itself sufficiently clear? If Lévi-Strauss has indeed discovered the message of myth, then is there some insufficiency in language that requires such an act of excavation, or is this defect of expressive power limited to the discourse of myth? Or do we refrain from making any such distinctions, and identify the same message in all discourses, including those of myth-maker and mythologist, the latter of which is then merely a translation into a different idiom of a message that was always already known from the beginning? Why, then, ought we bother to translate at all? Lévi-Strauss's distinction between "cold" and "hot" societies—that is, those with and without myth—simply restates the problem of historical difference in metaphorical terms, using a binary distinction characteristic of mythic thought.[31] If language is universal, then why isn't this true of myth, which ostensibly depends on the same procedures as language and addresses a similar problem, namely the arbitrariness of cultural institutions?

On the other hand, the dissolution of the category of myth that has been performed by a number of scholars of religion influenced by poststructuralism is equally problematic. Bruce Lincoln's masterful reappraisal of the meaning of the categories of *mythos* and *logos* in ancient Greece ends by concluding that these terms have no inherent meaning, but serve only to mark a difference between competing social groups: "myth" became a label of opprobrium for the discourse of one's opponents.[32] Implicitly, Lincoln is reprising Friedrich Nietzsche's argument, in *On the Genealogy of Morals*, that such distinctions of value are both socially constructed and linguistically encoded.[33] Combining Nietzsche's earlier abolition of the distinction between "truth" and "metaphor"[34] with Foucault's argument for the inseparability of power and knowledge,[35] Lincoln offers a radical deconstruction of a genre distinction—namely, that between myth and logic—that arguably has undergirded, not only studies of myth, but Western rationalism itself.

Lincoln's impulse to criticize the patterns of discourse that sustain, by masking, such inequalities of power is laudable. Yet what can it mean to speak truth to power if there is no such thing as truth, even in a relative sense? And there had better be such a thing as truth, or what weapon do the weak have against the powerful, except dissimulation, which is precisely what Nietzsche and, now, Lincoln refuse? This discloses an inconsistency in Lincoln's position. Even in the act of abolishing the hierarchical valuation of genres, he replicates such a hierarchy, by exempting himself from the general acquiescence to rhetoric. Moreover, elsewhere in his work on religion, he has identified certain features commonly found in religious discourse as especially coercive—such as "the tyranny of taxonomies," for example[36]—thus reintroducing the very distinction between truer and falser discourses that, in his critique of the *mythos–logos* distinction, he seeks to abolish.[37]

A similar difficulty is found in the work of another theorist of religion, Jonathan Z. Smith, who has perhaps done more than any other scholar to call into question the validity and durability of the category of "religion" and its subcategories, which are allegedly social artifacts discursively constructed for specific purposes. When it comes to the category of magic, for example, Smith dismisses James G. Frazer's argument that this category represents a discrete genre characterized by the mistaken application of the laws of association—namely, similarity and contiguity (see Chapter Two)—and embraces Franz Steiner's demonstration that Frazer's own discourse about magic is organized according to precisely such rhetorical devices.[38] While this implies the falsity of Frazer's argument and, thus, the untenability of his category of "magic," it does not finally resolve the issue, as Smith himself continues the characterization of such rhetorical devices as fraudulent reasoning, and merely places Frazer on the side of those infected by magical thought. The implicit privilege of the scholar to remain above and beyond such rhetorical errors, while surveying the whole, is maintained; and with this, too, the apparent impossibility of avoiding such distinctions as are concretized in such categories as magic and religion.

Unacknowledged in such self-contradictory positions is our apparent inability to escape the gravity of history, in particular, our displacement from and transcendence of such genres as myth, magic, and religion. Structuralism ignores history, by rendering everything into an example of a universal pattern. Poststructuralism accomplishes the same by reducing differences to social oppositions, and with this, abolishing any meaningful sense of "before" and "after," even when the shells of an historical narrative are provided. The structuralist privileging of the genre of myth and the poststructuralist deconstruction of the same are both neglectful of history. And even when a rigorous effort is made to deny the existence of a real distinction between religious and secular discourse, this effort is undermined by the scholar's implicit reinscription of such a distinction, which invokes once again the specter of evolutionism and the cultural chauvinism thought to be implied therein.

Semiotic recognition

As we see from the above examples, the development of an historical view of the semiotics of religion is of vital importance for the study of religion itself, which has reached an impasse when it comes to defining both its basic categories and our mode of relation to them. Although it has often been recognized that the definition of religion and its subcategories is inextricably bound up with the history of the West, this fact has seldom been related explicitly to another fact, namely, that the same is true of the category of rhetoric. What this suggests about the possible intersection of these two categories—religion and rhetoric—has not been investigated with the degree of attention it deserves. Yet part of the promise of a semiotics of religion lies precisely on this path. As I shall argue, an emphasis on the rhetorical dimensions of religious discourse offers a partial solution to the problem of earlier semiotic theories. Certain semio-techniques or modes of rhetoric, while widely dispersed in human communication, are especially prevalent in religion and its subcategories: ritual is in many cases an extreme form of what Jakobson called the "poetic function" in which such devices as rhyme, by emphasizing the density of their own semiotic structure, promote a certain self-reflexivity or "set toward the message as such,"[39] a phenomenon I am calling "semiotic recognition." This both highlights religious discourse as an act of communication, and contributes to the transmission of its message. Religion is not *sui generis*, but inhabits a cline or continuum with other discourses, as a more densely figurative or poetic discourse. Along the same continuum, modernity has defined itself through a distanciation from or transcendence of such rhetorical modes, as an "antirrhetic"[40] or polemic against myth, ritual, and the symbol. Secular modernity represents itself as an emergence from semiotic naïveté. Semiosis is therefore vital to the emergence of both of these categories—religion and modernity. Both of these categories depend on semiotic recognition, or the rise of an awareness of the processes that undergird language or communication as such.

The importance of semiotic recognition to an understanding of religion as co-emergent with the history of the West, and in particular of secular modernity, is indicated by the persistence with which the key cultural traditions that make up our genealogy have defined themselves in opposition to semiotic forms. Plato's critique of rhetoric and myth, the ancient Israelite attack on idolatry or image-worship, and Protestant iconoclasm and anti-ritualism exemplify this process of self-definition, as do other, more recent or local complaints against the rhetoric of magical thought, the "tyranny of taxonomies," etc. Indeed, it seems that many of our theories of the sign have developed out of this process of confronting the fact of rhetoric, specifying its principles of operation, and prescribing the bounds of their legitimate application. From this perspective, the rise of a consciousness of rhetoric appears to link several of those traditions that have been identified as "Axial," a category that also invokes the notions of a rise of critical consciousness and the transcendence of or disembedding from a prior condition below the threshold of such awareness.[41]

I want to illustrate the phenomenon of semiotic recognition by revisiting the debate over rhetoric in ancient Greece, specifically the debate between Plato and Gorgias, each of whom has a claim to be one of the earliest semioticians. Gorgias of Leontini (*c.* 480–375 BCE) is frequently regarded as the first systematic rhetorician. He authored a well-known *Encomium of Helen* in which he defended Helen of Troy against the charge of abandoning her husband Menelaus and going to Troy with Paris. Gorgias argued that she was blameless because "by Fate's will and gods' wishes and Necessity's decrees she did what she did, or by force reduced, or by words seduced, or by love induced."[42] The translation preserves Gorgias's pervasive use of rhyming endings (*homoioteleuton*). His defense proceeded by the exhaustive enumeration of alternatives: Helen was either compelled by the gods, forced by human violence (i.e. abducted and raped), persuaded by words, or seduced by the power of erotic love. Gorgias addressed each of these alternatives, and concluded in every case that Helen was blameless. There being no other alternatives, one must admit her innocence.

At a literal level, the *Helen* is a simple courtroom argument, an example of the type of forensic oratory that was central to the practice of rhetoric in ancient Greece. Closer examination suggests, however, that Gorgias's real argument was in defense of rhetoric itself. One of the four alternatives addressed was that Helen was persuaded by speech. This afforded an occasion for describing the power of language, and especially of a certain kind of rhetoric:

> Speech is a powerful lord that with the smallest and most invisible body accomplishes most god-like works . . . I shall show how this is so . . . All poetry I regard and name as speech having metre . . . Thus by entering into the opinion of the soul the force of incantation is wont to beguile and persuade and alter it by witchcraft, and the two arts of witchcraft and magic are errors of the soul and deceivers of opinion . . . What is there to prevent the conclusion that Helen, too, when still young, was carried off by speech just as if constrained by force?

Gorgias's definition of poetry as "speech having metre" was self-referential. It described his own rhetoric, which employed poetic devices such as rhyme: for example, "I shall show how this is so"; "reduced . . . seduced . . . induced." This was the "force of incantation" mentioned in the *Helen.* We may infer that Gorgias's real goal was not to defend Helen, a fictional defendant, but to defend the power of rhetoric and its status as an art or technique that may be taught. One suspects that, among the four alternative defenses of Helen, the defense that she was persuaded by (poetic) speech was the one that really mattered. The others served to establish analogies for the persuasive power of speech: it was like the irresistible commands of Fate or the gods; it was like physical violence; it was like the attractive pull of erotic love. Gorgias added the further analogies that speech was like magic and an intoxicating drug. There were no corresponding defenses that Helen was drugged or bewitched—unless if by speech itself.

Reinforcement for this interpretation comes from a consideration of the audience and context for Gorgias's speech. This was a show piece, a prepared example of oratory given in order to convince students to sign up with Gorgias for a course of training in rhetoric—for a suitable tuition, of course. The *Helen* is the equivalent of a commercial advertisement, complete with jingles. The choice of Helen as defendant had the advantage that everyone was familiar with the facts of her case, the recital of which could therefore be dispensed with. Gorgias's "commercial" had to convince its listeners not only of Helen's innocence, but above all of the power of rhetoric, or more particularly of his own brand of rhetoric.

Surely it was this defense of rhetoric, not the defense of Helen, that raised a controversy. As Jacqueline de Romilly showed, Gorgias's identification of his rhetoric as a form of magic was subsequently taken up by others and used as a basis for condemning that rhetoric.[43] This may be described as a two-step process: first, the legitimacy of employing "speech having metre" within the genre of forensic rhetoric was denied; then, as is well known,

Plato argued for excluding poetry as a form of imitation (*mimesis*) from authorized discourse. Both Plato and Aristotle agreed that the primary forms of imitation in poetry were rhythm and metre.[44] However, in his dialogue named after Gorgias, Plato characterized rhetoric as poetry without music, rhythm, and metre: namely, divested of these mimetic properties.[45] Aristotle noted Gorgias's use of poetic devices in his rhetoric, but regarded the language of prose, including that of rhetoric, as distinct from that of poetry.[46] Famously, Plato sought to exclude poetry, as a form of imitation, from the ideal Republic. He embraced Gorgias's analogy between poetry and magic, but found in this analogy another reason to suspect the deceptive power of poetry.[47]

There was, indeed, some precedent for regarding "metre" as not a characteristic of rhetoric, properly speaking. Gorgias's use of repetitive sound as a technique of forensic rhetoric was relatively novel, at least to the degree to which and self-consciousness with which he used it. This made this usage more obvious, and a clearer target. Such devices were understood to belong to the domain of poetry and magical incantation. When they intruded into the realm of public discourse, especially in the assertive manner illustrated by Gorgias's *Helen*, they crossed the threshold of propriety, and needed to be outlawed. The result is well summarized by Foucault's broader judgment about the rise of philosophy: "efficacious discourse, ritual discourse, discourse loaded with powers and perils, gradually came to conform to a division between true and false discourse."[48] We might note especially that it was "ritual discourse" of a certain form and function—an imitative or repetitive form, and a magical function—that was labeled false and distinguished from the true discourse of philosophers, whose speech was supposed, at least ideally, to conform to reality rather than to cause its hearers (and, in the case of magic, reality itself) to conform to it. In his own trial, Socrates disavowed any such power to persuade; the inefficaciousness of his speech was converted into a sign of its truthfulness.[49] At least, this was his defense.

We have to be the judges in this case. It seems to me that Gorgias's defense of rhetoric, or at least of the persuasive power of "speech having metre," has never been refuted successfully. Instead, this power has been cordoned off, compartmentalized, and controlled, above all in such a way as to prevent it from spilling over into truly important matters. Given this repression, the reemergence of such forms, when it does occur, can occasion a minor scandal. Johnnie Cochran's famous line from the O. J. Simpson case, referring to the murderer's glove—"If it does not fit, you must acquit"—strikes us as either savvy rhetoric, shameless manipulation, or both. Like the formula "If you do the crime, you do the time," this line displaces the question of justice into the realm of poetry, and answers this question with a rhyme. Everyone already seems to get the point of such formulas. They reinforce, poetically, the substantive conclusion they seek, whether acquittal or conviction. Such courtroom equivalents of Madison Avenue jingles seem positively simple, even naïve. As these modern examples indicate, far from such poetic devices having died out in forensic rhetoric or courtroom oratory, they continue to be part of the lawyer's repertoire: albeit a part that is rarely exercised, and with discretion, due to its obvious appeal to passion over reason. Rhetoric excluded from more authoritative legal discourse reappears in courtroom arguments, as a permitted if inferior supplement.

The debate between Plato and Gorgias—so central to the formation of the Western tradition—illustrates several of the themes that have been raised thus far. First, it represents an alternative approach to the distinction between *mythos* and *logos* that Lincoln attempted to deconstruct.[50] Where he observed a lack of real distinction of genres, which are instead labels used to attack one's opponents, we see something rather different. Neither Gorgias nor Plato adopts the view that such distinctions of genre are meaningless. Both agree that there are certain formal features that define rhetoric, despite Plato's skepticism regarding the possibility of elevating rhetoric to the status of a systematic technique or *techne*. They also agree that such forms can be effective, although for Plato this is what renders them dangerous. And indeed, if such formulas were not effective, would the corporations that patronize the advertising firms of Madison Avenue expend billions of dollars annually?

In each case, it is semiotic recognition—the conscious theorizing of the rhetorical power of poetic and magical performance—that qualifies both Gorgias and Plato as semioticians, albeit of very different types. Gorgias was not wrong about the prevalence of such devices as rhyme in magic, as the perusal of even a limited sample of spells will demonstrate (see Chapter Two). The fact that such devices appear prominently in the ritual traditions of many cultures implies a general recognition of the role that such devices play in communication. Even modern traditions of spell-making, such as Wicca, deploy such forms in the absence of any received tradition or prescriptive rule. To this extent, I would agree with Lévi-Strauss that certain forms of discourse, such as myth or in this case ritual, are more highly structured, as a means of transmitting a message that may be either subliminal or overt. The articulation of an explicit theoretical account of such devices developed through a reflection on communication is much rarer than the prevalence of such devices would suggest. In the case of Gorgias, such a reflection took the form of the deliberate and systematic application of such devices in the very context of theorizing their efficacy. Arguably, it was this rise of semiotic awareness that contributed, in turn, to Plato's critique, which articulated its own theoretical account of such modes of discourse (i.e. the concept of *mimesis*), while simultaneously distancing itself from such modes, and circumscribing the bounds of their application.[51]

While highlighting the violence of the philosophical critique of *mythos*, Lincoln has largely ignored the question of the violence of rhetoric itself that, as we see, was at the heart of the debate between Gorgias and Plato. Far from rejecting the violence of rhetoric, Gorgias accentuates this quality, by comparing it to divine compulsion, physical assault, and seduction or rape. It is the threat that rhetoric poses to human reason, and not merely to the state, that led Plato to condemn it. As we shall see, a number of similar complaints against the threat that rhetoric poses to human autonomy underlay polemics against religious discourse in the early modern period.

My brief comparison between Gorgias's rhetoric and modern advertising indicates that such forms of rhetoric have scarcely died out, and therefore calls into question any historical account of our evolution beyond them. However, at the same time, the debate between Plato and Gorgias demonstrates the centrality of the critique of rhetoric to the historical self-definition of the West as the rise of a certain semiotic consciousness and, with this, a social legislation of genre distinctions, beginning with that between philosophy and poetry. As noted earlier, such a historical self-definition appears difficult if not impossible to transcend, as a critical distanciation from the rhetoric of religion remains, often unexamined, in the approaches of a number of scholars who would abolish such genre distinctions. And this contradiction is evident, not only from their critiques, but also from their implicit acceptance and inhabitance of such genre distinctions in their own scholarly practice: Lincoln would never make an argument in rhyme, nor would Jonathan Z. Smith descend to the rhetoric of association; and the distinction between native discourse and ethnography is maintained by even the most sympathetic ethnographer.[52]

Semiotics has oscillated between two views of semiotics as either praxis or critique, embracing, alternatively and sometimes simultaneously, either Gorgias's or Plato's view of rhetoric. The task of semiotics is to elucidate the techniques of communication that have been employed in different cultures, and attempt, so far as possible, to specify the general principles that underlie such techniques. What is the normative goal of this descriptive project? Is it to prescribe the methods by which one may perfect communication? It often appears that an implicit claim is being made that semiotics not only explains "how language works," but also may actually make language more effective. In this regard, some contemporary semiotic theories resemble the efforts of many traditional cultures to create magical languages. Another view is that the task of semiotics is to distinguish between legitimate and illegitimate uses of communication, and thus to purify (or at least to police) semiosis: an aim that appears to be shared not only by Platonism and Jewish iconoclasm, but also by the Baconians and a number of more recent thinkers. The objective of this essay is to enable a deeper understanding of the rhetoric of both religion and the secular, and to this extent, it continues the Enlightenment critique of traditional rhetoric, while extending this critique to the Enlightenment itself.

Bringing history to the semiotics of religion

As the debate between Plato and Gorgias suggests, it is imperative to scrutinize with greater care the ways in which modernity has defined itself in semiotic terms against forms of rhetoric or communication regarded as having been outmoded or transcended. This project is of vital importance to our understanding of religion because such polemics not only were directed against forms that we identify as myth, ritual, or magic, but also were motivated by ideas and movements that themselves have been identified as religious. Many criticisms of magical thinking, ritual repetition (e.g. "vain repetitions" in prayer), and traditional Christian typology were centrally associated with the Protestant Reformation, which had as much influence, historically speaking, on the semiotic ideology of modernity as modern science ever did.[53] As soon as semiotics as a discipline begins to think historically, it must confront the role that religious traditions have played in mediating semiotic praxis, articulating semiotic ideologies, and even shaping the genealogy of notions of signification that reappear, unquestioned, in contemporary semiotic theories.

Mircea Eliade offered an account, albeit a highly problematic one, of these developments. According to Eliade, traditional cultures inhabit a world pervaded by signs of the Sacred, which can manifest itself in anything (and is therefore arbitrary), but particularly in such natural objects as rocks, trees, mountains, etc. Such objects then become "hierophanies," a word that translates literally as "showings of the Sacred."[54] Eliade also argued that myths and rituals referred to "archetypes," meaning events or actions that occurred among the gods or ancestors "in the beginning."[55] It was by relating back to such prior models that human actions were invested with sacrality; myths and rituals coincided with a view of time as retrospective and cyclical, or infinitely repeated. It was the new notion of linear time articulated in Judeo-Christian tradition, which emphasized progressive revelation and placed a positive value on history, that disrupted the older, cyclical notion and displaced the archetype, ushering in a profane modernity.[56]

Eliade's views of symbols and archetypes have been criticized on several grounds, many of them accurate. His theory of the symbol as suffused with meaning is fundamentally Romantic, a form of nostalgia for a vanished past. His account of hierophanies describes the appearance of the Sacred as something spontaneous, as a rupture in history, in which the human is a passive spectator. He ignores the role that historical traditions and individual human agency play in mediating such events. We may add that Eliade offers no detailed account of semiosis or the principles by which religious signs are constituted as such: no fine-grained analysis of the poetic form of religious discourse, and no explanation of what icons, indexes, and other signs contribute to the pragmatic function of ritual. As such, his theory of the religious symbol is scarcely systematic, much less scientific.

Despite these flaws, the idea of a general disenchantment of symbols in modernity, which Eliade inherited from Romanticism, cannot be easily dismissed. As he suggests, Judeo-Christian tradition was partly responsible for the demise of a more densely symbolic interpretation of the world.

However, this occurred more recently, with transformations in Christian typological readings of the Bible. The traditional theory according to which events and figures in the Hebrew Bible or "Old Testament" were "types" that prefigured "antitypes" in the New Testament was inherently progressive and forward-looking: with the appearance of its antitype, the purpose of a type was fulfilled, just as the sacrifices of the Jewish law foreshadowed the redemptive sacrifice of Christ on the Cross, following which the law prescribing sacrifice was abrogated.[57] This basic scheme developed into a much more elaborate system of interpretation according to which scripture could be read at three or four different levels simultaneously; the literal sense was only one such level. A good example is Dante's *Letter to Can Grande*, where the poet applies to his own *Comedy* a scheme of interpretation normally reserved for scripture.[58] With the emphasis on the literal sense by Protestants during the Reformation, the other senses were accordingly devalued. To some extent this represented merely a deepening of the traditional Christian critique of the "shadows" of the Old Testament, and an emphasis on their replacement by "plain speech."[59]

Like Protestant interpretations of Jewish ritual as symbolic and, therefore, of lesser value (see Chapter Six), the critique of vain repetitions in prayer evinced a greater critical focus on the semiotic dimensions of ritual discourse, and was associated with broader trends in the acceleration of semiotic reflexivity in Britain, including the rise of scriptural literalism, of philological science, and of nominalist and empiricist theories of language.

The anthropologist Webb Keane has presented a series of important studies of the semiotic ideology of Dutch Protestant missionaries in colonial Sumba, Indonesia, and of the contrast or conflict between this and various indigenous ideologies. Protestants condemned the "fetishizing" of certain forms of language, especially formalistic or performative ritual language, while emphasizing sincerity and spontaneity in speech. Keane argues for a Protestant genealogy of various modern efforts to "disenchant" language, and makes a compelling case for the co-emergence of such semiotic ideologies with modern notions of subjectivity and autonomy. Keane has argued that "the long religious background is crucial for any critical understanding of the terms by which we try to understand words, things, and agency . . . Certain aspects of the familiar narratives of modernity cannot be discerned unless we understand the persistence of [the] religious attack on semiotic form in the Western world."[60] Aspects of this attack are explored in this book.

The historical outline provided above raises again the question of a general disenchantment of culture, and reframes this as a question of the transformations in language and semiosis that characterize secularism. Both of the original myths of disenchantment—the silencing of the pagan oracles and the replacement of the "shadowy" symbolism of Jewish ritual by the "plain speech" of the Gospel—depicted disenchantment as a semiotic event. A genealogy of the idea of disenchantment calls into question the degree of dependence of the semiotic ideology of secular modernity on earlier Christian theologies. As we shall see, there is a close relationship between Reformation polemics against idolatry and some of the movements we regard as representative of the secular Enlightenment. Although there has been much fruitless debate over whether disenchantment, considered as an historical event, actually happened, reframing this debate around the question of the semiotic ideology of disenchantment offers a more constructive approach. Regarded from the perspective of the history of culture and ideas, including religious ideas, the disenchantment of language and of the symbol constitutes one of the characteristic features of an ostensibly secular modernity.

A correct understanding of these developments is crucial for the history of religions, as well as for semiotics. With the demise of evolutionary narratives of the development from "primitive" culture to "civilization," the history of religions has been left largely without any framework within which to compare and contrast different cultures, or without even the ability to define its own object of study. Semiotics offers the promise of such a framework, which allows for the meaningful distinction among different cultural traditions as semiotic ideologies without reinstating cultural chauvinism. However, as previously indicated, it is difficult if not impossible for modern scholars to avoid the perspective of privilege that comes with our distance from the rhetoric of other cultures.

Outline of chapters

In a short book such as this, it would of course be impossible to give equal attention to all of the important dimensions of the semiotics of religion. This is particularly true as one of the aims of this book is to thread the needle between the structural and historical aspects of the semiotics of religion, demonstrating both cross-cultural similarities and some important cultural and historical differences. There can be no question of surveying all of the different types of semiotic ideologies of the various religions as these have been described by scholars. Nor is this book a survey of approaches current within the widely dispersed field of semiotics of religion. Among other significant topics left out—many of which have received attention elsewhere—are the structure of mythic narratives; glossolalia; divination; secrecy, esotericism, and encryption; the relationship between semiotic exchange and other modes of exchange, such as sacrifice; and the hallmarks of religious conversion and saintliness. Rather, I have organized the essay around a carefully selected set of themes that are basic to the semiotics of religion, and that together serve to highlight some of the contrasts that appear most salient for describing the semiotic ideology of secular modernity. Earlier chapters focus on features commonly found in the rhetoric of traditional religions and ritual systems, while later chapters focus on the criticisms of these features leveled by British Protestants, and the ways in which these criticisms have shaped modern views of the sign. In each chapter, I have attempted to respond to an important set of debates in the scholarly literature, and to further those debates by bringing to bear a perspective informed by a study of the data and history of semiotics.

Chapter Two develops earlier efforts to account for the poetic features found in magic spells and rituals, including repetition, alliteration, and palindromes. Using examples drawn from a wide number of traditions, I illustrate the manner in which such poetic forms contribute to the pragmatic function of ritual as a mode of rhetorical performance. Such rituals may even depict or imitate, in elaborate detail, the very act of communication or translation that they seek to effect, demonstrating that ritual can be a mode of verisimilitude or virtuality. The recuperation of a poetics of ritual aims to counter the neglect of such forms of iconicity or resemblance by many current theories.

Chapter Three complicates the structuralist thesis of the arbitrary nature of the sign by illustrating the phenomenon of the naturalization of arbitrariness in ritual systems and in efforts to construct a perfect or universal language in both traditional Hinduism and the Baconian tradition. Two case studies—the practice of folk or fictitious etymologizing in Hinduism and claims for the status of gesture as a natural language in Hindu and European traditions—exemplify the contribution of iconicity to the rhetoric of culture.

Chapter Four begins to trace part of the theological genealogy of modern theories of the sign, by exploring the intersection of Protestant iconoclasm with the critique of taking words for things in the Baconian tradition. The Reformation emphasis on scriptural literalism coordinated with a critique of metaphysical language, exemplified by pagan mythology, the very words of which supposedly encouraged idolatry and polytheism. Such ideas contributed to various scientific projects for the reform of language, as illustrated by Jeremy Bentham's proposal to codify the English common law tradition by purging it of verbal "fictions."

Chapter Five considers the causes of the repudiation of ritual and transformations in attitudes toward poetic performance and ritual repetition that a number of scholars have regarded as characteristic of the early modern and modern eras. One dimension of this is the Puritan critique of vain repetitions in prayer, which was leveled against the types of rituals that, as Chapter Two demonstrates, were prominent in many traditional cultures. Puritans regarded such repetitions as rhetoric, magic, and idolatry. The proscription of such forms highlights the consequences of literalism with its associated privileging of the semantic over the pragmatic function of ritual discourse. Another factor contributing to the decline of such poetry was the rise of a culture of printing after the development of movable type, which coordinated with Protestant literalism in either rendering obsolete or proscribing the poetic devices more common in modes of oral performance.

Chapter Six extends the exploration of the Protestant repudiation of ritual while reappraising the structuralist doctrine of the arbitrary nature of the sign. That doctrine has antecedents in, among other things, seventeenth- and eighteenth-century Deist polemics against the ceremonial laws of the Jews such as circumcision, sacrifice, and dietary prohibitions. Early Christians had given these laws a symbolic value, as prefigurations of the Gospel. Now, even such a limited value was called into question, as Deists attacked the Mosaic ritual laws as "arbitrary" and "positive" because of their instituted and nonnatural, supposedly divine status. The notion that God would impose such commands by fiat disturbed the order of natural law and, with this, the sanctity of human reason. Deist semiotics displayed an aversion to a certain kind of arbitrariness that appeared to threaten human autonomy and agency. Mary Douglas's structuralist account of the Jewish dietary laws, which concludes that the Holy is opposed to "anomalies," ignores the fact that it is the modern and early modern opponents of the Jewish law, rather than the Hebrew Bible itself, that seem to have had an aversion to anomalies or rather to arbitrariness.

Collectively, these chapters aim to extend some of the key contributions of structuralist approaches to the semiotics of religion while interrogating and rethinking these approaches. Without pretending to have elaborated a new grand theory, I hope to have introduced some complexity, historical nuance, and flexibility into the semiotics of religion, and to have staked out some clear positions concerning the rhetoric of religion and of secular modernity that should inspire some fruitful debate.

CHAPTER TWO

The poetics of ritual performance

Toward a theory of poetic performance

Gorgias was right: speech is a powerful lord, with a force that can carry us away. Plato was also correct: poetry can be deceptive, and possibly even dangerous. How both the Sophist and the Philosopher could be correct, while disagreeing with each other, is the focus of this chapter.

An examination of spells, magic, and other rituals reveals certain formal features that cut across many different cultures and historical periods and that are found, to a lesser extent, in modern advertising, political slogans, and rhetoric. These features include, in addition to repetition in nonverbal registers (such as the performance of a sequence of gestures or other behaviors or the concatenation of resemblances such as items of similar color), various forms of verbal repetition such as rhyme, alliteration, tautology (the repetition of similar or identical words or phrases), and palindromes (phrases that read the same backwards as forwards) or chiasmus, meaning an inversion of phonemes, words, or other units of discourse which may be rough rather than exact. What accounts for these characteristic features of ritual and ritual language? The present chapter develops a theory that accounts for a number of these forms by demonstrating the contribution they make to ritual as a mode of rhetorical performance. A few basic principles go very far in rescuing the formal features of rituals—in particular, their use of poetry and repetition—from the neglect or even disparagement that these features have received from many existing approaches.

In many cultures, "ritual" and "repetitive performance" appear to be nearly synonymous, or at least so closely linked that to speak of ritual implies repetition or reiteration, and in more than one sense. Behavior that is "ritualistic" implies actions that are undertaken by force of habit or tradition, and in imitation of prior models. Within an individual performance of a ritual, too, there may be coordinated a variety of modes of behavior or expression, which leads to the characterization of ritual, as opposed to ordinary behavior, as involving redundancy, orchestration, and "sensory pageantry," meaning the coordination of expressions affecting multiple modes of perception.[1] The types of repetition found in ritual vary enormously, from verbatim repetition to rhyme in spoken registers, to rhythmical movement expressed in gesture or dance, to the simple multiplication of a ritual such as the Mass, or feast days, etc.

More than two millennia after the debate between Plato and Gorgias, we are still waiting for an adequate theory of the role that such forms of repetition play in ritual, in particular as modes of rhetoric. Scholars have proposed several, divergent explanations for these features of ritual. To mention only a few of the most prominent such explanations, Sigmund Freud argued that religious practices, like the obsessive acts of the neurotic or, as we would now term him, the person suffering from obsessive-compulsive disorder, are repeated because they are needed to fend off the perennial encroachments of anxiety.[2] Mircea Eliade focused his attention on the ways in which rituals often imitate the cosmogony or actions of the gods or primal ancestors, which serve as models for sacred human action.[3] Frits Staal contended that the mantras or verbal formulas, and the sequences of ritual behaviors, prescribed by the ancient *Vedas* and other Hindu traditions were repeated because they reflected a stage of culture that was "prelinguistic," possessing the rudiments of syntax but no semantics or meaning, just as the incessant warbling of birds and babes.[4]

The neglect or even condemnation of semiotic form and of the contribution this form makes to the function of spells, magic, and other rituals, mars a number of recent theories. Even some theories that have emphasized the power of religious signs have argued or merely assumed that this force stems only from convention. Émile Durkheim's insistence that the totems or *churinga* of Australian tribes were purely arbitrary and nonrepresentational in form was a necessary corollary of his conclusion that the force of such signs derives entirely from the social group: they are symbolic of the power of society, purely and simply.[5]

The current concept of ritualization, which has inherited the structuralist and poststructuralist emphasis on binary oppositions as constitutive of the sign, holds that ritual cannot be defined through any particular set of features, but is marked by its sheer difference from ordinary behavior. As Catherine Bell states:

> Clearly, ritual is not the same thing everywhere; it can vary in every feature. As practice, the most we can say is that it is a way of acting that distinguishes itself from other ways of acting in the very way it does what it does; . . . Among the most important strategies of ritualization is the inherent flexibility of the degree of ritualization invoked.[6]

According to this view, repetition would be simply one of a potentially limitless number of techniques by which ritual announces itself as such. Similarly, poetry, literature, and other genres would be based on a process of distinction and opposition. In my view, such an approach is inadequate, as it abdicates the responsibility to account for the regularities in ritual forms. The concept of ritualization does not help us much to distinguish ritual from other genres, nor to explain the heightening of poetic function in ritual and its contribution to the pragmatics of ritual performance. It is certainly true that rituals are marked off as special. In the case of spells, one way this happens is through the use of apparently nonsensical words—the so-called "magic words" (*voces magicae*) that are found in many traditions, including the Greek magical papyri (*abracadabra, aski kataski*), Sanskrit Tantric mantras (*oṃ, hrīṃ, śrīṃ*, and other "seed" (*bīja*) syllables), Bengali folk mantras, and English ("hocus pocus" *mumbo jumbo*). These add to what Bronislaw Malinowski referred to as the "coefficient of weirdness" in magic, the idea that this is special/ not ordinary language.[7] But such patterns, as we shall see, often do more than simply demarcate the boundaries of the ritual event.

Ritualization reduces semiosis to a question of social convention; ritual signs are supposedly arbitrary, like any others. This cannot explain the fact that many rituals, especially of the magical variety, deploy signs that are relatively nonarbitrary in the senses that they frequently either (1) construct an analogical relationship, that is one of similarity or contiguity, between the ritual and its target or objective (see Table 2.2 below) or (2) deploy poetic repetition, in both cases to an extent greater than can be explained by sheer randomness or cultural variation. Like the concept of ritualization, Jakobson's definition of the poetic function also recognizes that one of the aims of poetry is to announce itself as an act of communication. However, unlike the concept of ritualization, the concept of poetic function, especially as developed by Michael Silverstein, enables a careful analysis of the formal features of ritual and of the contribution made by such features to ritual as a mode of rhetorical performance.

Repetition is crucial to the "performance" of a ritual,[8] in a dual sense: the internal orchestration of the ritual as an unfolding dramatic or expressive performance, and the "worklike" function of ritual as an effective means for transforming the world—if only virtually—or influencing social action. The analogy between ritual and dramatic performances has been explored in recent decades, first by anthropologists and now also under the rubrics of discourse analysis and performance studies.[9] Anthropologists and scholars of religion have applied to ritual both J. L. Austin's concept of the "performative utterance" and John Searle's related concept of "speech acts."[10] Austin explained that certain utterances (such as "With this ring, I thee wed") do not merely make a statement about the world, but accomplish something in the act of being uttered. However, his theory of linguistic performance contained no explanation for the frequency of repetition in ritual, including especially ritual language.[11] Austin's neglect of semiotic form extended a long history in the English philosophical tradition of excluding poetic form as nonsense, or at least of no account.[12] Parts of this history are described in later chapters of this volume.

This defect was partly remedied in anthropologist Stanley Tambiah's essay "A Performative Approach to Ritual":

> Ritual is a culturally constructed system of symbolic communication. It is constituted of patterned and ordered sequences of words and acts, often expressed in multiple media, whose content and arrangement are characterized in varying degree by formality (conventionality), stereotypy (rigidity), condensation (fusion), and redundancy (repetition). Ritual action in its constitutive features is performative in these three senses: in the Austinian sense of performative, wherein saying something is also doing something; in the quite different sense of a staged performance that uses multiple media by which the participants experience the event intensively; and in the sense of indexical values—I derive this concept from Peirce—being attached to and inferred by actors during the performance.[13]

In defining what he meant by "a performative approach," Tambiah amalgamated the senses of theatrical performance and Austin's linguistic performatives with a third, less common sense of performance taken from Charles Sanders Peirce, namely the concept of ritual as an "indexical icon" that signals or points to some thing or event in its context.[14] Within this orientation toward performance, Tambiah highlighted several features of ritual, including especially its repetitiveness and use of multiple media. He attributed to these features a function that we might broadly term persuasion or the rhetorical function.[15] However, he associated this with other communicative functions, including "transmitting a message through redundancy, . . . storing vital technological knowledge in an oral culture, and . . . constructi[ng] the spell itself as a lengthy verbal form."[16] Different traditions of interpretation converged in this statement. One was the application of communication theory to explain how ritual repetition facilitates the conveyance of a message.[17] Another was Albert Lord's and Milman Parry's demonstrations of how poetic devices contribute to the recall and composition of epics in oral performance.[18] Jack Goody and others have also suggested that repetition is especially important as a mnemotechnic in oral cultures.[19] Recently, cognitive theories of religion, for example that of anthropologist Harvey Whitehouse, have also posited that ritual repetition contributes to memorization and cultural transmission.[20]

Tambiah's theory of ritual as a mode of rhetorical performance was a significant advance in the anthropological understanding of ritual. It suggested a function for many of the formal features commonly found in ritual, which had too often been dismissed as simply meaningless. However, it did not provide a careful analysis of these formal features, and of their contribution to the function of ritual. The burden of this chapter is to provide such an analysis, by extending Michael Silverstein's interpretation of ritual as an "indexical icon," a heightening of the poetic function that reinforces ritual as a mode of rhetorical performance.

The rhetoric of spells

Some of the poetic features of magic have been recognized for a long time. Both E. B. Tylor and James George Frazer argued that magic was based on a mistaken application of the laws of association of ideas.[21] There is a symbolic association between the ritual and its goal or effect that often depends on the principles of sympathy and contagion, or similarity and contiguity. Many cultures that lack an understanding of scientific causation misinterpret coincidental or artificially constructed, symbolic relationships as real relationships that may be deployed to practical effect.

For example, a Serbian spell against jaundice runs:

Yellow cock,
Beat your yellow wings three times
Over a yellow hen
A yellow hen in a yellow year
In a yellow month
In a yellow week
On a yellow day
Laid a yellow egg
In yellow hay
Let the yellow hay stay
And the yellow fever leave our Milan.[22]

The intent of the spell is clear: all of the yellow will stay where it belongs, in the hay and other things of yellow color with which the hay is connected physically or temporally, and depart from poor sick Milan. This spell is characteristic of one of the main types of "sympathetic magic" described by Frazer, following Tylor: it uses similarity, in this case the resemblance in color among different objects, to construct a symbolic connection between the ritual and its intended target (in this case jaundice, which turns the skin yellow), and to manipulate this connection so as to effect a transformation in the target. This spell also uses extensive repetition consisting not only of an accumulation of items of the same color, but also of times (year, month, etc.). The fact that the hen is supposed to beat her wings three times recalls similarly repetitive sequences in other rituals, not to mention nursery rhymes, folk tales, and modern movies such as *Beetlejuice* (1988), where the eponymous wicked spirit may be invoked by calling his name three times in succession.

Magic spells can deploy different types of resemblance. The so-called historiola—which Fritz Graf has defined as "a modern term describing brief tales built into magic formulas, providing a mythic precedent for a magically effective treatment"[23]—invokes a mythic archetype and harnesses this to the production of a similar effect in the here-and-now. Among some snakebite charms I collected in Bangladesh, there were references to the episode in which the god Krishna defeated the serpent Kaliya: in similar fashion, the victim was supposed to overcome the cobra's venom. Eliade provided an example of a healing charm from early-seventeenth-century England that uses a historiola:

> Hallowed be thou, Vervein [verbena], as thou growest on the ground,
>
> For in the Mount of Calvary, there thou wast first found.
>
> Thou healedst our Saviour Jesus Christ, and staunchest his bleeding wound;
>
> In the name of [Father, Son, Holy Ghost] I take thee from the ground.[24]

In some other magic rites or spells, the symbolic association between the ritual and its target is based on contiguity rather than similarity, as when a so-called "voodoo doll" incorporates the hair, nails, or an article of clothing from the intended victim. For example, a Swedish spell to make a couple into enemies instructs: "Take an egg and boil it hard and write the couple's names on it. Then cut the egg in two pieces and give one of the halves to a dog and the other half to a cat."[25] The association between the two halves and the couple is accomplished by writing their names, that is by contiguity. This having been done, the physical division of the halves of the egg, which is made permanent by feeding them to animals that (usually) fight with one another, is supposed to divide the two lovers in body and in spirit.

Frazer's principles of sympathy and contagion, or similarity and contiguity, have been identified by Thomas Sebeok, among others, as coinciding with the sign-types of icon and index defined by Charles Sanders Peirce.[26] Peirce elaborated a typology of different signs, which depended upon the fundamental triad of icon, index, and symbol, illustrated in Table 2.1 below.

Different types of signs may serve similar functions. For example, a red traffic light is a conventional index that signals us to stop at an intersection; while the same function may be performed by the iconic image of a pedestrian with a slashing line through it, or by the raised hand of a traffic cop, which is a natural index in the sense that the hand metonymically represents the physical act of stopping another person. Although Peirce's triadic typology has sometimes been deployed rigidly, the fact is that almost

Table 2.1 Types of sign, after Peirce[27]

Sign Type	Basis	Examples
Icon	similarity, including structural resemblance	portrait, statue, metaphor, onomatopoeia or "sound symbolism"[28]
Index	co-occurrence, spatiotemporal contiguity, or causal relation	smoke for fire (and vice versa), a weathervane, metonym
Symbol	convention or arbitrary determination	red light for a traffic stop, (almost all) language

Table 2.2 Sign relations in magic, after Frazer and Peirce[29]

Frazer's Laws of Magic	Ritual action	Sign relation	Intended goal
Law of Similarity	(a) image of victim (e.g. doll, picture) stuck with pin (b) water poured on ground (c) yellow substances cast out	index → motivated by iconicity (resemblance, metaphor)	(a) victim injured in corresponding limb[30] (b) rain falls on crops; drought ends (c) yellow jaundice leaves patient[31]
Law of Contact/ Contagion	(a) victim's clothing burned (b) weapon that injured victim destroyed	index → motivated by indexicality (contiguity, metonymy, *pars pro toto* or part for whole)	(a) victim burns (b) wound caused by weapon heals[32]

all signs are complex and fall into more than one of these three categories. The property of signs as complex becomes important in the analysis of rituals, especially of the magical variety, where certain icons or indexes may be taken as natural or causal indexes of events in their context, such as the goal of the ritual. Frazer's laws of symbolic association in magic can be glossed in Peircean terms as in Table 2.2 above.

Unlike symbols, icons and indexes are partly "motivated" signs,[33] meaning that the association between them and what they signify is not purely conventional, unlike the vast majority of words: the use of the word "cow" in English is no more natural than the use of the word *vache* in French to designate a type of bovine. The use of motivated signs in magic rhetorically reinforces the idea of an association between the ritual and its target. The very slipperyness and permeability—even fungibility—of different sign-types allows one type of sign to be taken for another, as resemblance (iconicity) or contiguity (which is one type of index) may be taken as, or may substitute for, a "real" or causal indexical relation. One or more symbolic associations is interpreted as an association-in-fact, that is an index that is natural or causal, which may then be manipulated in such a way as to produce an effect in the physical (nonsymbolic) world. As Edmund Leach explains:

> [T]he general consensus of most recent anthropologists is that what the magician usually does is to interpret an index as a signal, after the fashion of Pavlov's dog . . . [T]he sorcerer [who thinks to injure his victim by destroying a lock of said victim's hair] makes a triple error. He first mistakes a metaphoric symbol (i.e. the verbal label "this is the hair of X") for a metonymic sign. He then goes on to treat the imputed sign as if it were a natural index, and finally he interprets the supposed natural index as a signal capable of triggering off automatic consequences at a distance.[34]

Leach's analysis of this simplest case of sympathetic magic is a more precise restatement of what Tylor and Frazer already said. His explanation is good as far as it goes. But neither his restatement nor Frazer's earlier account, nor even Tambiah's "performative approach" explains many of the features commonly found in magic, including especially the extreme repetition and accumulation of poetic devices observable in many spells. Noteworthy in a number of examples already given, including the Serbian charm against jaundice and the English spell against bleeding, is how rhyme or repetition on the phonetic level combines with analogical associations on the semantic level. Spells in many cultures deploy such poetic devices as alliteration and rhyme; this informs the labeling of such as incantations and, in Latin, as *carmina*, which like chant means both spell and song.

Such examples require a more complex analysis, one that attends to the unfolding performance of the ritual and the manner in which this augments the ritual as an index. The notion of the indexical icon has been developed by the anthropologist Michael Silverstein, who followed his teacher Roman Jakobson in combining Saussurean semiology with Peircean semiotic.[35] According to Silverstein, ritual is a heightened case of a more general poetic function of language, in which repetition and metricalization in discourse communicate both the "entextualization" of the discourse—its emergence as a text—as well as its "co(n)textualization" within its pragmatic context, with which such metricalization establishes relations of presupposition and

entailment of a quasi-causal nature.[36] Poetic repetition or iconicity within
the text of a spell, for example, points toward resembling lines or other
units within the text, and even beyond the text, creating indexical relations
with these units. The concept of the indexical icon bridges the gap between
the analysis of the structural (i.e. phonetic, morphological, semantic, and
syntactic) features of a text or ritual performance and the analysis of the
interaction between such a text and its context.

Similar to Lévi-Straussian structuralism and Jakobsonian poetics, the
methodology applied in such analyses begins with a general segmentation
and notation of patterns evident in the emerging event of discourse.
Sequences of text, or of language or other semiotic modalities converted
into text, are broken down into their phonetic, semantic, and syntactic
components, which are then correlated with events and patterns in their
extra-linguistic context. A simple illustration of this technique appears
in Table 2.3 below; phonetic and semantic parallelisms and appositions
between segments of discourse are indicated by the use of capital letters.

The unfolding pattern of icons and antitheses creates a recognizable text
that bears also a pragmatic relation to its context (i.e. illness or burning).
The multiple indexes thus formed—including imperative verbs and deictics,
or "pointing" words such as spatial and temporal markers (e.g. "here" and
"now")—add up in a way that enhances the overall force of the spell as an
index of its goal. This illustrates also the complex character of such signs,
which are simultaneously icons and indexes (hence "indexical icons") and

Table 2.3 Analysis of the poetic function of folk charms

Text	Phonetic apposition/ iconicity	Semantic apposition/ iconicity and antithesis
(Charm against fever) Fever, fever, stay away, Don't come in my bed today![37]	FEVER, FEVER stAY AwAY todAY	STAY away (there) don't COME (here, now)
"How to Cure a Burn" Three holy men went out walking, They did bless the heat and the burning; They blessed that it might not increase; They blessed that it might quickly cease![38]	walkING, burnING incrEASE, cEASE	NOT INCREASE (but) CEASE
"Another Remedy for Burns" Clear out, brand, but never in; be thou cold or hot, thou must cease to burn. (etc.)[39]	IN, BURN	OUT, NEVER IN COLD, HOT

in which icons may be taken as indexes, and even regarded as actual causes of events in context.

Such phonetic associations may be interpreted as semantic (meaningful) or even pragmatic (effective).[40] They create associations of presupposition and entailment within the structure of a ritual performance, which associations can then be transferred to the goal of the ritual itself. Repetition and other sign-relations can accumulate to augment the overall indexical or pragmatic force of the ritual. Ritual illustrates with particular precision the permeability of the boundaries among different types of signs, as well as different levels of language: phonetic, semantic, and pragmatic. For similar reasons, Jakobson criticized the "bias of phonetic isolationism" that fails to recognize that poetic repetition operates on the semantic as well as the phonetic level of language.[41]

Some of these ideas help to account for the poetic features of Hindu Tantric mantras, which employ a wide range of forms of repetition, including simple reiteration of the basic formula, reduplication, alliteration and, last but not least, imitation of the cosmogony and other creative processes.[42] An example analyzed in Table 2.4 below is:

Oṃ hrīṃ śrīṃ klīṃ devadattaṃ mama vaśyaṃ kuru kuru klīṃ śrīṃ hrīṃ oṃ.	oṃ hrīṃ śrīṃ klīṃ, Make, make Devadatta (John Doe) my slave, klīṃ śrīṃ hrīṃ oṃ.

In this example, the repetition of imperative verbs—which are already a kind of index—strengthens the force of the spell, while the apparently nonsensical "seed" (bīja) mantras such as hrīṃ add poetic and rhythmic force. "Enveloping" (saṃpuṭa) the mantra with the same syllables both forward and backward at beginning and end, respectively, converts the mantra into a kind of palindrome or chiasmus. This is an attempt to diagram or model exemplary types of creation that are believed to have a similar, in-and-out shape: breathing, sexual intercourse, and the rhythmic cycle of cosmic creation as conceived by Hindus.

The goal of such imitative diagrams is to make the mantra more powerful. A mantra that mirrors creation is felt to be more creative. Iconicity is harnessed to the production of indexicality. Despite sharing superficial similarities with Staal's syntactical analysis of mantras and other rituals, this interpretation contests his claim that the proliferation of repetitive patterns in ritual and ritual discourse signifies "meaninglessness." In this case, redundancy makes the language of the mantra both more meaningful and, within the linguistic ideology of the Tantras, more powerful. Mantras are neither nonsense nor ordinary language, but rather especially sacred and effective language.

The sequence of vocables in the mantra is also of paramount importance. The order of bījas at the beginning of the mantra often depicts the evolution

Table 2.4 Analysis of chiasmus in Hindu Tantric mantras[43]

Sequence of mantra when enveloped (saṃpuṭita)	Forward order of enveloping	(Mantra/ sādhya)	Reverse order of enveloping
Sample mantra	oṃ hrīṃ śrīṃ klīṃ	make, make so-and-so my slave	klīṃ śrīṃ hrīṃ oṃ
Abstract schema	a-b-c→	X	→c-b-a
Cosmic cycle	creation	stability	destruction
Cycle of sexual reproduction	birth	life	death
haṃsa mantra[44] ha = Śiva, male god sa = Śakti, female consort	haṃsaḥ Śiva→Śakti male→female		so 'haṃ Śakti→Śiva female→male
Cycle of breath	out-breath	(rest)	in-breath

of life, breath, the body, and/or the elements, and therefore the coming-into-being of the material goal announced at the center of the mantra by the *sādhya*, a technical term that means literally "that which is to be accomplished" and that denotes the part of the mantra that names the objective. A mantra formed in this way is said to be *siddha* (accomplished, successful, or effective), a word related to *siddhi*, meaning the magical powers attained through yogic practice. At the point where such mimetic diagrams of creation give way to the announcement of the material goal, mantras represent the ability of ritually perfected, powerful speech to cross over the divide between language and physical reality. By diagramming the path of creation, in which sound is transformed into physical reality, mantras also depict the virtual causation of physical effects by means of sacred speech. These effects include such actions as killing or banishing one's enemies, but also the manifestation of different deities in physical form. This is especially clear in the case of mantras that deploy a special form of the alphabet called the script of the elements (*bhūtalipi*), which rearranges the letters to mimic the evolution of the five elements from space to earth, that is from the least tangible to the most concrete element, ending just before the announcement of the *sādhya* or material or mundane goal aimed at by the mantra. (See Table 2.5 below.) Such devices represent the overcoming of the perennial gap between language and reality from entirely within language, that is virtually. Mantras, like other spells, deploy poetic, imitative, or motivated language in order to index and call to mind their goal with increasing vividness.

Table 2.5 Enveloping a mantra with the script of the elements[45]

| Script of the elements | | | | | ... etc. → | sādhya |
ha	ya	ra	va	la	→	
Space → (intangible)		air →	fire →	water →	earth → (concrete)	material goal
Language ...					... etc. →	reality

Such heightened reflection on the structure of language is characteristic of what Jakobson called the poetic function of language, which promotes a "set toward the message as such." In the case of mantras, however, one is supposed to look beyond the message itself to the pragmatic consequences that it announces. The types of imitation found in mantras and similar spells can extend beyond simple rhythm and repetition, and reflect a deliberate effort to perfect language as an indexical icon of the natural world. That is why I have referred to mantras as a "natural language," in contrast to the common usage of this phrase to denote indigenous language traditions.

The principles of spell-construction

Several principles of the rhetoric of spells may be inferred from the above examples. The most important, and most general, concerns the manner in which such rituals depend on substitution: one sign is substituted for another, as when an artificial index is taken as natural. The voodoo doll, effigy, or victim's article of clothing is very obviously a substitute. More elaborately, relationships constructed within the text of the spell may be taken as an argument for a relationship between the spell and its real-world context, as when Tantric mantras represent in verbal form the evolution of intangible sound into a concrete result. The magician's mistake—or possibly art—is to create a certain sleight-of-hand, which shuffles these sign-relations in such a way that one may fail to notice.

Substitution is not unique to magic; it is absolutely general to the sign, which serves as a stand-in for its referent. Umberto Eco's famous designation of semiotics as a "theory of the lie" recognized that a sign may substitute or cover for a referent that is absent.[46] Indeed, it is when the referent is noticeably absent—as in the case of some goal not yet attained but fervently desired—that the sign is needed most. Nietzsche argued similarly that all signs are inherently metaphorical: displacements, at several steps' remove, from that which they represent, often in an altogether different medium, as when the sounds of language are substituted for a physical reality that has already been mediated through the doors of perception.[47]

Although such substitutions are arguably inherent in all semiosis, they are particularly evident in ritual, which constructs a separate domain that is often deliberately intended, as in the case of Tantric mantras, to function as a microcosm, one amenable to manipulation in a way that the larger world may not be. That this constricted world is often intended as a microcosm is indicated by the frequent invocation in ritual of the cardinal directions, elements, etc. The "doll's house" or ludic dimension of ritual enables a working-through, on a smaller scale, of problems that are obviously of larger import.[48] To some extent, this is no different from what we constantly do when we model problems, simplifying them by reducing them to a smaller set of pieces that can be rearranged, perhaps to achieve a solution that can have real-world application, as with Friedrich August Kekulé's discovery, in a dream, of the ringed structure of the Benzene molecule. What distinguishes the case of ritual is just that the model is often claimed or represented as convergent with reality, although its sign-relations are often blatantly artificial. It is not just a question of bad science. In an alternate universe, the operations performed by the magician might be found empirically to produce their intended effect; and the cosmology underlying the ritual might prove correct. But the fact that in ritual purely phonetic relationships, such as rhyme, may be taken as substitutes for truly causal or natural, indexical relationships demonstrates that there is, at bottom, a kind of displacement that has much more in common with rhetoric than it does with science, even of the bad or mistaken variety.

The second important principle that emerges from an examination of these spells is the manner in which they accumulate sign-relations, either by proliferating repetition in both phonetic and semantic registers, or by sensory pageantry, that is, orchestrating various semiotic modalities such as sound, gesture, smell, etc. The first spell given above, that to cure jaundice, exemplified this by multiplying the list of yellow things in which all of that color was supposed to remain, departing poor Milan. Tantric mantras frequently reduplicate the imperatives in the central part of the mantra that announces "what is to be accomplished" (sādhya): for example, "make, make so-and-so my slave." The spells in the Greek magical papyri also often repeat deictics such as "now, now, immediately, immediately."[49] Just as in ordinary discourse, such repetitions add emphasis. Ritual is not binary, is not simply either "on" or "off," but is a question of degree and quantity. The very fact that sign-relations can accumulate to motivate a spell as an index of its goal illustrates a basic defect of the concept of ritualization, and of poststructuralist interpretations of ritual more generally. According to such interpretations, repetition, accumulation, etc. are only devices to mark ritual off as a separate event of discourse or behavior. Yet when we examine the text of spells, we find that these devices are not merely marking off ritual, but are instead quite emphatically indexing some event orchestrated by the ritual. Ritual in these cases is less like a flashing neon sign, and more like a laser pointer, or the landing beacons at an airport, which may light up in sequence to indicate the appropriate direction.

Illustrating this point, a simple spell against consumption banishes this disease from the inside to the outside, to progressively further reaches of the patient's body, and finally out of the patient entirely: "Consumption, I order thee out of the bones into the flesh, out of the flesh upon the skin, out of the skin into the wilds of the forest."[50] Another form of spell that accomplishes the same thing is similar to children's counting-out rhymes such as "eenie meenie minie moe," or to the "A Hundred Bottles of Beer on the Wall" song.[51] Like the "ten-nine-eight" before rocket launch, certain spells count down to their goal in a way that heightens anticipation and makes the goal appear inevitable.[52] Such patterns are very common in the Greek magical papyri,[53] but are also found in other traditions. Joseph Frank Payne referred to these as "numerical charms," and provided several examples, including the following from the Anglo-Saxon charms:

> For Kernels (i.e. scrofulous glands).
> Nine were Noththe's sisters:
> then the nine came to be eight,
> and the eight seven,
> and the seven six,
> and the six five,
> and the five four,
> and the four three,
> and the three two,
> and the two one,
> and the one none.
> This may be medicine for thee from kernels, and from scrofulles, and from worm, and from every mischief.[54]

A special form of accumulation is what I termed in an earlier work "exhaustion": the complete enumeration of a particular set, such as the directions, the elements, the ritually significant colors, the groups of gods, etc.[55] Tambiah noted this feature in many of the Trobriand Island spells described by Malinowski.[56] A spell collected in the same area more recently by Gunter Senft is a good example; I provide an excerpt of both the original and the translation to show the coordination of exhaustion with accumulation in the phonetic register:

Bulivaleva bulivaleva	Wild pig, wild pig
Bulivaleva bulimalema	Wild pig, wild pig come
Bulimalema bulimalema	Wild pig come, wild pig come
Badududem	I will charm and kill you
Basobalem kwapusiga	I will call you over and kill you at your flank
Pusigam asamla	Your flank I kill
Asamla asamla	I kill, I kill
Amwala asamla	Your head I kill
Asamla kudum	I kill your tooth
Asamla asamla ampola	I kill I kill your brow
Asamla asamla togitem	I kill I kill your loin
Asamla asamla tobulumalem	I kill I kill your belly (streaky bacon)
Asamla asamla lopem	I kill I kill your stomach
Asamla asamla katem	I kill I kill your innards
(Etc.)	(Etc.)[57]

The function of spells

Such devices reinforce a conviction in the efficacy of the spell, by enumerating all contingencies and harnessing the spell to these as an index of its goal. In this regard, a spell often appears to be constructed like an insurance policy: it aims to provide coverage in the case of any or all of a range of related contingencies. An elaborate formula of ownership among the Anglo-Saxons, translated into modern English, runs: "So I hold it as he held it, who held it as saleable, and as I will own it / and never resign it / neither plot nor ploughland / nor turf nor tuft / nor furrow nor foot length / nor land nor leasow / nor fresh nor marsh / nor rough ground nor room / nor wold nor fold / land nor strand / wood nor water."[58] (The translation preserves the extreme alliteration and rhyming of the original.) Another Anglo-Saxon example is: "Find those kine [cattle], and fetch those kine, / And have those kine and hold those kine."[59] A basic function of signs is to produce certainty in the existence of the state of affairs of which they stand as a guarantee or certificate. In the case of spells and magical rituals, this function is especially difficult, given that the state of affairs that such rituals attempt to certify may be counterfactual: either unlikely, or the opposite of what is presently observable, and in any case prospective. The many devices deployed in spells are responses to their condition of use; they must produce certainty out of uncertainty, or security out of anxiety, for example, sun from a stormy sky, or rain in a drought. This is why such devices are commonly found in protection spells, as in the following "A Charm against Shooting, Cutting or Thrusting":[60]

> In the name of J.[esus] J. J. Amen. I (*name*); Jesus Christ is the true salvation; Jesus Christ governs, reigns, defeats and conquers every enemy, visible or invisible; Jesus, be thou with me at all times, forever and ever, upon all roads and ways, upon the water and the land, on the mountain and in the valley, in the house and in the yard, in the whole world wherever I am, stand, run, ride or drive; whether I sleep or wake, eat or drink, there be thou also, Lord Jesus Christ, at all times, late and early, every hour, every moment; and in all my goings in or goings out. Those five holy red wounds, oh, Lord Jesus Christ, may they guard me against all fire-arms, be they secret or public, that they cannot injure me or do me any harm whatever, in the name of + + + [Christ, or the Cross]. May Jesus, with his guardianship and protection, shield me (*name*) always from daily commission of sins, worldly injuries and injustice, from contempt, from pestilence and other diseases, from fear, torture, and great suffering, from all evil intentions, from false tongues and old clatter-brains; and that no kind of fire-arms can inflict any injury to my body, do thou take care of me. + + +. And that no band of thieves nor Gypsies, highway robbers, incendiaries, witches and other evil spirits may secretly enter my house or premises, nor break in; may the dear Virgin Mary, and all children who are in heaven with God, in eternal joys, protect and guard me against them; and the glory of God the father shall strengthen me, the wisdom of God the Son shall enlighten me, and the grace of God the Holy Ghost shall empower me from this hour unto all eternity. Amen.

Such devices function much like the language in a legal contract. Any contract seeks to be binding, and to maximize the probability of performance by the contracting parties. A contract is an insurance policy, which reassures and guards against unknown dangers. In other words, a contract is a kind of mechanism or machine for the production of certainty. That is why, in a sales contract, there are usually so few provisions regarding the buyer's performance, apart from some instructions prescribing the manner of transfer of funds. The reason for this is that we all know what money is. Money is an example of a completely fungible good; the only issue is the quantity. But in the case of goods being sold, we must know exactly what these are, and numerous provisions regarding their nature, extent, and quality are customary in a sales contract. When the sales contract details the goods sold by enumerating all of their parts, it is attempting to ensure that the entirety of the goods, without remainder, will be transferred. And toward that end, it may employ formulas that are repetitive and exhaustive, similar to the sayings "lock, stock, and barrel" and "hook, line, and sinker." The modern courtroom oath, "Do you promise to tell the truth, the whole truth, and nothing but the truth, so help you God?," also employs repetition and exhaustion which, presumably, maximize certainty and make the oath more binding than the simple promise "I won't lie."

This interpretation is admittedly functionalist, but that does not make it incorrect. Malinowski's hypothesis that magic is often applied in situations that are especially dangerous and there are no more effective alternatives for addressing such dangers may not always be true, but it is often true.[61] So, for example, the charms against snakebite I collected in Bangladesh in 1998 were being used in villages where there was little medical assistance of any kind available, much less antivenin. On the same trip, I spent Manasa Puja, the Hindu worship festival for the snake goddess Manasa, in a fishing village in Mymensingh. The propitiation of this goddess took place during the monsoon, at a time when the rivers were overflowing and fishermen were especially at risk from water-dwelling cobras. Given this context, and the heightened anxiety it would occasion, such rituals are entirely understandable, even if we don't believe they are effective.

My interpretation, then, is that the devices deployed in magic—substitution, accumulation, exhaustion, pointing, etc.—are designed to reinforce the status of magic as an index of its announced goal. This interpretation accords with the argument of Leach, et al., that sympathetic magic involves (mis)taking one type of index for another. However, it incorporates also the recognition that, on the textual level of spells and rituals, the sequence of words and actions and the intratextual relationships these construct also contribute to reinforce the ritual as an index of that which it seeks to bring about. Magic is a type of rhetoric that uses poetry for persuasion.

This explanation contrasts with some others that have been advanced. I have already noted deficiencies in the concept of ritualization and other poststructuralist theories. In a sense, these do no more than assert that ritual is sacred in the original sense of that term as "set apart," demarcated from ordinary behavior. Yet ritual is embedded in a context of use, and often attempts to obscure the gap between this context and its own text, which converge in the denouement of the ritual.

Another hypothesis regarding the function of poetic devices in ritual, suggested by Tambiah as noted above, is that they are mnemotechnics: they serve to make a spell more memorable, assisting recall and oral performance. This view is addressed at greater length in Chapter Five. For now, I will note only a few points. While such devices as rhyme may have a mnemonic function that is especially important in an oral culture, this explanation applies equally to all types of language and behavior; it is not distinctive of spells. Accordingly, this explanation cannot account for the proliferation of such devices in the text of spells and other magical rituals, where such devices are more commonly found than in other genres. Second, in the case of magic, these devices are not usually about recall: they are prospective, designed to accomplish something in the more or less immediate future. Even as Tantric mantras repeat the cosmogony, they do so not for mere recollection, but for another purpose: to construct a sequence of ritual indexes that bridges the gap between language and reality and brings about an event in the here-and-now. Therefore, their function is not limited to the mnemonic.

The production of certainty: analogical punishments and trials by ordeal

Two types of rituals that resemble magic in certain of their semiotic features are analogical punishments and trials by ordeal. A brief examination of how these work supports the hypotheses (1) that the function of many rituals is to produce certainty by reinforcing the status of the ritual as an index of its referent, and (2) that poetic devices can contribute to this function.

By analogical punishments I mean those punishments that establish, by means of similarity or contiguity, a certain symbolic fitness to the crime they aim to redress. Some of the most well known of these are punishments where there is a direct resemblance between crime and punishment, as in the so-called "law of talion" (*lex talionis*), that is "an eye for an eye, a tooth for a tooth" in the Hebrew Bible.[62] Cutting off the hand of a thief is an example of a punishment that invokes metonymy, as is the more specific injunction in the Hindu *Laws of Manu*: "When a lowest-born man uses a particular limb to injure a superior person, that very limb of his should be cut off."[63] In some cases the resemblance is more figurative. *Manu* prescribes, for the crime of sleeping with his guru's wife, that an upper-caste man must either lie down on a red-hot iron bed or embrace a red-hot iron image of a woman,[64] or be branded on the forehead with a representation of a vagina.[65] For drinking liquor, the brand would be a tavern sign.[66] Such punishments often closely resemble magic. Although the indexical relationship they reinforce is retrospective, it appears designed to achieve an association between the idea of the crime and the idea of the punishment, so that those witnessing the ritual of punishment will fear the same fate if they commit the same crime. (This is Jeremy Bentham's view, described below.) To this extent, analogical punishments function just as magical rites do, as indexes or signals of what will happen consequent to a certain action. Indeed, like some magic spells, a number of punishments bear a purely poetic relationship to their corresponding crimes. *Manu* 12.63 reads in part "*tailaṃ tailapakaḥ khagaḥ*"—by stealing oil (*tailaṃ*), (one becomes) a cockroach (*tailapakaḥ*)—and 12.64 reads "*godhā gāṃ vāggudo guḍam*"—by stealing a cow (*gāṃ*), (one becomes) a monitor lizard (*godhā*); by stealing molasses (*guḍam*), a flying fox (*vāgguda*).[67]

There is, admittedly, a difference between magical operations at a distance and analogical punishments, most of which act directly upon the body of the patient. However, it seems inadvisable to draw too sharp a distinction. In addition to imagined punishments in the afterlife, there are examples of magical punishment at a distance, such as the burning of criminals in effigy.[68] Frazer includes in his discussion of contagious magic an example of a thief being punished in absentia through destruction of his clothing.[69] Analogical punishments clearly fall under the broader interpretations of Frazer's laws proposed by semioticians. Both analogical punishments and sympathetic magic appear to be particular cases of very general semiotic phenomena.

How should we understand the function of such devices? One plausible explanation was given by the legal reformer and utilitarian philosopher Jeremy Bentham (1748–1832), who was also an accomplished semiotician. Bentham labeled such punishments "*characteristic*": "[O]f all punishments that can be imagined, there are none of which the connection with the offence is either so easily learnt, or so efficaciously remembered, as those of which the idea is already in part associated with the offence: which is the case when the one and the other have some circumstance that belongs to them in common. When this is the case with a punishment and an offence, the punishment is said to bear an *analogy* to, or to be *characteristic* of, the offence."[70] Bentham devoted extensive discussion to the law of talion,[71] including it in the class of characteristic punishments, and even identifying it as the best member of that class, as it produces the closest analogy between crime and punishment.[72] In cases where talion is too harsh or impracticable, Bentham allowed that "recourse must be had to other sources of analogy."[73] Therefore, the sources of analogy or "characteristic circumstances will be different in different crimes. In some cases they may arise from the instrument whereby the mischief has been done; in others, from the object to which the mischief has been done; in others, from the means employed to prevent detection."[74] Applying these principles, Bentham argued that arsonists should be burned and poisoners poisoned,[75] and in other cases there should be "Punishment of the Offending Member": "In punishing the crime of forgery, the hand of the offender may be transfixed by an iron instrument fashioned like a pen; and in this condition he may be exhibited to the public . . . In the utterance of calumny, and the dissemination of false reports, the tongue is the instrument employed. The offender might in the same manner be publicly exposed with his tongue pierced."[76] The punishments advocated by Bentham scarcely differ from those in so-called "primitive" law. *Manu* provides that if a lower-caste man insults an upper-caste man, "a red-hot iron nail ten fingers long should be driven into his mouth."[77]

What mattered to Bentham was the ability of punishment to function as a deterrent sign. Consequently, he advocated using various devices, including analogy, to increase the "exemplarity" or appearance of punishment while reducing its reality.[78] Toward this end, Bentham specifically advocated maximizing the ritual formalities of punishment:

> A mode of punishment is exemplary in proportion to its *apparent*, not to its *real* magnitude . . . The object of the legislator ought therefore to be, so far as it may be safely practicable, to select such modes of punishment as, at the expense of the least *real*, shall produce the greatest *apparent* suffering; and to accompany each particular mode of punishment with such *solemnities* as may be best calculated to further this object.[79]

Bentham stated that, in the cases of forgery and calumny mentioned previously, the punishments of piercing "may be made more formidable in appearance than in reality, by dividing the instrument in two parts, so that the part which should pierce the offending member need not be thicker than a pin, whilst the other part of the instrument may be much thicker, and appear to penetrate with all its thickness."[80] He took these ideas to their logical conclusion that "If hanging a man *in effigy* would produce the same salutary impression of terror upon the minds of the people, it would be folly or cruelty ever to hang a man *in person*."[81] Bentham's philosophy of punishment culminated in a self-conscious illusionism in which punishment becomes indistinguishable from magical performance. He displayed a clear appreciation for the rhetorical force of resemblance. Another quality of punishment closely related to its exemplarity is its "popularity," or quality of being nonobjectionable to the populace.[82] Here, too, analogy plays a role. Bentham contended that "the property of characteristicalness . . . seems to go as far towards conciliating the approbation of the people to a mode of punishment, as any; insomuch that popularity may be regarded as a kind of secondary quality, depending on that of characteristicalness."[83] Similarly, he stated that "The species of punishment that command the largest share of public approbation are such as are analogous to the offence," although he confessed not to know the reason for this.[84] Therefore, a punishment that bears an analogical relation to its crime is impressive not only to the individual prospective criminal as a deterrent but also to society as a whole.[85]

Among the factors Bentham enumerated that are capable of reinforcing the association between crime and punishment were not only relations of analogy, but also proximity in time and certainty; deficiencies in either or both of these qualities would require a compensating increase in the degree of punishment.[86] Prospective criminals had to believe that punishment was swift and certain so that they would be deterred from committing offenses. Given that, in his view, the religious sanction—meaning the belief in retribution in the afterlife—had declined to the point where it was no longer an effective deterrent,[87] Bentham sought to substitute a more effective human system of punishment. Certainty of enforcement was most important in this regard, whereas proximity functioned, much as Pavlov's dinner bell did for the dogs in his famous experiment, to reinforce the idea of a conjunction through timing.

Bentham's view that the function of punishment is related to its ability to produce an association between it and the crime to which it refers is an important insight that applies to signs in general, including ritual signs. It is true that there are many signs, including some we label "religious," that aim instead to promote ambiguity: such as the Romantic idea of symbols as pregnant, overflowing with meaning, or even enigmatic.[88] But the semiotic function of the rituals we have been considering throughout this chapter is just the opposite: it is to eliminate ambiguity and achieve conviction or clarity in the transmission of a signal. Consequently, the view of some literary theorists and semioticians that interpretation and/or semiosis is "limitless" or "indeterminate" obviously cannot be applied to such rituals.[89] This describes most magic and analogical punishments as little as it describes traditional literalist readings of scripture or projects to purify or perfect language. (Both of these cases are described in later chapters of this volume.) The poetry of ritual may depend on a certain ambiguity or displacement, to the extent that it encourages the substitution of signs for things, form for content, rhyme for reason. Yet such substitution often is in the service of the production of certainty.

This is evident also from trials by ordeal, which often deploy poetic devices such as analogy, rhyme, and nonverbal repetition to reinforce the status of the ritual as an index of guilt or innocence.[90] There are numerous examples in the sixteenth-century Hindu *Divyatattva* (Treatise on Ordeals or Sacred Trials),[91] which describes nine types of ordeal (*divya*) to be applied in various circumstances: by being weighed on the balance, by carrying a red-hot iron ball, by holding one's breath under water, by taking poison, by drinking water in which an image of a deity has been bathed, by chewing dry rice without bleeding, by retrieving a coin from a cauldron of boiling oil, by licking a red-hot iron plowshare, and, lastly, by the drawing of lots. Following these ordeals, there is an account of the trial by oath (*śapatha*), which historically was closely associated with the ordeal. In the ordeal by carrying the red-hot iron ball, the accused or person tested (*śodhya*) has to carry the ball across seven concentric circles, then stand in the eighth and throw the ball into the ninth.[92] Prior to that, his hand is wrapped with, among other things, seven leaves of each of the *aśvattha*, *śamī*, and *dūrvā* plants, tied with seven strings.[93] According to some accounts, afterward, while looking for burns, the hand is rubbed with rice seven times.[94] There is a clear relationship of symmetry among these procedures: just as the iron ball has to burn through seven layers, the accused has to cross seven circles. The race between the two was thus "equalized."

The iron ball has to be heated not once, but three times.[95] Similarly, in the ordeal by drinking holy water, the accused has to sip three times,[96] and in the ordeal by chewing dry rice without bleeding, he has to spit three times.[97] The ordeals employ other nonverbal forms of repetition. Before the ordeal by the iron ball, the god of fire is invoked by red flowers.[98] In the ordeal by the drawing of lots,[99] the accused selects from a jar the image of either Dharma, the god of Justice, or Adharma, Injustice. These images are, respectively, white and black, and are invoked by flowers of the same colors, as well as by the *pañcagavya* or five products of the cow: milk, curd, clarified butter, urine, and dung. The *pañcagavya* represent a different form of repetition, the exhaustive enumeration of all excretions of the sacred cow.

The repetitive and poetic nature of the Hindu ordeals is perhaps most evident in the various mantras or invocations with which they begin. Each ordeal is preceded by oblations to the 108 gods of all the directions. The following exhaustive formula is written on a leaf and attached to the head of the accused:[100]

āditya candrāv anilo 'nalaś ca	The Sun, the Moon, the Wind, the Fire,
dyaur bhūmir āpo hṛdayam yamaś ca	the Sky, the Earth, the Waters, the Heart, the God of Death,
ahaś ca rātriś ca ubhe ca sandhye	the Day, the Night, the Sunrise, and the Sunset,
dharmo hi jānāti narasya vṛttam	as well as Dharma, know the acts of men.

Invocations are then used to summon the particular god or element presiding over the ordeal. These invocations sometimes involve the use of alliteration or paronomasia, as in the formula in the ordeal by hot oil,[101] which begins with simple alliteration: "*param pavitram amṛtam . . .*" ("the best purifier, ambrosia . . .").

The invocation of fire in the ordeal of the heated iron ball adds extra alliteration to an otherwise proper etymology:[102] "You are called 'purifier' because you purify sin" (*pāpam punāsi vai yasmāt tasmāt pāvaka ucyate*). As with English "whence" and "thence," the relative-correlative markers appearing in this formula, *yasmāt tasmāt*, while semantically related, also rhyme. "Purifier" (*pāvaka*) bears a real etymological connection to "purify" (*punāsi*) through the verbal root "pū," but only a resemblance in sound to "sin" (*pāpa*). This formula is of the type that have sometimes been called "folk" or "fictitious etymologies." (See Chapter Three for a discussion of these.) The invocation in the ordeal by weighing on the balance is a clearer example of such devices. The word for balance is *dhaṭa*, the two consonants of which become the basis for the following invocation:[103]

> *dhakārād dharmamūrtis tvaṃ ṭakārāt kuṭilaṃ naram/ dhṛto dhārayase yasmād dhaṭas tenābhidhīyate*

From the letter "dha," you are the embodiment of justice (*dharma*); from the letter "ṭa," when raised (*dhṛta*), you raise (*dhārayase*) the dishonest (*kuṭilaṃ*) man, therefore you are called "dhaṭa."

Such etymologies have a venerable history in the context of Hindu ritual. In the *Brāhmaṇas* and *Upaniṣads*, they often describe the secret "relations" (*bandhu*) that are the ultimate meaning and source of efficacy of the ritual. (See Chapter Three.)

These poetic devices including fictitious etymologies appear in many cases designed to motivate or naturalize the ordeals and diminish the appearance of their arbitrariness. It is significant that, as in the ordeals found in other cultures, the power of determining the guilt or innocence of the accused is often given over to some elemental substance or entity such as fire or water. In this way, the contribution of arbitrary or human motivations to the result of the ordeal seems to be minimized, and the result may be regarded as a direct expression of natural or cosmic forces. To promote greater confidence in the outcome, the invocations of the *Divyatattva* exploit coincidental phonetic resemblances, repetition, and exhaustion to rhetorically reinforce the instruments of the ordeal, including fire and the balance, with respect to their ritual function of determining guilt or innocence.

The ordeal is a method of proof that is normally resorted to only in the absence of more direct evidence. Out of this basic condition of uncertainty, the ordeal must construct a clear determination of guilt or innocence. This is the source of the "binary" function of the ordeal, which is normally allowed to answer only "yes" or "no," not "maybe." The ordeal by drawing of lots is the simplest way of constructing such a binary system. In the *Divyatattva*, for example, the accused draws from a vessel either a black or a white figure indicating guilt or innocence. Temporal proximity, as in Bentham's theory of punishment, is also important: in the case of some trials, the person is checked after a certain period of time has elapsed from the performance of the ordeal. If there is no injury, sickness, burn, etc., the accused is found innocent, having been exonerated by the gods.[104] The semiotics of this type of ordeal depends also on establishing a "bright line" or absolute cutoff so that there can be a clear determination of guilt. Despite the general triumph of realism over formalism, modern law also includes such bright lines as statutes of limitations and arbitrary ages of majority (e.g. 18, 21), which contribute to certainty in the legal system.

It is significant that many ordeals, such as trials by fire, by submersion in water, or by poison, themselves establish through the operation of the ritual a situation in which it would be normal to be burned, drowned, or poisoned. The ordeal itself constructs a natural index of injury, which has to be defeated by a countervailing supernatural index.[105] If the accused emerges unscathed, divine intervention establishes his or her innocence. Such a sign of innocence has to overcome the "distortion" or static produced by the ordeal, thereby proving its power as a sign. Of course, the fact that many trials by ordeal would normally be expected to produce injury or even death is also a powerful deterrent to undergoing such rituals, and establishes a social sanction that favors negotiation or the alternative mediation of disputes. Nor is the choice of the accused ever free from social bias, as Evans-Pritchard's studies of witchcraft accusations emphasized.[106] Yet such aspects of social context do not account for the formal features of the ordeal, which are often best understood in semiotic terms.

The most common reaction to ordeals has been to declare them a species of superstition that reflects a belief in the supernatural and its power to suspend the natural order. However, a minority opinion has sought to uphold the rationality of these rituals through naturalistic, scientific, or physiological principles.[107] The medieval ritual of the corsned involved eating a morsel of dry bread; some have argued that an accused who was guilty would have a dry mouth and be unable to perform this trial.[108] Similarly, J. Duncan M. Derrett argued that, in the Hindu trial by fire,[109] an innocent person would supposedly perspire less and escape blisters; in the water ordeal,[110] an innocent person would have a lower rate of pulse and respiration and be able to remain submerged longer; and in the ordeal of chewing uncooked dry rice without bleeding,[111] the dry mouth of a guilty person would "make failure inevitable."[112] Such attempts to rationalize ordeals appear strained. One can imagine them being extended with some plausibility to certain cases, such as those involving a waiting period, in which the guilty mind might eventually break down and suffer psychosomatic illness or, perhaps, produce a confession. However, in the case of other ordeals—such as drinking the poison[113] or drawing lots[114]—no physiological explanation appears adequate. In these and other cases, attention to the basic semiotic function of the ordeal to achieve certainty or "conviction"—in a double sense—often provides a more adequate explanation.

Chiasmus and communication

One curious feature of a number of rituals, including Tantric mantras, is their deployment of palindromes or chiasmus. Arguably, talion and similar analogical punishments are already a form of inversion: "what goes around, comes around." In some cases, explicitly chiastic formulas are used to depict retaliation. *Manu 5.55* promotes vegetarianism by describing the retribution for eating meat:

māṃ sa bhakṣayitāmutra yasya māṃsam ihādmy aham

etan māṃsasya māṃsatvaṃ pravadanti manīṣinaḥ

Which translates as:

"Me he (*māṃ sa*) will eat in the next world, whose meat (*māṃsa*) I eat in this world"– this, the wise declare, is what gave the name to and discloses the true nature of "meat" (*māṃsa*).[115]

The karmic punishment expressed in this verse is in the form of a folk etymology, where the word for a thing is supposed to disclose the true nature of that thing. This is another example of the belief in the consubstantiality of speech with physical reality, or an essential connection between words and things. Like some other examples of karma described previously, this punishment relies on alliteration. There is also a parallelism between the first and second halves of the first line: "*māṃ sa . . . yasya māṃsam*" etc. Substantively, this has the logical form of an inverted "if-then" proposition, in which the consequence is spelled out first, followed by its condition of occurrence. This indexical relationship is reinforced and rendered more symmetrical by the addition of a pair of indexical phrases marking spatiotemporal location ("in the next world" vs "in this world").

Examples can be found in other cultures, as in the Hebrew Bible's formulations of the law of talion. As many scholars have noted, Leviticus 24:13–23 encloses the basic talionic formula ("eye for eye, tooth for tooth") within an elaborate chiasmus.[116] The letters to the left of the verses have been added to highlight this chiastic structure:

A1	13 And the Lord said to Moses,
B1	14 "Bring out of the camp him who cursed; and let all who heard him lay their hands upon his head, and let all the congregation stone him.
C1	15 And say to the people of Israel, Whoever curses his God shall bear his sin.
D1	16 He who blasphemes the name of the Lord shall be put to death; all the congregation shall stone him; the sojourner as well as the native, when he blasphemes the Name, shall be put to death.

E1	17 He who kills a man shall be put to death.
F1	18 He who kills a beast shall make it good, life for life.
G1	19 When a man causes a disfigurement in his neighbor, as he has done it shall be done to him,
H	20 fracture for fracture, eye for eye, tooth for tooth;
G2	as he has disfigured a man, he shall be disfigured.
F2	21 He who kills a beast shall make it good;
E2	and he who kills a man shall be put to death.
D2	22 You shall have one law for the sojourner and for the native; for I am the Lord your God."
C2	23 So Moses spoke to the people of Israel;
B2	and they brought him who had cursed out of the camp, and stoned him with stones.
A2	Thus the people of Israel did as the Lord commanded Moses.[117]

As John Welch notes, "the [basic] talionic formula [i.e. "eye for eye, tooth for tooth"] stands squarely at the physical and conceptual center" of the chiasmus, which "lends itself formally to the substantive content of talionic justice."[118] Such literary forms appear to serve both a rhetorical and a mnemonic function, by simultaneously reinforcing the idea of retribution and making it more memorable. Both persuasion and memorability, however, are only specialized aspects of a more general function of communication. In Leviticus 24, God lays down the law, in the form of a verbal command, and at the end of the passage, what God has commanded is performed. This is a representation of successful communication between the divine and human realms. The same appears to be true of *Manu* 5.55, which also uses parallelism to depict a reciprocity between this world and the next. Such examples denote the belief in a justice that is immanent in the world, or at least certain in the next world. They also mirror, on the level of language, the relationship of reciprocity or quid-pro-quo that seems particularly appropriate to the concept of retribution. As Mary Douglas said of such punishments, "They chime with justice."[119]

Chiasmus is often employed in situations in which the act of communication or dialogue is itself highlighted. The inversion of word order is quite common, not only in English but in other languages as well, in framing questions. This inversion calls forth an answer that reverses the word order of the question:

Will you wash the dishes?

I will wash the dishes.

What sort of dog does Lucinda have?

Lucinda has a toy dog.

In the first example, the auxiliary verb ("will") comes before the pronoun to signal a question, and the answer then reestablishes the normal order of pronoun-verb-object. In the second example, the object comes before the subject and verb. The dialogical rhythm of question-and-answer is reinforced by the inversion of word order.

Similar inversions characterize and help to define the structure of some other communicative acts, such as call-and-response, as in the following English and Arabic greetings:

How are you?

I am fine.

as-salām 'alē-kum (Peace be upon you.)

wa 'alē-kum as-salām (And upon you be peace.)

The reciprocal relationship between the person giving and the one receiving the Arabic greeting is mirrored in the chiasmic form of the greeting itself.[120]

In the case of Tantric mantras, as noted above, one of the common ways of making these effective is by enveloping them with certain seed-mantras in forward and reverse order at beginning and end. This has the effect of converting them into quasi-palindromes, at the syllabic level. It also converts the mantra into a diagram of speech itself, as is most evident when the entire Sanskrit alphabet is used to envelop a mantra. This alphabet is organized in such a way that the vowels are enumerated first, followed by the consonants. The order of enumeration follows the path of speech along the vocal pathway, from the back of the throat (a-ka) to the front of the lips (u-ma). It is possible that the sacred syllable *om* (or "a-u-m") represents a condensed diagram of speech. Therefore, when *om*, or the entire alphabet, is pronounced in forward and reverse order at the beginning and end of the mantra, it figuratively diagrams the act of communication itself. The *haṃsa* mantra (*haṃsaḥ so 'haṃ*), which incorporates the sound *om* sandwiched in between the seed mantras representing the god Śiva (*ha*) and his consort Śakti (*sa*), represents a different sort of communication: sexual intercourse, which becomes the paradigm for rendering the mantra effective. (See Table 2.4 above.) The *haṃsa* mantra echoes earlier male-female palindromes found as far back as the *Vedas*.[121]

Tantric mantras provide the most elaborate and explicit case of the poetic function—understood as a self-reflexive announcement of the event of communication—of which I am aware. However, they are not unique.

Many spells in the Greek magical papyri deploy palindromes, including magic words such as *ablanathanalba* (which is similar to *abracadabra*), or the sequence of seven Greek vowels, as in the example given below, which repeats each vowel a certain number of times in accordance with its position in the sequence of seven, then does the same in reverse order.[122] These vowels (from alpha to omega) also roughly follow the path of speech from throat to lips, suggesting an attempt to mimic the act of speech and to harness it for pragmatic purposes, although this must remain speculation.[123]

α	ωωωωωωω
εε	υυυυυυ
ηηη	οοοοο
ιιιι	ιιιι
οοοοο	ηηη
υυυυυυ	εε
ωωωωωωω	α

An interesting feature of some of these chiasmi is that they cannot be explained as an effect of oral culture. Bernard Jackson refers to Leviticus 24 as a "literary chiasmus":[124] because the pattern is too elaborate to be evident upon hearing, presumably it was designed in written form, which allows for backward scanning and the recognition of more complex structures. Similarly, the repetition of the entire Sanskrit alphabet both forward and backward, combined with other vocables, would seem to require visualization if not actual writing; and we know also that these formulas were sometimes written down. The analogous patterns in the Greek magical papyri, as the one given above, were certainly written when used in magic.

Like related symbolic forms, chiasmus employs imitation to establish a reciprocity or symmetry between two qualities. Such forms of imitation are basic to human communication and cognition. They may also be used to reinforce a spell as an indexical sign, and even to represent or depict the act of communication itself. This is a key example of the phenomenon of semiotic recognition described in Chapter One.

Repetition, chiasmus, and salvation

A final example of the contributions made by repetition and chiasmus to the reinforcement of indexical relationships brings us somewhat outside the domain of ritual, though still within the domain of religion. The thirteenth-century Italian poet Dante Alighieri's *Comedy* expresses throughout its structure the idea of the Holy Trinity that appears at the end of the poem. The poet devised an elaborate trinitarian structure for the *Comedy* so as best to express the nature of the Triune God, and to that end even created the verse form of rhymed tercets (*terza rima*), with their progressive rhyme scheme: ABA, BCB, CDC, and so on. From beginning to end, the *Comedy* consists of a series of trinities, each looking backward to the one immediately preceding and forward to the one immediately following. Ultimately all such trinities anticipate, and achieve their consummation in, the Holy Trinity. As August Schlegel argued:

> It would be a mistake to see th[e] numerical symmetry [in the *Comedy*] simply as an idle game in Gothic taste; it is just as important as similar interrelations in Gothic architecture. The number three constitutes a mysterious and in itself perfect unity which can be traced through the whole of the work, from the mystery of the Trinity to the form of the *terza rima* itself.[125]

The Trinity is expressed also at larger structural levels of the *Comedy*: each of its three major divisions or canticles (*cantiche*)—the *Inferno, Purgatory,* and *Paradise*—ends with the word "stars" (*stelle*). The three canticles are in this way made to rhyme, as if they represented separate poetic lines joined in a single verse. Within each of these three major divisions, there is a different threefold structure.[126] As Mark Musa notes: "The poem consists of one hundred cantos, divided into three major sections: *Inferno, Purgatory,* and *Paradise*. The *Purgatory* and the *Paradise* contain 33 cantos each, while the *Inferno* has 34, the opening canto serving as an introduction to the work as a whole. The structural formula for the great masterpiece is, then, 1 + 33 + 33 + 33."[127] Although there is no fixed number of tercets in each canto, there are 33 syllables in each tercet: three lines of 11 syllables each, indicating a parallelism among the three members of this smallest trinity that mirrors the parallelism among the three canticles in respect of the number of cantos each contains.

Table 2.6 Structure of Dante's *Comedy*

Division					Totals
First	canticles	*Inferno*	*Purgatory*	*Paradise*	3 canticles
Second	cantos	1 + 33	33	33	100 cantos
Third	tercets				3 lines of 11 = 33 syllables each

In addition to such elaborate numerical repetitions, the *Comedy* deploys inversion or semantic chiasmus, most obviously in the graphic retributions imposed on sinners in Hell. Those who have committed violent crimes against others are immersed in boiling blood.[128] In the circle of traitors, Count Ugolino gnaws upon the head of the man who starved him to death.[129] The hypocrites are crushed by robes golden on the outside, but leaden within.[130] One headless inmate explains: "Because I parted [a father from his son] I carry my brain, alas, parted from its root in this trunk; thus is observed in me the retribution."[131] And there is a more elaborate literary chiasmus that depicts the talion imposed on the ultimate sinner. Satan, who has three heads, is lodged upside-down in the center of the ninth and last circle of Hell. Satan is both a likeness and an inversion of the Holy Trinity, which rests precisely at the opposite end of the cosmos, at the top of the Empyrean. The trinitarian "rhyme" is also a "palindrome." Satan and the Holy Trinity appear in the final cantos of their respective canticles (*Inferno* 34 and *Paradise* 33), constructing a kind of rhyme between the first and third canticles which parallels that occurring between the first and third lines of each rhymed tercet, similar to Schlegel's prescient suggestion:

> Seen from a different point of view, the *terza rima* again mirrors the three spiritual levels: Paradise and Hell are absolute opposites and hence evince a certain similarity and symmetry, as though they were meant to constitute a rhyme for one another; Purgatory, on the other hand, represents the transitional space between them and functions as a kind of negative, exactly like the middle line inserted between the two rhyming lines of the *terza rima*.[132]

The Holy Trinity completes and perfects the trinitarian ideal that Satan had imperfectly reflected, both by being upside-down and by being placed in the thirty-fourth rather than thirty-third canto of the *Inferno*. This device also allows the Holy Trinity to mirror precisely the trinitarian ideal by appearing in the thirty-third and final canto of its canticle, and to "square the circle" by rounding up the number of cantos in the *Comedy* to 100.

Dante's exhaustive, even obsessive network of trinitarian equivalences certainly indexes his reverence for God. However, this network also points beyond the poet's particular theological views to some general features of poetry. Through the use of diagrams based on the number three, qualitatively different structural levels of the *Comedy* are brought into equivalence. Numerical equivalences are projected beyond the phonetic level of the poem to encompass the parallel and simultaneous semantic level of the narrative. Precisely such narrative "semes" as Satan and the Holy Trinity, sequenced by the parallel poetic structure, constitute the "rhyming" units of the canticles as poetic "lines." The progressive accumulation, through poetic performance, of such trinitarian equivalences directs (if only from the perspective of one who is clued in to this device) the reader's journey to the Holy Trinity, and so to salvation, which is maximally indexed as the terminus of both poetic form and narrative content. In this regard, the *Comedy* functions like many of the poetic spells analyzed earlier in this chapter.

The reality of magic

The reader may regard my rhetorical theory of poetic performance as a more elaborate (and, I believe, more comprehensive and explanatory) version of the old theory that magic is a form of deception; and on this basis, he or she might be skeptical of my explanation, on the grounds that it appears to reinstate the old distinction between "primitive" and "scientific" (not to mention "false" and "true") modes of thought. A great deal of ink has been spilled over the question of whether magic, understood in this sense, is really believed in; can or ought to be distinguished from other genres; or is instead a projection of our own biases onto cultures that used to be called "primitive."[133] Many anthropologists now regard "magic" as a pejorative category that precludes a proper understanding of the practices of other cultures. Certainly, any behavior that is apparently symbolic should be taken as an invitation to deeper inquiry into the cosmology and social context that renders such behavior understandable. Following E. E. Evans-Pritchard's nuanced account of witchcraft among the Azande—a set of practices that differs entirely from Frazer's category of magic, and that is amenable to explanation in terms of the social motivations for accusations of witchcraft[134]—the very category of magic has been discredited. Intellectualist explanations of magic as mistaken reasoning have largely given way to an emphasis on the social function of such practices, or on the nature of such practices as aesthetic or expressive, or even to rejections of the category of magic as a projection with no basis in social reality.[135]

Like many scholars, including Edmund Leach and Keith Thomas, I believe that the category of "magic" remains useful to describe certain practices.[136] Given that this category has become so controversial, it is appropriate to give some of my reasons for invoking it. First, although it is true that such practices are not universal—as Evans-Pritchard's account of the Azande already demonstrated—they are widely distributed across cultures. We have to provide some account of such regularities, or abandon the project of a general anthropology or science of humanity. Second, while it is true that it is always better to investigate carefully all beliefs and practices in their context of meaning, as Evans-Pritchard did, when we attempt to do so we by no means find that magic vanishes like an illusion. Instead, what we frequently encounter, as I did both while reconstructing centuries-old Hindu *Tantras* composed in Sanskrit and while collecting Bengali charms from an *ojha* or snakebite healer in Bangladesh in 1998, is an apparent belief in the efficacy of magic, meaning the ability of such formulas to alter physical reality. In the case of the *Tantras*, this view is based upon a sophisticated cosmology that maintains the consubstantiality of language with both nature and the divine, an idea that is rendered quite explicitly in such claims as "The body of the god arises immediately upon pronunciation of the seed mantra."[137] Unless we dismiss such beliefs as nonsense, which seems to me a worse form of cultural imperialism than taking them at face value, we are stuck with a hard puzzle: How is it that such practices reinforce the belief in their own efficacy? What explains the regular or at least nonrandom association of poetic devices with magical practices?

Jonathan Z. Smith contends that ritual is, above all, an ordinary form of behavior, a mode of working through certain problems.[138] Expressions of so-called magic supposedly reflect an awareness precisely of the incongruity or gap between the actual state of affairs and the ideal situation of which the ritual constitutes an expression, rather than any belief in the ability of ritual to overcome that gap. Rituals are performed in conscious contemplation of the gap that obtains between them and the actual state of affairs: they are done out of recognition rather than misrecognition. The magician or ritualist does not believe that magic works, but constructs an ideal world that deviates from reality precisely out of the awareness that things are not as we would like them to be.

This is an ingenious explanation, which I find myself unable to agree with. First, it requires us to discount apparently clear assertions of the efficacy of magic. It projects our own recognition of the counterfactual status of such statements or operations onto others. And it ignores the fact that human beings often believe what is false, or behave in ways that run counter to reality, out of motives that are sometimes evident to outside observers more than they are to those who engage in such behavior. Where, indeed, would religion be without a sincere belief in the counterfactual? As argued above, it is true that the devices used to "supercharge" ritual signs are deployed in response precisely to the very counterfactual status of that state of affairs which ritual is supposed to bring about. However, this is not the same thing as a full recognition of, much less an acquiescence to, reality. Second, as we have seen, what magic often attempts is precisely to bridge the gap between the actual and a projected state of affairs—sometimes by tracing a continuity between the ritual and an event-in-context—rather than to counsel acceptance of things as they are.

Smith's effort to rehabilitate ritual as a mode of work that focuses reflection on the gap between the real and the imagined is a fruitful move that helps us to recognize the performative dimensions of ritual. However, we must recognize also how the manner in which ritual works as a mode of performance has been transformed in modernity. This transformation is highlighted by a difference in views toward ritual repetition. Indigenous accounts of repetition often claim or imply that repetition "works" in the sense of producing a result. The more one repeats the words of a certain prayer, or performs some other ritual action, the more effective the ritual supposedly becomes. The paradigm case or extreme form of this belief is the spell or incantation. Take, for example, the opinion of Hindu Tantra that the more one repeats a mantra, the more successful it will be.[139]

The Tantric view of ritual repetition exposes the wide gulf that separates us from what Eliade called the "archaic ontology,"[140] in which imitation and other forms of repetition are understood to contribute to the effectiveness of the ritual. To put it simply, we no longer share this understanding. Many contemporary scholars have attempted to rehabilitate these rituals from the charge that they are mere superstition. However, the contemporary truism that such practices are meaningful "in context" still leaves the problem of how to account for such pervasive, cross-cultural features of ritual as repetition, which is precisely not "arbitrary," in the twin senses that it is found to be nonrandomly associated with ritual (i.e. with greater frequency than in other modes of discourse) and that it often, as in the case of Hindu Tantric mantras, constitutes an attempt to construct ritual as a kind of "natural language" that imitates reality and can influence it prospectively. Ritual discourse frequently reflects an attempt to overcome the arbitrariness of the sign through imitation and other forms of repetition, which therefore function as a kind of rhetoric to produce conviction in the efficacy of ritual. The Tantric techniques for making mantras effective (*siddha*) by converting them into diagrams of creation represent an indigenous theory of ritual performance. However, in its insistence on the real, physical effects produced by mantras, this theory is far removed from modern theories of ritual performance, which emphasize, to the contrary, the aesthetic, psychological, parasympathetic, or rhetorical dimensions of ritual practice.

As we saw, although Smith is skeptical concerning the category of "magic," he accepts the idea that there is a rhetoric of association of ideas, and generalizes this rhetoric beyond the primitive, by identifying it in Frazer's own discourse. If the conclusion is simply that magical thinking cannot be confined to premodern or traditional cultures, then we should happily agree. Indeed, the type of rhetoric found in magic is much more broadly distributed, and has affinities especially with advertising and political slogans.[141] Yet this does not prevent us from taking the category of magic as an exemplary case of a broader phenomenon, so long as we do not use this category to argue for an unbridgeable difference between "primitive" and "scientific" thought, in a manner that repeats the worst sins of European ethnocentrism and social Darwinism.

Stanley Tambiah's account of ritual performance recognized that repetition and analogical devices help to produce persuasion. However, in his desire to rehabilitate the "magical power of words" from the charge of falsity or meaninglessness,[142] he minimized the divide between emic (insider's) and etic (outsider's) views of performance," deftly substituting a new version of the latter for the former. Tambiah attributed to ritual traditions an awareness of the nature of ritual as a rhetorical performance, an awareness that often appears to be absent from the overt expressions of native informants or the evidence afforded by textual traditions, such as the Hindu *Tantras*, which assert the ability of verbal and other forms of ritual repetition to work magic or heal the sick. Tambiah therefore arrived at a conclusion similar to Smith's. Tambiah's explanation of ritual as a form of aesthetic expression appears to be an anachronism, a projection of modern attitudes onto the past. The difference between magic, on the one hand, and dance, music, and other forms of art, on the other, is that magic is not simply about aesthetics: it makes a claim on the world, and competes with the indexical form of the syllogism, while invoking substitute sign-relations to point, with increasing urgency, at a state of affairs that it seeks to bring about. As such, magic makes a truth claim that cannot be separated from its evaluation as an aesthetic object.

Despite the analogy that has frequently been drawn, by Tambiah and others, between magical rituals and those culturally effective modes of expression that Austin labeled "performatives," the former, unlike the latter, are not automatically effective. The types of rhetoric employed in both cases do converge, indicating that the use in magic of culturally effective forms of speech may be parasitic upon the ordinary use of such forms. Although the pronunciation of a precise formula in fulfillment of other conventional ceremonial conditions may serve, from a cultural standpoint, to alter, even irrevocably, one's legal or social status, the same cannot be said of a magical ritual where the goal is to influence physical reality. Repeated imperatives designed to command or persuade our neighbor may turn out to be no more effective than those directed at the gods; but at least they have a chance to work. This is one reason why the category of magic, as a special mode of expressive action, remains so stubbornly useful, despite efforts to discard it.

Another reason for retaining the category of magic as such is that it does appear to mark a certain relative difference from modern thought. Long before Frazer, there were polemics against "vain repetitions" in prayer as a form of illicit and fraudulent magic, and against the idea that ritual signs could function to bring about or embody that which they signified. To some extent, as described in Chapter Five, these polemics reflected developments internal to European Christianity during the Protestant Reformation. Although such polemics might be dismissed as evidence of a theological bias shaping the category of "magic," it appears that such Puritan complaints astutely singled out some of the features and functions of magic and other rituals.[143] The relative exclusion of such ritual practices from certain genres (such as science, law, and other authorized discourses) is evidence of the Protestant contribution to the semiotic ideology of modernity, a contribution described in later chapters of this book.

It should be pointed out that, under the flag of respecting cultural differences, what some scholars have done is to suppress such differences, by denying clear evidence of magical thought and retrospectively projecting their own cosmologies, anthropologies, and concepts of agency onto other peoples. Sadly, this has had the effect of extending rather than interrogating the hegemony of modern thought, and rendering one of the important dimensions of modernity, namely disenchantment, and in particular the decline of magic, unintelligible.

The question of deception: Pavlov's dogs and dirty dancing

I appreciate the impulse to avoid the conclusion that magic is false. Reaching this conclusion raises once again the prospect of a hierarchy of discourses, and perhaps even of cultures. Yet some of the logic that has been deployed to avoid this conclusion is itself exemplary of the universal human capacity for tortured logic and self-deception. Even a modestly observant student of human nature should recognize that deception is more common than honesty. While it may be easier to recognize others' fallacies than our own, as long as we preserve a certain humility, the comparative study of cultures offers an open laboratory for the study of rhetoric.

As Leach noted, what the magician does is similar to what Pavlov, or perhaps Pavlov's dogs, did: misrepresent or mistake a coincidental, extraneous sign as a cause. Constant conjunction or co-occurrence are frequently interpreted as signifying a causal relationship. The magician constructs, in some cases, a whole series of adventitious causes, and harnesses them to the prospective goal of the ritual by deictics or "pointers," in order to create a rhetorically effective illusion.

Godfrey Lienhardt has argued against this interpretation:

> [T]hose symbolic acts which are regularly performed, like the sacrifices made after the harvest, take place at a time when people are already beginning to experience naturally (as we should say) something of the result which the ceremony is intended to bring about, or at least may soon expect to do so. . . . In these [their regular ceremonies] their human symbolic action moves with the rhythm of the natural world around them, re-creating that rhythm in moral terms and not merely attempting to coerce it to conformity with human desires.[144]

Lienhardt observed that the Dinka perform the rain-dance ritual at the end of the season of drought, just on the verge of the rains. They do not perform the ritual in the middle of the drought. Supposedly, this indicates that they are aware of the weather, and the periodicity of the seasons, and adjust their behavior accordingly so that the ritual is precisely not counterfactual, but rather an instance of careful planning. (This interpretation appears to contradict Jonathan Z. Smith's argument that ritual highlights the gap between itself and reality as, according to Lienhardt, an effort is made to avoid said gap.)

Lienhardt's example actually proves my point. Here's why. The timing of the rain dance can be viewed as parasitic, a piggybacking on the natural cycle of rains, in the same way that the bell in Pavlov's experiment was parasitically attached to the dogs' mealtimes. What made this experiment noteworthy, of course, was that it demonstrated that the parasitic index had the power to make the dogs salivate in anticipation even when no food was brought. Constant conjunction had led them to associate the two events so strongly that, even when they were separated, the dogs behaved as if their meal was about to arrive. In the same way, the magician deploys a variety of indexes to create anticipation, which is always counterfactual until satisfied.

What may have thrown off some scholars is the label of deception. This is a loaded term that carries a profoundly negative connotation for many people. But what I am here calling "deception" exists on a broader continuum with a range of human behaviors that are utterly normal. This mitigates any negative value judgment that would otherwise attach to the label. For example, there are ritualized behaviors of courtship that resemble magic in a number of respects. Dancing is a kind of ritual. Especially in a number of its modern forms, it also is an imitation of sexual intercourse involving physical contact, gyrations, etc. Dance both simulates and stimulates erotic activity. Although dance can be a prelude to actual intercourse, it need not be. Dance is defeasible as a predictor of greater levels of social intimacy; as such, it is like magic, which is similarly defeasible if the event that it predicts and seeks to bring about fails to occur. Only the most extreme prude or Puritan would label dance as such a form of deception. However, I think it can be recognized that in dance there is maintained a certain plausible deniability such that the expectation of something further can always be disavowed by either or both parties.

A recent experiment studied the sounds women make during sex with their male partners.[145] It turns out that these sounds have nothing to do with whether the woman is having an orgasm. The timing, frequency, and intensity of the sounds were a response to the women's male partners, and were interpreted quite reasonably by the researchers as a way of encouraging the men to "hurry up and finish." One, uncharitable way of interpreting such behavior, then, is as a form of deception: a "fake orgasm." But that would be too harsh. It is really more like Pavlov's dinner bell, only that there is no intention of depriving the dog of his dinner. "Encouragement" or "anticipation" seems about right.

The magician's deployment of signals may be similarly well-intentioned. Of course, if it is clearly understood that such signals have no chance of working, then the term "deception" may be more appropriate. But I am not invested in proving the magician a liar, no more than I am in condemning human beings for other, similar behaviors.

Excursus: encounter with a fakir

My encounter with a fakir or Muslim holy man in Dhaka, Bangladesh in 1998 provides a further illustration of how magic works through the manipulation of indexical signs. After engaging in some small talk, the fakir asked a series of questions of the form: "Have you ever been to country X (e.g. Russia)?" etc. If the answer was "Yes," he could appear to know the history of his targeted client. If the answer was "No," then his question could be reframed as a suggestion: "You should go to country X." The illusion of mind-reading depends on some of the same semiotic processes as the more outright forms of magic. The fakir's question was an ambivalent index that could be interpreted retrospectively and strategically in accordance with his target's answer; this afforded the fakir plausible deniability. The fakir's track record as a mind reader was terrible: he had no accuracy in predicting which countries I had visited, nor how many siblings, nor whether I was married, etc. He cultivated the appearance of randomness in his topics of discussion, an appearance which was supposed to indicate wisdom (the wisdom of fools and children?), but which we can see had other functions, as a random "hit," like an apparent violation of the laws of nature, appears especially significant.

The fakir had agreed to meet with me on one condition: that I not drink any alcohol. He didn't object to cigarettes. In Bangladesh, which is a dry country, his taboos were rather convenient for the locals. Note, again, the sign-function of this taboo: all of the time I was meeting with him, I was "not drinking alcohol." The fakir invited me to go with him and his partner, an engineer fluent in English, to a kabab restaurant on the north side of town, toward the airport. His accomplice having excused himself after eating on the grounds that he had prayers to attend to, I was left alone with the fakir. This was deliberate, as I was asked later by my host (not the engineer/fakir's accomplice, but the person who had arranged my meeting with the fakir) if I had been shown a "sign." The fakir had arranged the place carefully, as he began to show me what he afterward called his "remote control": he claimed to be able to make the wind move through the trees. After explaining that he would do this, he started saying *Jore, jore* (stronger, stronger), usually in couplets like that, over and over. Then he would point somewhere else and say *Dekho* (look), and repeat the process. After some initial encouragement from me, he continued to demonstrate his ability to control the wind. However, in subsequent attempts the wind often failed to strengthen; and once I caught him saying *Dekho, jore, jore* after the wind had already picked up. The fakir had a better view of his side of the thatch-roofed booth, as well as of spots behind me, and made his selection from among these. He could witness, to some extent, the wind's progression through the leaves of the trees before it became visible to me. This increased his ability to predict when the wind would be strong; but if the wind was slow, he could always keep repeating *Jore, jore* until it finally picked up. Even this leeway did not suffice in a few instances, when his predictions proved inaccurate.

It is clear that the "magic" of this business consists in creating an indexical relation in which the imperative (*jore, jore*) appeared to precede, and entail, the increase in wind. But there was strategic latitude in the construction of this relationship, a latitude produced by a tendency to see the event for what the magician signaled it to be, through his use of the imperative. The indexical relation thus created or inferred was a cognitive illusion based on the idea that the imperative both preceded the natural phenomenon and caused it. This was a complete reversal of the actual indexical relation, as the magician's prediction was made when it was likely to be followed by the phenomenon, that is, when the phenomenon had already been signaled by other trees, by the passage of time, etc. This is analogous to the performance of rain-making ceremonies on the eve of the rainy season.

CHAPTER THREE

Natural, arbitrary, and divine languages

The naturalization of arbitrariness

The question of whether signs are natural or, on the other hand, arbitrary and instituted by cultures and individuals, is one of the fundamental questions of semiotics. This question was already proposed, though not resolved, in Plato's dialogue *Cratylus*, in which the debate was over whether language is based on nature (*physis*) or cultural laws (*nomos*).[1] According to the common structuralist view, Ferdinand de Saussure's resolution of this question in favor of the arbitrariness of linguistic signs allowed him to arrive at the fundamental principles of a science of language.[2] It is an axiom of modern semiotic theory that signs—or at least cultural signs, which include all language—are arbitrary. They bear no necessary connection to that which they signify, and are not motivated by some special relationship of fitness to their referents. From this perspective, the belief of many cultures in a natural language, one that perfectly reflects and may even influence reality, is a form of naïveté.

The present chapter considers a number of claims for the naturalness of language and other modes of expression. While upholding the structuralist axiom of the arbitrariness of the sign, I suggest that we may view such claims, although not literally true, as important instances of rhetoric that reveal significant dimensions of cultural imagination and practice. More than merely a scientific doctrine, the arbitrariness of the sign poses a human predicament that is arguably universal: the problem of how to communicate in a world of crossed signals and uncertain meanings. To understand how human beings respond to this challenge, which is as much existential as practical, we need to move beyond the doctrine of arbitrariness to account for the role that particular types of signs—including especially icons, such as those described in the preceding chapter—play in the rhetoric of culture.

Current approaches to the semiotic divide between nature and culture have been strongly influenced by structuralism. The impossibility of establishing a direct, one-to-one connection between signifier and signified requires an alternative solution to the production of meaning, the creation of distinctions within an originally undifferentiated field of sounds (in the case of language) and the arbitrary mapping of such distinctions onto the world, so as to establish a relationship between words and things. Therefore, meaning is never isolated but always consists of a value which is positional and relational. Hence the importance of "structure."

Lévi-Strauss's application of these principles to myth grew out of his earlier study of the incest prohibition in different cultures. Anthropology has struggled with the question of whether there are any values that are held or practices that are observed universally across different cultures. The amazing variety of human activity and expression generally suggests a negative answer to this question. The incest prohibition is among the very few candidates for the status of a "universal." Even so, there is a diversity of kinship rules and regulations in different societies. The degree of consanguinity or familial relation that serves to establish the threshold for the prohibition of sexual relations varies from culture to culture; and there is also of course the fact that such incest taboos are not always observed.

Lévi-Strauss concluded his study by arguing for an analogy or even an identity between two apparent human universals—the incest prohibition and language—as systems of communication and exchange, whether of women or of words.[3] The network of kinship distinctions establishes patterns similar to those found in language, which also operates by creating distinctions. Lévi-Strauss went on to apply these principles to myth; it was no accident that his early essay "The Structural Study of Myth" focused on the Oedipus legend, which concerns incest.[4] Just as the incest prohibition represents arguably the primal intervention of culture into merely biological nature, which observes no such restrictions on sexual relations, Lévi-Strauss concluded that myths express and struggle with the fundamental tension between nature and culture. By implication, the myth-maker is just as concerned with the "problem" of arbitrariness as the interpreter of myth: the discourse of myth reflects an awareness, however subliminal, of the fact that such cultural distinctions as the incest prohibition are precisely neither natural nor universal.

In the case of many spells and magical rituals, the very fact that the event that such behaviors index prospectively has not yet come to pass underlines the arbitrariness of such signs. This is why they must be motivated or rendered apparently natural through the deployment of various poetic devices. The nonoccurrence of the event signaled by the ritual is tantamount to a form of distortion, that stands in the way of the successful transmission of the message of the ritual. One of the common ways of transmitting a message through layers of distortion is to repeat it, also in different registers. In Edmund Leach's example, if I shout the same declaration in a windstorm several times, I will more likely be heard.[5] The repetition of imperatives and deictics in ritual functions analogously. Yet it may also serve another purpose. Freud argued that the symbolism of dreams is designed to overcome a different kind of distortion: the refusal of the censor to permit the fully conscious recognition of that which the dream represents, namely, a form of wish-fulfillment.[6] Working against such barriers, something of the message may nevertheless be transmitted, as in the Oedipus story, which reveals certain prohibited desires. Lévi-Strauss's argument was that the repetitive devices deployed in myth function in similar fashion, to express a recognition of the fundamental tension between nature and culture that may not be fully acknowledged.

The rule of the arbitrariness of the sign admits of very few exceptions. One potential exception concerns the phenomenon of sound symbolism, which includes onomatopoeia: sounds that supposedly resemble what they represent, as with some words for animal cries (e.g. cock-a-doodle-doo) or some words for sounds (e.g. smash, crack). Yet the variability of even these few supposedly onomatopoetic words across cultures (e.g. a German rooster says *kiki-riki*) has sustained a vigorous debate as to whether any words may truly be referred to as natural or iconic. Roman Jakobson devoted a long essay to exploring this topic, and to countering the normative view that language is wholly arbitrary.[7] Although the existence of iconic signs has been disputed in recent times,[8] many contemporary investigators agree that there exists a certain, limited number of sound symbolic or in some sense "natural" words.[9] In certain modes of cultural expression, including poetry, magic, and ritual, as we have seen, it is arguable that such signs assume a greater proportion of the total. Signs of the types Peirce termed icons and indexes, which roughly correspond to the cognitive associations of resemblance and contiguity respectively, are more common in these modes of expression.[10] These signs are, if not natural, at least not wholly arbitrary. Observation of this fact often, especially from an emic or native perspective, reinforces the conviction that such modes as poetry and ritual may constitute what, borrowing from the *Cratylus*, we might call natural languages, ones that possess a special ability to convey meaning or, in the case of magic, to influence reality.

Many rituals deploy poetic devices to create the appearance that they perform as natural indexes of their intended goals. Certain rituals, such as Tantric mantras, may even iconically represent natural processes in order to augment these rituals' pragmatic function or performative efficacy. These uses of iconicity are forms of verisimilitude, or what Plato called *mimesis*. As such cases suggest, the view that all signs, without exception, are arbitrary and depend wholly upon conventional distinctions for their value is, at the very least, incomplete. Such a view fails to account for the proliferation of poetic devices in ritual, where, if we accepted such a view, we should expect to find a random distribution of such devices, similar to that found in other genres of discourse. Not all signs are equal; some appear to be more effective as rhetoric. Moreover, often such ritual icons are precisely in the service of a "naturalization of the cultural." There is a substitution or sleight-of-hand that allows cultural signs—such as language—to be taken as natural, or even consubstantial with physical reality. Religious discourse, rather than highlighting the distinction between nature and culture through discursive oppositions as Lévi-Strauss suggested, in many cases uses iconicity to suppress or gloss over this distinction.

However, more critical etic or objective investigation suggests that many of these ostensibly natural signs are motivated only in relation to a linguistic or other cultural code, in terms of which resemblance may be constructed and communicated. Resemblance or iconicity, rather than demonstrating the naturalness of discourse, indicates instead its rhetorical function. This conclusion accords with that of the editors of a recent volume on iconicity in language:

> [I]conicity is a cultural phenomenon. . . . The study of iconicity will therefore be directly linked with cultural studies because it allows us to understand how different cultures mentally represent their worlds and values. Because iconicity has cultural implications, it also constitutes a rhetorical means for justifying values and therefore one's own culture. By seeing (or presenting) such signs as iconic, we imply that those values are not conventional but natural. We can thus believe in an iconic dimension or manipulate others by presenting certain things as iconic.[11]

The fact that we observe this as the ruse that it is indicates the gulf between the modern acceptance of the arbitrary nature of the sign and the belief of many traditional cultures that, on the contrary, certain signs (one's own language, as opposed to that of other tribes, or possibly some subset of language as perfected by ritualists) are precisely not arbitrary, but natural and even endowed with special power. Even in the midst of his effort to counter Friedrich Max Müller's negative judgment that myth is a "disease of language," Ernst Cassirer acknowledged that traditional cultures often believe in "word magic," or "the essential identity between the word and what it denotes."[12] Not that we are ourselves immune from such beliefs, as Müller already acknowledged with his concept of "modern mythology."[13] Yet the rejection of word magic in favor of a conviction in the arbitrariness of the sign is a characteristic feature of modernity.

Structuralists regard "arbitrariness" as a scientific concept that applies universally, even to those cultures that do not recognize or acknowledge the arbitrariness of their own signs, or do everything they can to motivate signs for particular purposes. Such a view has contributed to a neglect of the co-emergence of the notion of arbitrariness with a particular, modern semiotic ideology. Brian Vickers has described this emergence as the shift from "identity" to "analogy": from the belief in the identity of words with things to the belief that the status of words is merely analogical or metaphorical.[14] Vickers regards this shift as having arisen from the struggle of the Baconian tradition against magical beliefs in the seventeenth century. Different aspects of this struggle will be considered in subsequent chapters. To preview some of these findings, the rise of the notion of the arbitrariness of the sign as the dominant ideology of language appears to have come about, in England at least, with the triumph of the Baconian tradition, or of nominalism and empiricism more generally.[15] This doctrine was partly connected, as Vickers suggests, with the triumph of science over magic. Yet it also had a great deal to do with Protestant literalism and associated critiques of mythological and ritual discourse.

The belief in the power of language to capture reality—not only in the sense of imaging or picturing it, but also of influencing or directing it—is grounded in the idea that language is ontologically prior to that which it describes. Many traditions depict speech as central to the creation of the world: the Hindu *Vedas* are one example;[16] the Memphite Egyptian cosmogony involving the god Ptah another.[17] Mircea Eliade gave the example of the Finnish magician Väinämöinen, who cured himself of a wound from an iron weapon after reciting the story of the origin of that metal.[18] By rehearsing the story of the time of beginnings, when things were first fashioned, one achieves power over the things themselves. The reiteration of the cosmogony in Tantric mantras also depends on this basis.[19] In the Hebrew Bible, there is not only God's generative pronouncement "Let there be light" (Genesis 1:3), but also the idea that Adam spoke a perfect language. The power of Hebrew, at least before the fall of the Tower of Babel, to express and influence nature was often extolled, and efforts made, even in recent centuries, to remedy the loss of such a perfect language.[20] Some of these efforts are described in later sections of this chapter.

The Hindu *Vedas* reflect such a view of the ontological priority of language. Within the Brahmanical system of ritual correspondences or *bandhu*, a word that literally means affinity or kinship, various forms of iconicity are deployed in order to reinforce the status of ritual as a natural sign with pragmatic efficacy.[21] In the early *Upaniṣads*, the refrain is that one who knows these correspondences will be able to make the ritual work.[22] Often, it is the division of different things into a similar number of parts that establishes their correspondence.[23] Or a connection may be indicated by a similarity in the names for different things:

> Death . . . undertook a liturgical recitation (*arc*), and as he was engaged in liturgical recitation water sprang from him. And he thought: "While I was engaged in liturgical recitation (*arc*), water (*ka*) sprang up for me." This is what gave the name to and discloses the true nature of recitation (*arka*). Water undoubtedly springs up for him who knows the name and nature of recitation in this way. So, recitation is water.[24]

This technique of argument is sometimes referred to as "folk" or "fictitious etymology," but this is really a misnomer, as the point is not etymology at all—not historical derivation or even semantics in a narrow sense—but rather the assertion of a substantive connection that may be exploited for pragmatic purposes. Such practices are described more fully below in this chapter.

The preference of each culture for its own language as a description of reality is expressed in condemnations of the languages of others as inferior or subhuman. The Greek term *barbaroi*—source of our word "barbarian"—may be an onomatopoeia that mocks the speech of non-Greeks as a form of stuttering or chattering. Words like "stammer," "murmur," and "mutter" all suggest the reduplicated speech of infants, animals, or others who cannot speak distinctly. Frits Staal has placed the language of mantras in the same category, comparing them to baby talk and birdsongs. However, as we have seen, the goal of repetition in Tantric mantras is to heighten the power of language as an index of nature.

Rather than mere nature, ritual represents an effort to correct or supplement nature by means of human art. The aporia or contradiction in magical thought is that what is presented as natural is actually the height of artifice. The basic principle of substitution described in the last chapter applies also to the concealment of arbitrariness in language: indexical and iconic relationships that exist merely on the phonetic level, and are expressed through rhyme or alliteration, can substitute for and give the appearance of a causal relationship between the spell and its goal. Intralinguistic sign relations are represented as or taken for a relation between language and the world.

In the case of Tantric mantras, as we have seen, this extends to the creation of elaborate diagrams of various natural creative processes, such as the cosmogony, sexual reproduction, and breathing. The more elaborate these diagrams, it seems, the more aligned the mantra is with physical nature, and the more capable the mantra is of bringing about its goal. Ignoring such a deliberate investment of effort, the artificiality of these formulas is denied. The mantra is represented as natural, spontaneous, and creative, on par with the cosmogony and human reproduction. Rendering the mantra magically effective in this way is called "birthing" (*jīvana*).[25] Similarly, the seven vowels of the alphabet used in many Greek spells were, like other letters, referred to as *stoicheia*—a word that also denoted the "elements" out of which nature was composed[26]—and apparently were regarded as consubstantial with, and therefore capable of influencing, reality.

Like many rituals, Tantric mantras also reflect what I have labeled the "scripting of spontaneity":[27] the deliberate imitation of ostensibly natural or spontaneous processes in highly orchestrated fashion. An example of this is the *haṃsa* mantra described in the last chapter, a palindrome that supposedly represents the path of breath in and out of the body. This mantra is called *ajapā*, or unspoken: the practitioner is supposed to get in the habit of constantly repeating the mantra with each in- and out-breath, naturally and silently, throughout the course of the day.[28]

Such illustrations of the manner in which ritual obscures its own function as a form of rhetoric require a modification of some well-known theories of poetry. The classical theory of poetry as mimesis or imitation has to take account of the manner in which poetry doubles back on itself—as an autocommentary or performance on its own text, which repeats its own sounds etc.—even while claiming to represent, with verisimilitude, a nature that lies outside of it. On the other hand, Jakobson's definition of the poetic function as the "set toward the message as such" must be qualified if it is to be extended to those cases where the poetry of ritual is designed to deflect attention from its own mechanism of operation, even as it engages in an increasingly elaborate orchestration of natural activities, such as speech or breathing.

The ruse of many ritual traditions is that their tightly scripted movements and utterances are claimed to be not a form of art, but an evacuation of an artificiality that pervades human behavior and a return to a more natural, native, or primal condition. So, for example, in the Zen tradition the practice of drawing "emptiness" in the form of a circle is supposed to be utterly spontaneous, like the state of mind it represents ("beginner's mind").[29] In this case, the thinness of the rice paper forbids retracing a shape, so that one must act with decisiveness and deliberateness, which can of course only be done with practice. The contradiction here, as with so many forms of Zen practice, is that such a "natural" state is in fact the product of extensive training and cultural imitation.

This points us to a function of ritual that applies much more broadly, beyond spells and other manifestations of the poetic function. In many traditions the belief in the natural status of ritual coexists with an equally sincere belief that mere nature is imperfect, and that ritual is what perfects it. Ritual supplements the defects of nature by creating a second-order, ideal nature, not so much a supernature as a hypernature. This belief is illustrated by the Vedic tradition of *saṃskāras*, or life-cycle rituals, which are performed for Hindu males of the upper castes, who are said to be "twice born" (*dvīja*) as a result of these rites. The word *saṃskāra* is related etymologically to *saṃskṛta*, or Sanskrit, the word for the language, which means "perfected," "cultivated," "polished." The same root is used for the *mantra-saṃskāra*, the rituals that render the mantra effective (*siddha*).[30] In the case of the life-cycle rituals, there is a similar suggestion that physical birth is itself inadequate, incomplete until perfected by the ritual process. This parallels those forms of Tantric initiation (*dīkṣā*) that involve the imparting, from male teacher to student, of "seed" mantras, a word that, in Sanskrit as in English, refers also to human semen. Such initiations symbolize the process of birth or sexual reproduction. As in many traditions that privilege the male sex, such forms of ritual transmission implicitly reject the adequacy of female or natural birth. There is even an ancient mythological charter for such ideas. In the

Puruṣa Sūkta (*Rig Veda* 10.90), the Brahmin or priest is said to be born from the mouth of the primal man, who created the world through his sacrifice, an eminently cultural institution here conflated with the cosmogony.[31] There is the suggestion here of an organic connection between birth and speech, or the primary modes of natural and cultural production.

Such cases of a "second birth" through ritual add evidence for Nancy Jay's thesis that the institution of sacrifice is designed to replace transmission through a female lineage with transmission through a male lineage, which must also be birthed in many instances through blood.[32] The conflict between natural birth, marked as female, and ritual birth, marked as male, parallels the conflict between nature and culture that Lévi-Strauss identified as the central tension in many mythological traditions. Far from being a property only of the savage mind, this conflict is expressed also in Western traditions, including not only the Oedipus legend but also the Hebrew Bible and New Testament. Seth Kunin argues that the Jewish tradition struggled with the contradiction between natural and divine birth.[33] This is reflected textually, according to Kunin, in a strategic ambivalence regarding Isaac's parentage. Isaac is born when his parents are at an age that normally precludes childbearing; this signifies divine intervention, but also, potentially, the divinity of Isaac's parentage. The rejection of a merely natural genealogy is suggested by Abraham's favoring of Isaac over Ishmael, Abraham's older son by his concubine Hagar. Finally, after Isaac's rescue from sacrifice on Mt Moriah by the last-minute substitution of a ram, the story refers to Abraham—but not Isaac—returning down the mountain: an omission that, Kunin suggests, may imply that Isaac actually was sacrificed[34] and then, presumably, reborn, which would imply his divine status. A similar ambivalence concerning the paternity of Jesus—who was simultaneously Joseph's legal son and conceived of the Holy Spirit— suggests that such stories may be about the effort to reconcile apparently irreconcilable alternatives, whether expressed as human and divine, nature and culture, or, as Lévi-Strauss suggested long ago, "birth from one or birth from two?"[35] As if not only the myths but also the sacrifices and other rituals as well were designed to give an answer to the question: "Who's your daddy?" It seems indisputable that arbitrariness (whether of human institutions such as sacrifice, or of natural birth as an event regarded as meaningless until sanctified by ceremony) is a stubborn fact acknowledged, however subliminally, in many cultures, which respond to this fact in different ways with only partial success.

"The tyranny of taxonomies"

One of the most common forms of the naturalization of arbitrariness found in many cultural and religious traditions is the classification of a number of unrelated domains in terms of a basic number of elements.[36] Examples are the four elements and humors of classical Greek tradition; the three qualities (*guna*) or five elements of classical Hindu tradition; the duality of Yin and Yang and the five elements of classical Chinese tradition; etc. Such systems purport to represent qualities that are essential to creation, are often implicated in the cosmogony, and are manifested in a wide variety of domains including not only the physical, but also the social and moral orders. As such, they provide a natural or cosmic genealogy for practices and institutions that are cultural and arbitrary. Yet the natural status of such taxonomies can be maintained only for so long as they are not challenged by either empirical observation or the recognition that other cultures divide up the universe in quite different ways.

As we saw, magical operations often involve the manipulation and accumulation of various forms of iconicity or resemblance. The fact that different domains may share no common qualities or direct resemblance complicates such an effort. The easiest way of circumventing this problem is to construct a quantitative or numerical resemblance by dividing each domain into an equal number of parts, and then matching these parts up one-for-one. The kind of resemblance thus created is what semioticians refer to as a "diagram" or "diagrammatic icon."[37] When we are talking about such different domains as colors, sounds, etc., that are frequently coordinated in ritual, such modes of iconicity allow the correlation of disparate dimensions of experience that otherwise have nothing in common. Often, these taxonomies claim to enumerate exhaustively the various domains with which they are correlated: the directions or the elements, for example. The principle of exhaustion described in the last chapter reinforces the rhetoric of such lists. Color is one of the qualities that is often enumerated. The three Hindu *gunas* are all identified by their basic colors—white, dark, and red[38]—as are the four humors of Galenic medicine: black bile, yellow bile, (red) blood, and (white) phlegm. Victor Turner, who noted the importance of the color triad black-white-red among the Ndembu, argued that there was a biological basis for these colors, which supposedly represented basic bodily substances, such as blood and semen.[39] However, when we look cross-culturally, the variability among such taxonomies contradicts any naturalistic explanation. Instead, they serve as organizing rubrics or metaphors that, by means of artificial associations, permit the coordination of different dimensions of both nature and culture into a comprehensive cosmology.

When anthropologists began to study these taxonomies, they were focused especially on the systems of so-called "totemism" according to which every member of a social group was assigned to a particular sub-group that has its own symbol or totem, usually an animal, as well as a cardinal direction, sacred plant, color, etc.[40] The focus on what such taxonomies contribute to social organization inspired a creative interpretation by Émile Durkheim and Marcel Mauss, who called them systems of "primitive classification."[41] According to Durkheim and Mauss, such systems establish the basic categories of thought, grounding mythology and ritual as well as philosophical speculation. The question, however, was the source and function of these lists. Given that they are founded on neither a priori reason nor empirical observation of the world, how is it that they originated? Durkheim and Mauss argued that these taxonomies derived from the divisions of the social order itself. This division was primary; all others were secondary. In this way, they argued that society itself, and not mere abstract speculation, had given rise to what we think of as primitive philosophy.

This was a powerful argument that unfortunately ignored the cases where there was no evidence that such taxonomies had ever reflected a preexisting or even a subsequent division into tribes. In the case of Yin and Yang, perhaps, one might argue that the association of these qualities with female and male respectively might conform to the thesis. However, in the case of Empedocles's elements, there was not a shred of evidence to support the contention that the Greeks had divided themselves into four tribes, each with an element as its totem.[42] More recently, both Pierre Bourdieu and Bruce Lincoln have made claims similar to Durkheim's and Mauss's respecting the social origin of such taxonomies in cases where there is no evidence supporting such claims.[43]

In Durkheim's case, and possibly in the case of some of his contemporary followers as well, one observes a kind of obsessive tracing of everything to society. The same propensity was evident also in Durkheim's insistence that the "original" totems—the *churinga* of the Australian aboriginals—were merely arbitrary, nonrepresentational signs.[44] Supposedly, such signs were invested with force in the primal scene of a group ritual, which supercharged them as "collective representations" of the group's own identity and self-awareness. Every subsequent remove from this primal scene meant a loss of the force of such representations, which therefore had to be recharged periodically by reconvening the group in public rituals. This primal scene is, however, as much a fiction as those of earlier theories of the state of nature. The idea of a group ritual as applied to any society larger than a tribe can only be a metaphor. Of course, all taxonomies are conventional and socially constructed; that is not the question. What I mean is that the Durkheimians often ignore the role of semiotic mediation—the role that symbolic forms and modes of cultural expression—can play in constructing sign-systems and contributing to a rhetoric of culture.[45] In the case of taxonomies, various forms of iconicity create an illusion that facilitates the naturalization of arbitrary cultural institutions. If the force of such signs derived entirely from the fact that they were culturally instituted by convention and habit, then such elaborate symbolic systems would add nothing to reinforce the social distinctions with which they are associated and would in fact be entirely superfluous. But this is not the case. Such taxonomies instead provide crucial evidence for the power of rhetoric to reinforce social ideology, and they deserve to be studied in their own right, in light of a general semiotic.

Indeed, the power of such forms of rhetoric has long been recognized. The vast system of correspondences that formed a part of the "Great Chain of Being" in medieval Europe was powerful enough to stymie for centuries the development of alternative, empirically based modes of categorizing the world.[46] The Galenic theory of four humors long held its ground against contenders, and the received theories of astronomy posed nearly insuperable barriers to discoverers like Kepler and Galileo. It is the power of such correspondences that inspired the following scholastic argument against Galileo's discovery of the moons of Jupiter, which suggested that there might be more than the seven planets recognized by the prevailing Aristotelian cosmology:

> There are seven windows given to animals in the domicile of the head, through which the air is admitted to the tabernacle of the body, to enlighten, to warm and to nourish it. What are these parts of the microcosmos: Two nostrils, two eyes, two ears and a mouth. So in the heavens, as in a macrocosmos, there are two favourable stars, two unpropitious, two luminaries, and Mercury undecided and indifferent. From this and from many other similarities in nature, such as the seven metals etc., which it were tedious to enumerate, we gather that the number of planets is necessarily seven.[47]

We see that such arguments by analogy function in a manner entirely parallel to the manner in which many rituals work, not to mention many false syllogisms. The accumulation of resemblances "adds up" to index what appears increasingly as an inevitable conclusion, that there can be only seven planets.

"I pooh-pooh the purity": etymologies in Hindu and British traditions

The belief in a natural language is evidenced by the practice of "folk" or "fictitious etymologies" in classical Hinduism. Scholars of Hinduism have paid greater attention recently to the function of etymologizing and related language practices within this tradition, in part because these practices are prominent and distinctive features of Hinduism, and in part to correct earlier dismissals of such verbal forms by Western scholars. Friedrich Max Müller's statement that "a sound etymology has nothing to do with sound,"[48] although directed at unscientific linguists in Europe, also captured an attitude common among some European scholars toward etymological speculations within the Hindu tradition. Beginning in the *Brāhmaṇas* (*c*. 1000 BCE), certain forms of Hinduism used coincidental resemblances among words to argue for deeper connections among the things these words denoted. For example, *Chāndogya Upaniṣad* 1.4.2 states that "When the gods feared death, what they did was to enter the triple Veda. They covered it with the meters. The fact that the gods covered (*chad*) it with them gave the name to and discloses the true nature of the meters (*chandas*)."[49]

Disputing earlier views that tended to dismiss such etymologies out of hand, more recent scholarship has done much to show that these etymologies were not simply mistaken attempts to reconstruct the historical relations among words, crude anticipations of modern etymological science. They were instead deliberate attempts to exploit the poetic properties of language for philosophical and ritual purposes. Referring to the cosmological connections (*bandhu*) that were a key part of the esoteric knowledge communicated in the *Upaniṣads*, as in the earlier *Brāhmaṇas*, Patrick Olivelle has argued that

> An important basis for these connections . . . is the phonetic similarity between the Sanskrit words for two things or even the fact that the two terms may have the same number of syllables. One finds with an almost annoying frequency such "etymological" connections in these documents. . . . These are clearly not "folk" etymologies; the authors of these documents were learned men, and these documents themselves demonstrate that the science of grammar had already reached a high degree of sophistication. These men clearly knew the philological etymologies of the terms they deal with, but their quest was not for such common and well-known connections but for deeper and hidden ones, and they found in the sounds of the names a clue to those connections.[50]

Johannes Bronkhorst prefers to call these devices "semantic etymologies," which "connect one word with one or more others which are believed to elucidate its meaning."[51] Both scholars make clear that, within the Indian tradition at least, these devices were not regarded as true, historical etymologies in the strict sense. Consequently, they were not failed attempts to discover etymological relationships, but culturally successful attempts to argue poetically for relationships that extended deeper than the verbal level, into the structure of the world itself.

Indeed, the very use of the term "etymology" to describe such linguistic devices may be inherently misleading. It would be more accurate to say that we are talking about a range of uses of phonetic resemblances among words that, at first glance, appear to exhibit kinship with modern etymologies. One can immediately suggest a range of functions for such devices, such as: revealing a true (historical) etymology; defining or fixing the meaning of a word; developing poetic associations; arguing, whether seriously or facetiously, for a point (i.e. functioning rhetorically); producing humor, as in the case of puns; serving memory, as with an acronym; and exploiting a connection of imitation or resemblance for magical purposes. Only the first of these uses coincides with modern practices of etymologizing.

Bronkhorst also notes that such devices have often been connected with magic,[52] and may therefore do more than create meaning by contributing to the efficacy of ritual performance: "The practical advantage of these etymologies is that they allow man to obtain knowledge about these connections with the hidden reality. This knowledge—the texts emphasize it repeatedly—is of great importance: it can convey a number of advantages to him who knows."[53] Indeed, in the early *Upaniṣads*, it is often said that "For one who knows thus" (*ya evaṃ veda*), that is, understands the bandhu or cosmological associations of the ritual, the ritual will be effective. Despite this, Bronkhorst argues that "semantic etymologies are not performative acts and have no persuasive validity, as far as I can see; they certainly don't in early and classical Indian literature.[54]

In the later tradition, however, there are examples of such forms of wordplay, including some Tantric mantras, that do function as true performatives: that is, they are thought to bring about, by virtue of being uttered and as if by magic, the state of affairs that they declare and describe. In the *Tantras*, a number of different linguistic devices are employed that bear a distinct resemblance to the etymologies found in the *Brāhmaṇas* and early *Upaniṣads*, as well as in the *Nirukta*.[55] The entire seventeenth chapter of the *Kulārṇava Tantra* consists of semantic etymologies.[56] Many of these explicate the various implements or technical terminology of Tantric ritual, such as chanting (*japa*), esoteric gestures (*mudrā*), and sacred designs (*maṇḍala*). The etymology for mantra—"It is called 'mantra' because, from contemplating (*mananāt*) the true form of the deity, which is boundlessly radiant, it preserves (*trāyate*) one from all fears"[57]—echoes that found in a number of other *Tantras*. Some of these etymologies were traditional, and not idiosyncratic to the *Kulārṇava Tantra*.

Apart from such more or less direct continuations of earlier practices of *nirvacana*, we find in later Hinduism a number of other, related practices in which the phonetic relations among words are exploited or words are analyzed down to their component sounds, as in the *Śatanāmas* and *Sahasranāmas*, lists of a hundred or a thousand names of the deity, which occasionally use wordplay, as in the *Lalitāsahasranāma*: "She who is worshipped by heroes (*vīra*), She who is the cosmogenetrix (*virāj*), She who is without stain (*virajas*)."[58] Wordplay involving the name of the deity is also found in certain seed mantras in which the first letter of the name of the deity (e.g. "g" for *Gaṇapati*) is converted into a seed (e.g. *gaṃ*) and prefixed to the name of the deity invoked by the mantra: for example, *oṃ gāṃ* (or *gāṃ gīṃ gūṃ*, etc.) *ganapataye namaḥ*" (reverence to *Gaṇapati*).[59] *Lakṣmī Tantra* 21.22–5 specifically instructs that a seed mantra may be formed from the first letter of a word in this way.[60] What is important about such examples is the cosmological theory that underlies them: the idea that sound, more specifically language or the alphabet that is the matrix (*mātṛkā*) out of which the universe evolved, is ontologically prior to physical reality and may be manipulated as a means of altering that reality. Within the structural sequence of a mantra, the *bīja* is the seed out of which physical reality—whether the objective form of the deity or some other physical manifestation—evolves.

In Tantra, words are not "mere" words, but clues to a hidden reality that is, ultimately, both divine and physical. There is a continuum, rather than a sharp distinction, between language and physical reality. Arthur Avalon correctly identified Tantra as a theory of "natural name,"[61] although he did not recognize the extent of influence this idea had on the very structure of the mantras. Without an appreciation of this underlying linguistic ideology, it is impossible to understand fully the uses of semantic etymologies and related devices within the Hindu tradition.

Like other traditions, of course, the Hindu tradition was not monolithic in its views of language. For example, one of the main systems of Hindu philosophy, *Mīmāṃsā*, held that Sanskrit, or at least the language of the *Vedas*, was not conventional and created, but rather eternal or without origin (*autpattika*).[62] However, Śabara's commentary distinguishes this claim from the erroneous view that, upon the pronunciation of a word, the thing denoted by that word will be physically produced. The rejected view sounds suspiciously close to the later Tantric view of mantras. Other Hindus used etymological wordplay for polemical or satirical purposes. Eivind Kahrs provides two examples from Ksemaraja's *Deśopadeśa*:[63] "'*Guru*' (teacher) is so called because he is devoid of qualities (*guṇa*) and always lusting (*rutakārī*) after the wives of his students. '*Dīkṣā*' (initiation) is so called because it leads to the loss (*kṣayakaraṇād*) of money (*dīnāra-*) (i.e. costs money)." In such cases etymologizing serves as a form of parody. Such cases were the exception, rather than the rule, in Tantra and most of the rest of the Hindu ritual tradition. Nothing like this satirical use of semantic etymologizing occurs in *Kulārṇava Tantra* 17.7–9, where we find more reverent etymologies of guru.

The linguistic ideology thus expressed by semantic etymologies in the Hindu tradition is remarkably different from the views of language affirmed by modern, Western linguistics, where language is treated by and large as an arbitrary social institution, which is created rather than creative. However, the dream of a natural language, that is, one that has a direct and immediate connection with reality, as reflected in its etymology, was not uncommon in European culture also prior to modernity, and even into modernity as an increasingly marginalized minority opinion. Bronkhorst points to the *locus classicus* of such theories, Plato's *Cratylus*, which debates whether language is dependent on nature or human laws. Like some Hindu texts, the *Cratylus* engages in extensive use of semantic etymologies to reveal the "natural" meanings of Greek words, although in the process the text casts doubt upon the validity of such etymologies, and it is not even clear where

Socrates, or rather Plato, stands with respect to the central question of the natural status of language.

Bronkhorst notes that, unlike the Brahmins, the Greek philosophers did not regard their language as the only true one.[64] He does not note, however, the deeper levels of irony in Plato's dialogue, which pokes fun at the theory of a natural correspondence between language and reality. The very name of one of the interlocutors, Hermogenes, means "born of Hermes," that is, a rich person, but the man himself is poor.[65] Friedrich Nietzsche later exploited this very example in the course of arguing that language is always inherently unnatural, artificial, and misleading, a "metaphor of a metaphor."[66] This example, combined with the rejections of Gorgias's efforts to bring poetic magic into rhetorical discourse, suggests a deeper suspicion within the Greek philosophical tradition toward the deceptive potentialities of language than anything we have observed in the Vedic or Tantric traditions.

Despite this, as Bronkhorst notes, Neoplatonists and other groups in the ancient and medieval Mediterranean and European environments employed word magic along with other types of magic. The modern doctrine of the conventional status of language was elaborated in the sixteenth and seventeenth centuries partly in order to refute magicians who exploited the supposedly natural status of language.[67] Bronkhorst does not develop an account of these movements, which produced what amounted to a disenchantment of language. For now, a brief sketch of British nominalism within the Baconian tradition will illustrate the importance to this movement of controlling etymology and, through this, language itself. The linguistic ideology of this movement was in some respects directly opposed to that of Hindu Tantra, and in other respects exhibited some interesting parallels to that tradition. Later chapters of this book will extend the study of this British tradition and its links with Protestant literalism.

The main tradition of British linguistics inaugurated in the seventeenth century by Francis Bacon, Thomas Hobbes, and John Locke was both nominalist and empiricist in its orientation. Its nominalism was reflected in the critique of the habit of taking words for things, or believing that the abstract entities denoted by some words enjoyed a real, rather than merely verbal, existence.[68] Its empiricism was reflected in the complementary insistence that our words should be made to conform, so far as possible, to the real world. Science, or empirical investigation, was to purge language of metaphysical notions and approach the goal of a language that mirrored the world perfectly. This tradition tended to overemphasize the role of substantives, or nouns, in language, in part because such words could be identified with concrete entities in the real world.

Etymology played an important role in these projects of linguistic purification. Hobbes, for example, employed etymological analysis as one of the main supports for his nominalist reduction of metaphysical language. Significantly, he selected the terms "spirit" and "angel" for his analyses.

Tracing each back to its roots revealed a concrete meaning: Latin *spiritus* originally denoted breath, while Greek *angelus* meant a messenger.[69] All language ultimately referred to the physical world. At the same time, Hobbes was a strong proponent of the view that linguistic reference is a matter of convention, equivalent to an act of legislation. In both of these positions— his empiricism and his nominalism—Hobbes was largely followed by Locke, the etymological philosopher John Horne Tooke (1736–1812), and subsequent British theorists.

The linguistic ideology of the British tradition as thus outlined constituted both a radical break with the earlier, magical idea of a natural language and, in some respects, a continuation of this idea.[70] Language was decidedly not natural, in the twin senses that it did not conform to the reality of the world, and was a product of social legislation. However, language could be made to conform to reality through empirical investigation and philosophical fiat. As in magical versions of the ideal of a natural language, the goal of the new, scientific ideal was eminently practical, as it would facilitate the manipulation of nature.

Friedrich Max Müller (1823–1900) reflected this British tradition, which he combined with German Romanticism, comparative philology, and observations gleaned from his study of Sanskrit and other languages.[71] Like that of some of his British predecessors, Müller's nominalism was most conspicuous in his etymological analysis of the names of deities, which traced these back to substantive terms (*nomina*) that, in course of time, had been mistaken for the names of gods (*numina*). Following Locke, Müller argued that the basic roots of language were themselves ultimately concrete, material, or experiential.

Müller's theory of language and mythology represented the survival, in attenuated form, of the dream of a natural language.[72] Although language per se was not natural except in a very limited sense, it could be traced back through scientific etymology to a limited number of roots that were, in some sense, based in the natural or physical world. And these etymological meanings were, for Müller, still the key to understanding language and especially mythology, which etymology served to debunk. He was, of course, familiar with Plato's *Cratylus*,[73] and with more contemporary Western theories affirming the natural origin of words or language. However, Müller subjected most of these theories to intense criticism, referring to them derisively as the "bow wow" and "pooh pooh" theories.[74] These were, respectively, the theories that words were derived originally either from the imitation of animal cries and other natural sounds, or from the instinctive cries or interjections of human beings in certain situations. Müller did not reject the possibility that some words were derived in this way, but he objected to the notion that many could have been so derived.

Consideration of a particular set of examples involving the Sanskrit roots *pu* (to cleanse) and *puy* (to stink) will help to elucidate the differences in the understanding of etymology, and in the idea of a natural language, between

Hindus and British. Although, as we have seen, Bronkhorst rejected the idea that etymologies were used as speech acts in the classical Hindu tradition, the *Divyatattva*, a sixteenth-century Sanskrit *dharmaśāstra* text authored by the Bengali Raghunandana Bhaṭṭāchārya, employs etymologies in the operative portion of its rituals of ordeal.[75] One of these is the invocation of fire, given previously, in the ordeal of carrying the heated iron ball: "You are called 'purifier' (*pāvaka*) because you purify (*punāsi*) sin (*pāpam*)."[76] The form of the invocation, which is taken from Pitāmaha (*c.* 400–700 CE), refers to a real etymological connection between "purifier" (*pāvaka*) and "purify" (*punāsi*) through the verbal root "to purify" (*pū*). It also exploits the resemblance in sound between *pāvaka* and *pāpam*, or sin. Overall, the formula is supposed to disclose the truth about fire so that that natural element, personified as a god, will reveal the truth about the guilt or innocence of the person undergoing the ordeal. The etymology invokes the presence of the god of fire and requests his contribution to the efficacious operation of the ceremony. It therefore functions as a kind of performative utterance, by establishing an identification between the rites of purification in which fire is employed, and the moral purity of the agent in question, thus affirming for morality a basis that is, at once, both natural and divine.

By comparison, this sort of thinking was antithetical to much of British nominalism. In his critique of linguistic fictions, Jeremy Bentham singled out for opprobrium various abuses of the word "purity," and especially "the inference that has been made of the existence of moral impurity from that of physical impurity—of impurity in a moral sense, from that of impurity in a physical sense."[77] This coordinated with his critique of linguistic "fictions," described in Chapter Four of this volume.

The classicist Theodor Gomperz (1832–1912) addressed the case of "purity" and related words in the course of a discussion of ancient Greek theories of the natural basis of language, including the *Cratylus*. Gomperz's chief example of the natural basis of some words was the Indo-European root *pu*, meaning "to cleanse":

> If we employ the mouth itself, the organ of speech, to perform an act of cleansing, this is done by blowing away the particles of dust, straw, etc., which cover and pollute any superficial plane. If we do this energetically by a determined narrowing of our protruded lips, we produce sounds like *p*, *pf*, or *pu*. In this way the last-named sound might at least have obtained its primitive significance. Presuming our conjecture to be correct, a definite position and movement of the organs of speech formed in this instance, as doubtless in countless others, the bond between sound and meaning.[78]

However, with the passage of time, more and more words, including Latin *purus* (pure) and *pœna* (punishment), would be derived from this root through the admixture of purely arbitrary cultural elements, until at last, as with the modern English word "punishment," the relationship to the natural root has become so attenuated as to be unrecognizable to anyone except an etymologist.[79] Closer to the origins of language, however, grew up a range of uses that were somehow, given their proximity to their source, more natural: "the conception of punishment as a religious atonement or purification would be more appropriately expressed by the derivatives of *pu* than by descendants of other roots . . ."[80] Thus far, Gomperz's attempt to rehabilitate some portion of the traditional, natural theory of language origins resembles somewhat the *Divyatattva*'s ritual invocation of *pu* and, more broadly, the Hindu tradition's approach to etymology. However, Gomperz immediately adds that, even assuming a natural basis for some linguistic forms, that basis may lead in conflicting directions: the same operation of blowing may constitute an act of cleansing or, conversely, an expression of disgust, as in *pooh-pooh* or *pfui*, as reflected in verbal derivatives such as "putrid." Both, diametrically opposed uses of onomatopoeia occur in his pun, "I pooh-pooh the purity of your intentions."[81] Gomperz cites Heraclitus's observation that the "same" word (the homonyms *bíos* and *biós*) could mean opposite things, in this case, both life (*bíos*) and the bow (*biós*) that shoots arrows that cause death.[82] As with the example of Hermogenes in the *Cratylus*, we sense in this example a skepticism concerning the ability of language to signify naturally, a skepticism that, although not uniquely Western, contrasts sharply with the sort of thinking found in the *Divyatattva*, the *Vedas*, and the *Tantras*.

Although he does not name Müller as his target, Gomperz's extended discussion of *pu* was intended as a comment on and partial refutation of his predecessor's dismissal of theories of language as onomatopoeic, including the "pooh pooh" theory. Müller addressed the examples of *pu* and *puy* and their derivatives several times in his writings on language. He explicitly rejected the attempt to derive many words from their immediate resemblance to certain, supposedly natural interjections such as *pu*, *piff* and *pfui*.[83] The proper connection was an indirect one, through historical etymology, which took into account the transformation of words over time so that their connection with their original, historical roots was often no longer recognizable, but could be known only through the established laws of comparative etymology: "Sound etymology has nothing to do with sound." Müller allowed only that, at the basis of all of these far-flung derivatives, "the root PÛY was very likely the residuum of a number of sounds accompanying the acts of primitive men when rejecting something unpleasant and expressing their disgust."[84]

On the other hand, Müller on several occasions emphasized that the etymological connection of the root *pu* with the notions of both purity and punishment "shows us that when the word *pœna* was first framed, punishment was conceived from a higher moral and religious point of view, as a purification from sin . . .":[85]

Do we want to know what was uppermost in the minds of those who formed the word for punishment, the Latin *pœna*, or *punio*, to punish; the root "pû" in Sanskrit, which means to cleanse, to purify, tells us that the Latin derivative was originally formed, not to express mere striking or torturing, but cleansing, correcting, delivering from the stain of sin. In Sanskrit many a god is implored to cleanse away ("punîhi") the sins of men, and the substantive "pâvana," though it did not come to mean punishment, . . . took in later times the sense of purification and penance. Now, it is clear that the train of thought which leads from purification to penance or from purification to punishment reveals a moral and even a religious sentiment in the conception and naming of *pœna*; and it shows us that in the very infancy of criminal justice punishment was looked upon, not simply as a retribution or revenge, but as a correction, as a removal of guilt. . . . And here we perceive the difference between etymology and definition, which has so often been overlooked. The etymology of a word can never give us its definition; it can only supply us with historical evidence that at the time when a word was formed, its predicative power represented one out of many characteristic features of the object to which it was applied. We are not justified in saying that because *punire* meant originally to purify, therefore the Roman conception of punishment was exclusively that of purification. All we can say is that one aspect of punishment, which struck the earliest framers of the language of Italy, was that of *expiation*.[86]

Müller affirmed the value of etymology, which reveals the historical meaning of words. However, he maintained that, although some roots may have a basis in nature, including instinctive human reactions, they are inevitably cultural constructs. Moreover, the value of etymology is limited, as it cannot reveal the true or current definition or meaning of a word, although it may point to one of its original meanings. All of this shows how far Müller's attitude is from that of the *Divyatattva*, despite his recognition of the religious and moral dimensions of purification. Indeed, Müller's debunking of mythological language elsewhere focused on the same Sanskrit root:

The name of [the Greek god] Pan is connected with the Sanskrit name for wind, namely, "pavana." The root from which it is derived means, in Sanskrit, to purify . . . [w]e have from "pû," to purify, the Greek "Pân," "Pânos," the purifying or sweeping wind, strictly corresponding to a possible Sanskrit form "pav-an." . . . It is thus that mythology arose . . .[87]

Mythology proceeded through a mistaken personification of terms that had originally a natural reference. This etymological reduction of Pan is entirely in keeping with Müller's nominalism, which echoed Hobbes's in contending that spirit "meant originally no more than a puff or whiff, a breeze, a breath."[88] A true science of etymology would reveal, not that nature is divine, but that so much of what we regard as divine is merely natural, or rather human and linguistic. For Müller as for some other nominalists, the project of purifying language of its demons also had religious dimensions, as it expressed a form of verbal iconoclasm.[89] However, his idea of a natural language was diametrically opposed to that of much of the Hindu tradition prior to modernity.

"Natural language[s] of the hand": gesture and the question of arbitrariness

If language cannot be regarded as natural, might there not be some other discourse that reflects and expresses nature immediately and directly, so as to be capable of serving as a universal medium of communication? Some have thought to find such a medium in gesture and bodily movement. Kinesics and the semiotics of dance are recognized subdisciplines of communication studies that have embraced a scientific view of the sign.[90] Yet some older theories of gesture, including some in more recent centuries, regarded gesture as a natural or even a divine language. The remainder of this chapter will focus on the religious dimensions of a few such theories.

The idea that there is a natural language of gesture need not be religious, of course. When asked to explain the meaning of a dance performance, Isadora Duncan stated: "If I could say it, I wouldn't have to dance it."[91] Her point was that dance is self-sufficient as a mode of expression. It neither needs speech to convey its message, nor is it replaceable by a verbal gloss. The dance requires no "libretto." At first blush, this appears to lend support to those who have affirmed the dignity of gesture as a mode of expression which, although it coordinates with speech (usually in a subordinate role), is not reducible to the latter, and may even communicate on its own. However, Duncan's response may be interpreted differently. The disjunction she posits between verbal and bodily modes of expression may be taken to undermine the possibility of recovering a natural language of gesture, such as could be embodied in dictionary form. If the significance of gestures, or of any particular gesture, is natural, then why isn't this significance immediately apparent? Why should it need to be recovered through study, and elaborated in words? Duncan would preserve the dignity of dance as a medium, at the price of any ability to communicate, in words, the message of that medium. This opposes any attempt to redescribe the meaning of gesture in words. If, on the other hand, gesture remains mute until it is glossed, then it cannot be regarded as a self-sufficient mode of communication, such as speech is. In that case, gesture would be similar to the fashion system in which, as Roland Barthes noted, particular changes in *couture* possess no meaning in and by themselves, and must be given meaning through a caption or verbal gloss.[92] It would appear that gestures do not, after all, speak for themselves; for if they did, they would do so without our assistance.

A review of some earlier attempts to recover a natural language of gesture reveals a cross-cultural human propensity to mistake culture for nature, and arbitrary signs for iconic ones. Instead of a science of gesture, we uncover theories of gesture that are rhetorical or ideological. In this respect, the history of attempts to recover a natural language of gesture parallels the history of attempts to recover or create a perfect or universal language that is spoken or written.

To preview the conclusions of this analysis: First, there is no significant unanimity as to the meaning of gestures across different cultural systems. Second, the very attempt to recover a natural language of gesture appears to be a response to fundamental problems of communication, especially the most fundamental problem: the perennial gap between discourse and reality known as the "arbitrariness of the sign." Efforts to avoid this gap end up reinstating it, by locating the meaning of gesture not in gesture itself, but in nature, or in a lost classical tradition, or even in some primeval moment of revelation. The reason why we do not understand at present the meaning of gesture is that this meaning has somehow been misplaced, or displaced. We live in exile from the natural language of gesture. Gesture appears as a potential substitute or supplement for the defects of our spoken and written languages, a supplement that highlights the inadequacy and arbitrariness of these modes of expression.

In his discussion of gesture in *Institutio oratoria*, the most important treatment of the topic in Western culture until modern times, the first-century CE Roman rhetorician Quintilian claimed that the art of manual gesture or "chironomy" "may almost be said to speak. . . . In fact, though the peoples and nations of the earth speak a multitude of tongues, they share in common the universal language of the hands."[93] The English physician John Bulwer (1606–56), whose system is discussed below, similarly maintained that the signs of gesture, as opposed to those of speech, were natural rather than conventional.[94] Gilbert Austin, in his *Chironomia* (1806), still affirmed something like a natural language of gesture when he argued that spoken language "derives all its significancy from compact only," but that there are "such external signs as indicate universally," among which are certain gestures.[95] Less cautious claims have been made in even more recent times. Little more than a century ago, Florence Adams stated that "All expression is but *the manifestation of the being by the body and its agents* . . . The student must develop the element of spontaneity as all manifestations of the being are spontaneous. . . . Pantomimic expression is the language of the soul . . . Pantomime mimics the *cause*, of which speech is the *effect* . . ."[96]

Closely connected with the question of the existence of a natural language of gesture is the question of the relation of gesture to imitation. This is because the basis for the claim that particular gestures enjoy a natural rather than merely arbitrary significance is made to depend upon the further claim of an iconic or mimetic relationship between gesture and reality. Quintilian notes the importance of gesture in the art of imitation, which he distinguishes from oratory proper.[97] The question of the connection between imitation or pantomime and oratorical gesture has been a common theme within the Western rhetorical tradition. Bulwer took the term "chironomon," meaning a master of rhetorical gesture, to be synonymous with "pantomime."[98] Imitation of a certain sort, namely, the imitation of the speech and mannerisms of particular individuals, was recognized already by Plato as a branch of rhetoric or sophistry.[99] Other arts also employed imitation, including imitative gesture. Aristotle noted that dance uses rhythm to imitate human behavior and experience.[100] The concept of mimesis or imitation has even been traced to ritual dance.[101] The close connection between gesture and imitation raises some difficult, and possibly insoluble, problems. In the case of certain gestures associated especially with pantomime, the imitation may indeed communicate without further gloss. However, in the case of dance or music, it is often difficult to see how the means of imitation employed, such as rhythm, represent anything in nature. Moreover, as Plato's attack on mimesis already suggested, imitation may be a form of artifice, rather than a proof of naturalness.

Other candidates for a natural language of movement include the distinction between the gestures of the right and left hands, and the distinction between gestures based on the vertical plane, or raising and lowering. Bulwer stated that "the right hand signifieth *liberality*, and for that cause [is] chosen to be the hieroglyphic of a most *beneficent* and *plentiful largesse*; whereas the left hand hath a contrary genius and is observed to be of a close and retired nature . . . of a skulking disposition affecting secrecy and the subtle leisure of a thrifty vacation."[102] (As a southpaw, I of course disagree.) Similarly regarding gestures of raising the body, Lord Kames (1696–1782) argued that "Joy, which produceth a cheerful elevation of mind, is expressed by an elevation of body . . . Pride, magnanimity, courage, and the whole tribe of elevating passions, are expressed by external gestures that are the same as to the circumstance of elevation . . . Hence it comes that an erect posture is a sign or expression of dignity."[103] Despite such assertions, Durkheimian Robert Hertz's essay on the sociocultural significance of right and left showed that these categories are, after all, overlaid with meanings that are anything but natural, and that stem from a more basic social opposition between the Sacred and the Profane.[104] More recently, Barry Schwartz has made a similar argument with respect to the distinction between higher and lower.[105] Demonstrations of the relativity of the meanings of these gestures or positions coordinate with the structuralist axiom that signs, being arbitrary, are often invested with significance through systems of binary opposition. "Right" has no meaning without "left"; and "high" has no meaning without "low." These oppositions are given additional, cultural meanings by being homologized with other, socially determined oppositions. The demonizing of the left hand, and the divinization of the right, are examples of such nonnatural meanings which, although found cross-culturally, are by no means universal. Neurological studies of the bilateral brain may shed further light on the tendency of such categories to carry particular meanings, although most likely the valorization of right- over left- handedness is simply an example of the ideological reinforcement of the norm: statistically speaking, more people are right-handed. If even such basic parameters of movement, not yet reduced to specific gestures, carry no natural significance, then what is the hope that one will ever be able to elaborate a universal language of gesture? This does not call into question the existence of gestures or reflexes that signify naturally as symptoms, only of those that purport to signify meanings, as the words and sentences of a language do, without the prior institution of a cultural code, such as that on which language is based.

John Bulwer's *Chirologia* and *Chironomia*

The recognition that language is imperfect—in the sense of not reflecting the natural order in a nondistorting way—as well as the desire to overcome the communication barrier among different linguistic traditions, inspired one of the more fascinating developments in theories of language in the modern period: the attempt to construct a perfect language or system of writing that would bypass language and communicate ideas directly.[106] Stemming from Francis Bacon's polymathic effort to delineate the tasks that lay before the new science, these projects burgeoned in the second half of the seventeenth century in England and continued into the nineteenth century along Baconian lines. Such efforts are the predecessors of contemporary projects for a universal language: Esperanto, Globish (Global English), etc. Utopian in aspiration, such artificial languages have often promised to be a panacea for a range of communicative, social, economic, and even religious ills.[107]

The topic of universal languages is of importance for the semiotics of religion for several reasons. First, while various scientific proposals for a universal language competed initially with magical views of language and occasionally made claims for the pragmatic benefits of their projects that bordered on the magical, these proposals also demonstrated a growing awareness of the gap between language and reality, or culture and nature. Consequently, they participated in the critique of the habit of taking words for things that, as described more fully in Chapter Four of this volume, was associated with Protestant literalism. Second, such projects often had specifically religious motivations. From a practical perspective, they were frequently inspired by the motive to communicate the Gospel in foreign lands: to construct an alphabet that missionaries could use first to record the unfamiliar words of native tribes, and then to translate the scriptures.

Discussions of the benefits of a universal language or system of writing often bordered on the utopian or even the soteriological. Such languages were seen as providing at least partial redress for the curse of confusion of tongues that had occurred at the fall of the Tower of Babel, and of repeating the miracle of Pentecost, when the Holy Spirit inspired the Apostles with the power to preach to all nations.[108] Already in his *New Atlantis* (1624), Bacon described a fictional book capable of translating the Gospel into all languages.[109]

Bacon's original proposal for a "real character" or universal system of writing, presented in his *Advancement of Learning* (1605), allowed that some linguistic signs might have a natural or iconic basis. Most of his followers, including Bishop John Wilkins (1614–1672), proposed to institute a universal language by convention.[110] However, some more enthusiastic figures continued well into the nineteenth century to promote or pursue the idea of a language that was natural or even divine.[111]

John Bulwer's vision of a language of gesture illustrates some of the motivations as well as contradictions of such schemes. In 1644, Bulwer published *Chirologia: Or the Natural Language of the Hand* and *Chironomia: Or the Art of Manual Rhetoric*, one of the first and most extensive treatments of gesture in the English language in early modern times.[112] The first book, the *Chirologia*, is descriptive: it reconstructs the natural and universal significance of certain manual gestures. The second book, the *Chironomia*, is prescriptive: it teaches the art of gesture for the benefit of different classes of orators. As his title indicates, Bulwer followed Quintilian's lead in delineating a "chironomy" or law of gesture, and attempting to fill a major lacuna in the arts of rhetoric. Bulwer's double title may also allude to Plato's *Cratylus*, or at least to the question of a natural language as framed in that dialogue. The dependence of Bulwer's two books on reason (*logos*) and law (*nomos*), respectively, replicates Plato's distinction between nature (*physis*) and law (*nomos*). That Bulwer possibly had this earlier distinction in mind is further indicated by his statement in the *Chirologia* that "gestures (being natural signs) have no dependence on any ordinance or statute of art . . . [b]ut . . . [are] part of the unalterable laws and institutes of nature . . . [and] are by their own personal constitution and by a native consequence significant."[113]

Bulwer's treatise reflects a fundamental problem raised earlier: If the language of gesture is natural, then why should it need to be learned? Many ritual and rhetorical practices are plagued by a basic contradiction, the scripting of spontaneity. Despite the fact that these practices are supposed to be unmediated and natural, facility in their use is something that can be acquired only through a long course of training. The gap between nature and art signaled already in the bipartite structure of Bulwer's treatise is complemented by other gaps that serve to undermine his claim for a natural language of gesture. One such gap is disclosed by his manner of evidencing the natural significance of gestures. He adduces copious, and sometimes conflicting, quotations from classical authors and from scripture to demonstrate the meaning of each gesture. The amount of book-learning Bulwer assembles is truly prodigious, and amounts to a kind of textual empiricism. Yet it does not avoid the problem raised earlier, namely, that gestures are not shown to have the power to speak by themselves. Only through massive erudition is one enabled to, as it were, hear the speech of gesture. This directly contradicts the capacity of gesture to function as a universal language for, if only truly bookish savants are capable of understanding gestures before being instructed, then even were the meaning of gestures able to be ascertained in this way, it would still limit their use to a small group.

Apart from the gaps between nature and art, and between gesture and speech, implicit in Bulwer's system, there is another gap that further separates gestures from any natural meaning: namely, that between the past and the present. His appeal to classical and biblical sources exemplifies a certain mode of textual authority. The ancients supposedly possessed all knowledge, which we have lost, and can now recover only by examining their remains. For Bulwer, the key to the universal code is gesture itself, which is "the only speech and general language of human nature."[114] This is because speech itself is no longer able to serve as a universal language, due to the separation of tongues at the fall of the Tower of Babel. As one of the poems dedicated to Bulwer's treatise states: "Chirologie redeems from Babel's doom, / And is the universal idiom."[115] Bulwer himself connects his chirology with the work of redemption:

> And indeed it is a kind of knowledge that Adam partly lost with his innocency, yet might be repaired in us by a diligent observation and marking of the outward effects of the inward and secret motions of beasts. This natural language of the hand as it had the happiness to escape the curse at the confusion of Babel, so it hath since been sanctified and made a holy language by the expressions of our Savior's hands whose gestures have given a sacred allowance to the natural significations of ours.[116]

Bulwer here draws on several well-known scriptural themes. Adam, the original sinner, is said in Genesis 2:19 to have called the animals "by their own names" (*nominibus suis*).[117] This had two possible meanings: either he established their names by convention, or he somehow knew their true names. Interpreters often embraced the latter position, and held that Adam spoke a perfect, natural language.[118] Bulwer does the same here, but with a twist. Whereas most would attribute the loss of that primeval, natural language to the fall of the Tower of Babel, he says that this language was already "partly lost" with Adam's fall into original sin. Accordingly, Bulwer connects the recovery of the natural language of gesture with humanity's redemption from sin. He therefore locates his treatise as part of the ongoing work of salvation.

Jeffrey Wollock has described some of the historical context of the *Chirologia* and *Chironomia*. Bulwer was explicitly responding to Bacon's calls for both a scientific study of gesture and a real character.[119] Bulwer combined or conflated these two projects, maintaining that gesture was a "universal character of reason" that could communicate to speakers of all languages.[120] He extended the term "character" to his manual language which, although not written, was, like writing, visible. Bulwer, John Wilkins, and other seekers of a universal character also authored systems of sign language for the deaf.[121]

As Wollock notes, Bulwer regarded his gestural character as naturally significant, unlike Bacon and Wilkins, who held that a "real character" could only be an arbitrary institution, tantamount to a cipher or code. Revealingly, however, Bulwer retained the analogy with a code. His pictorial illustration of the gestures described in the *Chirologia* adds the caption that these "Gestures, besides their typicall significations, are so ordered to serve for privy cyphers for any secret intimation."[122] The analogous caption in the *Chironomia* adds that "This following Table doth not only serve to expresse the Rhetoricall postures of the *Fingers*; but may be used as Cyphers for private wayes of Discourse or Intelligence."[123] To refer to the cryptographic use of such gestures seems logical as, like any code, they had to be learned, and could serve as a medium of communication only among persons all of whom already knew the code. However, as applied to gestures that are supposedly natural, the analogy of a cipher exposes the contradiction that these gestures are anything but spontaneously self-communicating. Ultimately, this contradiction vitiates Bulwer's project for uncovering a natural language of gesture.

The political and social context for these projects for a universal language is illuminating. They followed the decline of Latin and the rise of the vernaculars, and appear to have accepted the impossibility of instituting a universal spoken language. However, they retained the utopian promise of a common medium of communication capable of overcoming the deleterious social consequences associated with the breakdown of a common religious culture previously embodied in the Catholic Church. The lack of any standard for determining the meaning of words was blamed for theological disputes and consequent civil strife.[124] Bulwer's *Chirologia* and *Chironomia* were written during the English Civil War, as one of the dedicatory poems notes.[125] In the middle of such conflict, one might be excused for escaping into an idealistic vision of a harmony induced by better communication. Ultimately, however, the search for a universal character had no practical success. Even assuming one could produce a workable language of this sort, the effort involved in learning it would be sufficient to preclude its widespread adoption. This is the same problem that plagues Esperanto today. Although Esperanto draws extensively upon existing European languages, it is sufficiently unnatural that it constitutes a new, conventional idiom that, like any such code, has to be learned.

Hindu dance: gesture in the *Nāṭyaśāstra*

Hindu systems of gesture illustrate many of the issues already raised in connection with Western systems. Two traditions of gesture that have evolved in South Asia are that of the dramatic arts (*nāṭya*), and that of the religious movement known as Tantra. The use of gestures in drama and dance can be traced to the text called *Nāṭyaśāstra* composed by Bhārata sometime between 200 BCE and 200 CE. Tantra arose at a later date, around the sixth century CE, and developed its own system of gestures used for purposes of ritual worship and magic. Although the two traditions are independent, their gestures bear some resemblance to each other. Presumably, there may have been some reciprocal influence, especially by the existing dramatic tradition on the later Tantric tradition. The *Nāṭyaśāstra* uses the term *hasta* or "hand" for its gestures, whereas Tantra uses *mudrā*. This word has several meanings, especially that of a sign or seal. In later centuries, the term *mudrā* has come to be applied to dramatic gestures as well.[126] Mudrās have long played an important role in Buddhist iconography, and may be traced back to the still-disputed origins of that artistic tradition centuries before Tantra.

The *Nāṭyaśāstra* or "Science of Drama" is the foundational and most important text of the Indian aesthetic tradition. Dramatic gesture, together with other aspects of delivery, receives extensive treatment in the text, which elaborates sets of gestures (*abhinaya*) for the head, hands, and other limbs. The chapter on the basic 64 hand gestures (*hasta*) divides these into gestures for single hands, for both hands in combination, and for dance (*nṛtta*) as opposed to drama (*nāṭya*).[127] This last distinction is of some importance, and will be revisited later. The names for the hand gestures are frequently iconic, as are their meanings. For example, in the gesture called "flag" (*patāka*) the fingers are extended. This can be used to represent numbers such as ten, one hundred, or one thousand. If the fingers are made to tremble or to move up and down, they can depict flames, waves, or a waterfall. The gesture called "half-moon" (*ardhacandra*) can, naturally enough, be used to represent the crescent moon. Similarly, a number of the gestures in the thirteenth-century *Abhinayadarpaṇa* or "Mirror of Gesture" have iconic meanings: for example, the *Śivaliṅga* gesture, with the thumb sticking up, denotes the *liṅga* or phallus of the god Śiva.[128] However, apart from such iconic meanings, the *Nāṭyaśāstra* gives many that are conventional. The gesture called "clever" (*catura*) is supposed to represent not only such diverse qualities as merit (*guṇa*), demerit (*aguṇa*), and youth (*yauvana*), but even different colors.[129]

In general terms, the goal of Sanskrit drama is to convey certain sentiments (*rasa*: literally, "flavor") and emotions (*bhāva*). As the *Abhinayadarpaṇa* says: "Where the hand [of the dancer] goes, the eyes go. Where the eyes go, the mind goes. Where the mind goes, the emotion (*bhāva*) goes. Where there is the emotion, there the sentiment (*rasa*) arises."[130] How this communication of sentiments is achieved and, in particular, what gesture contributes to this achievement is, however, uncertain. The sentiments and emotions are exhaustively classified, as are the gestures. Yet particular gestures are not generally correlated with particular sentiments or emotions. Instead, the *Nāṭyaśāstra* gives detailed verbal descriptions of how to perform the gestures, and of their different meanings. The tasks of choreography and composition are left to the dancer, who presumably relied upon both practical training and an oral tradition.

The concept of imitation (*anukaraṇa*) is important in *Nāṭya* tradition, although less important than the theory of sentiments and emotions. The actor is supposed to imitate the actions of everyday life.[131] This, of course, is similar to the concept of imitation in the Western aesthetic tradition, in which art is supposed to be like life, only heightened. The various gestures and other accompaniments of art serve to produce this heightening effect. But the problem of imitation should be connected with another concept, that of representation. The *Nāṭyaśāstra* distinguishes dance (*nṛtta*) from dramatic acting (*nāṭya*). Dance, unlike acting, is not regarded as representational, nor as conveying meaning. (The later tradition also distinguishes a third type of patterned movement called *nṛtya*, which is supposed to be partly representational.[132]) Bhārata explains that the purpose of dance is instead to "produce beauty" (*śobhāṃ prajanayet*).[133]

In such Hindu traditions we observe the same conundrum posed by Western aesthetic traditions: apart from a few simple iconic gestures or pantomimic actions, how precisely do the gestures of drama signify?[134] The answer seems to be, once again, that gestures refer to a conventional code that purports to constitute a natural language. In the case of Indian drama, the very elaborateness and sophistication of this code contradicts its ostensibly natural status. As Ananda Coomaraswamy stated:

> Excellent acting wears the air of perfect spontaneity, but that is the art which conceals art. It is exactly the same with painting. The Ajantâ frescoes seem to show unstudied gestures and spontaneous pose, but actually there is hardly a position of the hands or of the body which has not a recognized name and a precise significance. The more deeply we penetrate the technique of any typical Oriental art, the more we find that what appears to be individual, impulsive, and "natural," is actually long-inherited, well-considered, and well-bred. Under these conditions life itself becomes a ritual.[135]

Indeed, the same could be said of any art. Yet in the case of Indian dance traditions, it is especially true. The more numerous and complex the gestures and other movements deployed, and the more elaborate the cultural code required to interpret them, the more such traditions depart from nature. Phillip Zarrilli has made a similar observation concerning the later South

Indian dance tradition called Kathakali: "For audience members, there is a great variety of levels for understanding *mudrās*, depending upon whether an individual has been 'initiated' into the intricacies of the gesture language. For the common man who does not 'read' the language, the generalized decorative use of gesture in pure dance can be appreciated for its own sake."[136] Zarrilli states that an actor must be able to communicate every single word of the drama through *mudrās*. Even grammatical forms such as case-endings may be indicated through gesture.[137] This approaches the ideal of a true gestural language or character, yet it is, for that reason, anything but natural.

In many premodern South Asian traditions, the origins of the arts and sciences were attributed to the gods or sages. The prototypes of all significant actions were given in a primordial moment of revelation, as Eliade suggested.[138] The *Nātyaśāstra* is no exception to this rule. The four *Vedas* are revealed ritual texts of the greatest antiquity and authority, if not present practical application, in Hinduism. The *Nātyaśāstra* explicitly declares itself a "fifth Veda" that combines elements of the original four.[139] Its first chapter relates that the creator god Brahmā taught the dramatic art to the sage Bhārata.[140] The first performance enacted the victory of the gods over the demons, which displeased the latter greatly, so that they paralyzed the faculties of speech, action, and memory of the dancers.[141] The gods overcame this obstacle, yet henceforth every performance had to be protected by means of the proper ritual observances.

Such references to a primeval, divine creation of the arts, despite their mythological status, have something in common with Bulwer's system of gesture. The myth of origins characterizes his system as well, inasmuch as he refers the beginnings of the art of gesture to classical rhetoric or to some vanished, golden past or Eden. These are all attempts to establish the temporal, ontological, and semiological priority of gesture. Although such attempts seek to secure the foundations of a science of gesture by placing them beyond the domain of the mundane and changeable, they actually disclose the gap that exists between an absent prototype and its present instantiation. They acknowledge, if only implicitly, the impossibility of grounding the significance of the gestures they describe. To this extent, they represent a latent awareness of the arbitrariness of the sign that has been brought explicitly to consciousness in modern semiotics. It is tempting to interpret the episode in the *Nātyaśāstra* in which the demons paralyze the dance as a kind of narrative admission of the arbitrariness of what are, after all, human institutions. However, this admission, if such it is, is immediately repressed. In contemporary India, the claim of divine origins is no longer tenable. However, the claim that modern Indian dance traditions are perfectly congruent with the ancient *Nātyaśāstra* is sometimes advanced.[142] The idea of a pure, changeless tradition is, in a way, a perpetuation of the myth of origins found in the *Nātyaśāstra*. Yet Mandakranta Bose assures us that the link between these ancient and modern dance traditions is not one of unbroken continuity.[143]

Mudrās in Hindu Tantra

Hindu Tantra employs numerous types of hand gestures called mudrās, together with the verbal formulas called mantras, to worship the gods and perform practical magic. Although the French Sanskritist André Padoux indicated the desirability of a semiological study of the relation between ritual words and gestures in Tantra,[144] this has not yet been done, and only a few preliminary suggestions can be provided here. Mudrās, which have been extensively developed in both Buddhist and Hindu Tantric traditions, sometimes have partly iconic or other natural significance, although they are often assigned to particular deities or purposes in a manner that is purely conventional. Their coordination with language poses a particular problem, for between language and gesture there is no immediately obvious resemblance. Language and gesture are fused in the Tantric rites of *nyāsa* or "laying down" the syllables of the mantra on the body of the ritual practitioner. Often this is done in forward and reverse order, representing the cosmic cycle with its phases of creation (*sṛṣṭi*) and destruction (*saṃhāra*). This is a type of diagrammatic icon, in which speech and gesture are coordinated.

Although Tantra gives to speech the leading role in creation and in ritual, sometimes gesture appears to be equivalent in authority and ritual efficacy. The *yonimudrā* or "womb sign" is an iconic gesture produced by the complete interlocking of the hands, as if to duplicate the embrace of the womb.[145] The use of this mudrā is one device for making mantras magically effective; another is the practice, described in the last chapter, of enveloping the syllables of the mantra with other syllables that are added in forward and reverse order. There are associated forms of yoga or meditation in which this back-and-forth movement of the syllables is visualized as taking place within the body. The womb-gesture, like its verbal analogues, constructs a diagram or iconic map of the cycle of creation, including not only the cosmic round of creation and destruction, but also the cycle of sexual reproduction, a fact that explains the reference to the womb. The *mudrā* or mantra is made to imitate nature. Yet this imitation is highly stylized and conventionalized, and depicts nature as Hindus conceive it: as a cycle of expansion and contraction, rather than a single "big bang."

The *Tantras* fall into a contradiction analogous to that into which Bulwer fell, by extolling simultaneously both the naturalness and the secrecy of the language of gesture. Although the *yonimudrā* is supposed to represent universal processes of creation, it is said to be "most hidden" (*ati gopyam*).[146] Like many other cultural traditions, Hindu Tantra wants to have its cake and eat it too: meaning, it wants to maintain that what is particular or proprietary to it is actually universal.

The Tantric reference to origins, which in this case means the creation of the world by the gods, is not unique to ancient, mythological traditions.

Ultimately, all such claims of naturalness, spontaneity, and temporal priority are forms of rhetoric designed precisely to cover up the fact that, after all, we cannot achieve salvation, or perform real magic, by manipulating syllables and digits. Nor may we even presume to be successful in more mundane, interpersonal communications. The dream of a natural language is a very powerful form of rhetoric, one that transcends any particular culture, and that continues to appear in some more recent systems, such as Bulwer's, that purport to be scientific.

The various systems of gesture summarized above demonstrate that most claims for a natural language of gesture resolve, upon further scrutiny, into conventional systems of purely cultural significance. The interpretation of gestures depends upon the knowledge of the appropriate cultural code, possession of which is either coextensive with an entire culture, as in the case of basic gestures of greeting, or limited to a much smaller subgroup of savants or esoteric initiates, as in the case of Hindu Tantra. Ignoring this obvious limitation, some enthusiasts have argued that gestures have a natural meaning, one that ostensibly reposes in nature, or in some lost tradition of the classical age, or even in mythic times. This displacement of meaning describes a gap between the past and the present, so that interpreting the language of gesture becomes an act of recall or remembrance, colored by the authority of tradition and the sentiment of nostalgia. Bulwer sought to return to a time before the Tower of Babel fell, by substituting a language of the hand for the lost universal spoken language. The Hindu *Tantras* attempted a complete fusion between past and present, so that their rituals would attain the power of the cosmogony. What is central to such theories is the idea that time's arrow points downward. History is devolution. Something is lost through time. The most that we may hope for is to emulate the past in its own forms. The act of interpretation is an uphill battle to recall a meaning that was present, in its fullness, at the beginning. The tropes of loss, and of the struggle of memory against forgetfulness, that mark each of these earlier systems of gesture identify them as rhetorical or ideological systems, rather than scientific approaches to the study of gesture.

CHAPTER FOUR

Literalism, iconoclasm, and the question of the secular

Literalism: what is old and what new?

Despite the stubborn persistence of the dream of a natural or perfect language, one of the chief divides separating the modern condition from its predecessors is the rise of a certain skepticism concerning the sign: its ability to represent nature, to communicate with the deity, or to alter the course of events by symbolic magic. As indicated in Chapter One, some of this skepticism has antecedents in the religious movement, complex and multifarious, that for simplicity's sake we refer to as "Protestant literalism." When English Protestants insisted that the Gospel was a form of plain speech, as contrasted with the figurative and misleading discourses of both Jewish ceremonial and pagan oracles, they were drawing on ancient Christian tropes that already characterized the present moment—post-Crucifixion—as the dawn of semiotic transparency or enlightenment. And these originally theological narratives, which expressed the Christian notion of salvation as having superseded earlier, misguided traditions, deeply influenced what we characterize, with imprecision, as "science," "rationality," or the "Enlightenment."[1] Secular reason is neither perfectly rational, nor fully secular.

Max Weber described part of this paradox: the manner in which a theological impetus, which he identified with the Puritan reappropriation and development of Jewish iconoclasm, contributed to disenchantment and the rise of secularism.[2] Although secularization is often thought of erroneously as the decline of religion—meaning, in part, the loss of faith in mythological narratives and the efficacy of ritual practices—it would more accurately be described as the replacement of one sort of religious cosmology by another. This new cosmology insisted on a rigorous separation between sign and referent, or word and thing. Exemplary of this development was Bacon's critique of various "idols" or mental errors, including the "idols of the marketplace," believing in "names of things which do not exist . . . to which nothing in reality corresponds."[3] It would be mistaken to represent this transition as effecting a complete divide between "primitive" and "modern" thought. For one thing, the attempt to perfect language by establishing a closer adequation between word and thing was, as we have seen, central to many premodern religious traditions. Implicit in these efforts was at least a partial awareness of the gap between nature and language, at least of that language that had not been perfected by ritual techniques and manipulation. Rather than ordinary language, it was special language—the language of scripture, of the Bible or the *Vedas*—that accorded with both divinity and reality.

With the secular Enlightenment, as represented by the Baconian tradition, such efforts to perfect language, as a response to a recognition of language's inherent failings, arguably intensified and accelerated. Also the means used to perfect language were utterly different. Rather than ritual manipulation or the discovery of a correct key to scripture, it was scientific observation and experiment that were supposed to make words conform to nature. This was partly a repudiation of the idea that words and things could constitute what we might call "reversible indexes" of the causal variety. Words could, indeed must, follow and conform to nature. Yet there was no possibility of using words to transform reality prospectively. The repudiation of symbolic magic contributed a key part of the polemic that the Enlightenment, in both its religious and its secular versions, conducted against earlier and other religious traditions. Language became ontologically and temporally subordinate to physical nature.

This does not of course mean that symbolic discourses disappeared. Rather, the line between fiction and literalism, like that between word and thing, was sharpened. One illustration is Huldrych Zwingli's (1484–1531) proclamation that the "is" (*est*) in "This is my body" (*hoc est enim corpus meum*) was merely symbolic: that the Eucharistic host "signified" Christ, without actually transubstantiating into His flesh and blood.[4] This was a debate over semantics, over hermeneutics or the interpretation of the Bible, to be sure; but it was also, as evidenced by the extent and duration of the controversy over the Eucharist between Catholics and Protestants of different stripes, much more than that. It was also a debate over cosmology, salvation, the Incarnation (which was reprised, in some sense, with every act of transubstantiation), over the possibility of miracles, and more generally, over the possibility of communication between humanity and divinity.

Although Zwingli's interpretation of the Eucharist represented one of the critical moments in the development of what we call "Protestant literalism," and one that exemplifies Vickers's account of the shift from "identity" to "analogy," it should be emphasized again how much continuity there was between before and after. Zwingli was hardly excluding the possibility of symbolic interpretation; indeed, he was insisting that some passages in the Bible *must* be read symbolically. Traditional Christian typological interpretation of the Bible had also insisted on this, and thus valorized the symbol to an often astonishing degree. To some extent, however, this had always been associated with an interpretation of certain parts of the Bible—in particular, the ceremonies of the Old Testament—as having value merely insofar as they foreshadowed events in the New Testament. Declaring such passages as symbolic—as prophesying and preparing the way for a more transparent message—was a way of finding meaning in the apparently meaningless. It was also a way for orthodox Christians to defend the relative value of the Mosaic dispensation, a move that preserved these texts while also subordinating them to the Gospel.[5] Together with the insistence on "scripture alone" (*sola scriptura*) as the source of authority in matters of religion, Martin Luther emphasized the primacy of the literal sense of the Bible. This tendency to subordinate the symbolic dimensions of scripture was given new emphasis in Protestant polemics against the excesses of traditional Catholic modes of typology and against Jewish ceremonial as a series of figures, shadows, and "hieroglyphs."[6]

There were, moreover, many forms of Protestant literalism, ranging from the one that is now almost exclusively taken to represent this movement—a fundamentalist insistence on the factual accuracy of scripture—to a vast range of orthodoxies, heterodoxies, even modes of religious skepticism. Protestants afforded varying degrees of latitude to the symbolic interpretation of scripture, in ways that conserved certain elements of the older typological approach, particularly its emphasis on the prophetic value of the Bible and condemnation of Jewish ceremonial. For more radical thinkers, especially Deists such as John Toland, the idea of the Gospel as revealing a plain and "natural religion" that eschewed "mystery" (as in the title of his *Christianity Not Mysterious* (1696)) coordinated with a devaluation of symbolism that went further than most older forms of Christianity. Toland mocked modes of biblical interpretation that referred to "type, symbol, parable, shadow, figure, sign and mystery,"[7] and argued that "in the New Testament *Mystery* is always us'd in the first Sense of the Word, . . . for *things naturally very intelligible, but so cover'd by figurative Words or Rites, that Reason could not discover them without special Revelation*; and that the Vail is actually taken away; then it will manifestly follow that the Doctrines so reveal'd cannot now be properly call'd *Mysteries*."[8] In other words, precisely because the plain speech of the Gospel had removed the veil of Mosaic ritual, symbolic readings of scripture had been rendered obsolete or superfluous. In such interpretations, the demise of the symbol is directly linked with Christian salvation and the idea of supersession, or the transcendence of and evolution beyond pagan and Jewish traditions.

At the far end of the spectrum, Thomas Hobbes's insistence on a literal interpretation of biblical references to "angels" and "spirits" in natural rather than supernatural terms was in the service of a hermeneutic of disenchantment.[9] All words ultimately must have a concrete reference, Hobbes insisted; the phrase "incorporeal being" is an oxymoron, therefore disembodied spirits do not exist.[10] While the nature of Hobbes's private religious convictions is unclear, and has been the focus of much debate, it is easy to imagine him, tongue in cheek, meeting more orthodox biblical literalists tit-for-tat by going back to the etymological meaning of scriptural references.

Through such diffuse and complex transformations, new lines came to be established dividing literal from symbolic discourses. Hobbes's arguments, along with Bacon's earlier complaint against the abuse of words as "idols of the mind," influenced the self-segregation of the discourse of science as founded precisely on the proper distinction between words and things. The motto of the Royal Society of London, the preeminent body for the promotion of the new science in the later seventeenth century, was *nullius in verba*, which translates loosely as "we place no faith in the authority of words." This was matched by a vigorous polemic carried forward by members and affiliates of this society against the deceptive power of language, conceived as a new form of idolatry—the worship of words— which went hand in hand with the glorification of tradition for its own sake.[11] Already in 1667, long before the sociologist Robert Merton argued, following Max Weber, that Puritanism had provided a crucial impetus to the development of science in England,[12] the historian of the Royal Society, Thomas Sprat, made a similar claim:

> [I]t is now the fittest season for *Experiments* to arise, to teach us a Wisdome, which springs from the depths of *Knowledge*, to shake off the shadows, and to scatter the mists, which fill the minds of men with a vain consternation. This is a *work* well-becoming the most *Christian Profession*. For the most apparent effect, which attended the passion of *Christ*, was the putting of an eternal silence, on all the false oracles, and dissembled inspirations of *Antient Times*.[13]

The affinities between the religious and scientific reformations extended also to a common style of discourse. Early in the last century, Richard Foster Jones recognized some of these affinities, and stressed the contribution of the scientific movement to the birth of a plain style of speech.[14] However, the plain style appears to have originated not in science, but in Puritanism. Calvin was the source of the critique of "vain repetitions" in prayer, described further in Chapter Five of this volume. The phrases "plain style" and "plain way" that Jones used to describe the new literary style[15] were used first to refer to the style of the Gospels or of Paul's preaching.[16] Many Puritans came to condemn forms of adornment and ornamentation, whether in speech, church decoration, architecture, theatrical display, or personal attire. John Sommerville has also emphasized the contribution of Protestantism to the "secularization of language," stating that Keith Thomas was "surprise[d], in studying the decline of a mystic faith in words, that it was caused more by Protestantism than by science. Protestant writers associated 'magical' philosophies and technologies with the Catholic Church and disparaged them at a time when scientists were still maintaining open minds."[17]

When we consider the influence of Protestant literalism, therefore, we have to consider not merely its legacy for fundamentalist interpretations of scripture, but also its legacy for many discourses thought to be secular or scientific, which defined themselves against the symbolic, poetic, or metaphorical in much the same way that many Protestants had already defined the Gospel against figurative language. A case in point is the legal reformer Jeremy Bentham's long war against the tyranny of verbal "fictions," considered in detail in this chapter.

In reconsidering the "Great Divide" between modernity and whatever came before, it is necessary to acknowledge also the many continuities. Not only did the new literalism draw on older theological modes of interpretation, but its advent scarcely represented the outright demise of the symbolic. What we are talking about is instead a sequestering, segregation, or compartmentalization of the figurative, one that often amounted to a demotion of its value, but which did not prevent but in some cases actually facilitated the development of new modes of antiliteralist discourse, such as the modern novel. This division of labor among genres is also characteristic of the secular. Fictional literature has grown up alongside the increasing insistence on literalism in ostensibly more rational, public, or utilitarian discourses, partly as an escape from such modes.

One example of the influence of Protestant literalism on the division of genres concerns the history of the literary device we call "foreshadowing." The older Christian notion was that some events in the Bible, and particularly the Old Testament, typified, in the sense of prophesying, later events, particularly those in the New Testament. The word "to foreshadow" or "to shadow forth" first appeared precisely in connection with Christian typology: the type or figure was also called a "shadow" (*umbra*) that pointed dimly toward an event in the future that would illuminate its significance retrospectively. Typology retained a belief in the connection between words and things. Everything was a part of God's plan, which was revealed gradually through sacred writ, albeit in a veiled form. So, although there was no general correspondence between words and things, some of God's words and other modes of expression could in fact predict the future. It would be just as accurate to say that, according to typology, one event could symbolize and signify, and even predict though perhaps not cause (in the sense that this signification was, being derived from God, indefeasible), a future event. This semiotic ideology, by granting ontological and temporal priority to certain signs, shared much with those other cultures that believed in the possibility of a natural or perfect language.

The further development of such notions outside of Christian orthodoxy describes part of the difference of the semiotic ideology of modernity. Foreshadowing is now a recognized literary technique. However, whenever it appears, it marks a literary work, a film, or other text as precisely counterfactual, fictive, even surreal. The use of foreshadowing has an air of the uncanny that specifically precludes its use in fictional realism. This marks a significant departure from the older Christian view that foreshadowing is not a mere literary device, but supernatural: a divine language. In the same way, the contemporary notion of "fiction" is an anachronism when it is applied to scripture.

Iconoclasm and literalism

Despite the tremendous variation among different Protestant and secular literalisms, we can identify certain general tendencies that enable us to characterize both the location and the direction of the semiotic ideology of modernity. This ideology had its roots in a broader, theologically inspired critique of the sign, the most obvious manifestation of which was Protestant iconoclasm. The connection between iconoclasm and literalism has been noted previously, by the historian of religions Peter Harrison[18] and by the anthropologist Webb Keane, who has focused attention on the manner in which the semiotic ideology of modernity continued a Protestant attack on the sign as a "fetish."[19] Keane has in mind as well Weber's account of the manner in which ancient Jewish iconoclasm was reprised and emphasized by Protestants.

Recognition of the continuity between modern and older, often explicitly theological modes of iconoclasm calls into question the newness of the semiotic ideology of modernity that Keane argues for. In broader perspective, what we see is arguably not a sharp distinction—much less a "Great Divide"—between modernity and everything that came before, but rather an ebb and flow between a position of semiotic naïveté and one of semiotic critique. If the West is distinguished by the critique of semiotic form, as exemplified by Plato's attack on poetry and sophistry, and by the iconoclasm of Abraham and Moses—which gives one answer to Tertullian's question "What has Athens to do with Jerusalem?"[20]—then this distinction is precisely not one between past and present, except to the extent that post-Reformation modes of iconoclasm must, like earlier modes, have their own specificities. Moreover, we have examples of iconoclasm, and of other polemics against verbal and plastic images, in other cultures, including Islam. Perhaps the best way of thinking about these relationships, then, is to recognize that modernity exists on a continuum with other semiotic ideologies, including many that are customarily labeled "religions," and that on this continuum modernity may be grouped with those types of religion that have been identified as "iconoclastic."[21]

Iconoclasm—literally, the "breaking of images"—may have many motivations. It may be a form of political critique or social revolt against an existing regime, the power and authority of which are represented, concentrated, and communicated by particular images. The attack on the image in this case is a symbolic dismantling of the existing order, as well as a practical move toward revolt, given the effectiveness of signs (and of their destruction) as a form of social action.[22] But in many cases there is also a deeper theological basis for iconoclasm, which reflects a conviction that the divine may not be captured or depicted adequately in material form. The representation of the deity by means of a statue or other image may also be taken as the arrogation to oneself of the power of creation, as well as of control or authority over God, especially as images are often deployed as instruments in magical rites. The prohibition against idolatry has to be understood in this context. So, for example, when Puritans condemned the "vain repetitions" of Catholic prayers, they objected to, among other things, the use of such devices to influence the deity.[23] Iconoclasm can be part of a larger complex of ideas according to which the divine is placed beyond human imagination and influence, as a means of asserting the omnipotence of God and His utter distance from the merely human. At the same time, this is a bid for universality, as any embodied image is bounded, circumscribed, by its particular shape and form. Paradoxically, only a God who is beyond our capacity to image or describe is fully "translatable" into all cultures. This aspect of iconoclasm appears to be shared by the universalizing monotheistic traditions.

In the case of certain schemes for a universal language that were inspired by Bacon, the demand that each thing be represented by one and only one word expressed an analogy between monotheism and the idea of a precise, univocal language.[24] The monovalence of the sign—beginning with the name of God—was a foundation for the creation of a universal language. No longer would metaphors and poetry be allowed to render language ambiguous, as this could undermine not merely communication but also salvation. This applied especially to Christian texts and categories. The fixing of both scripture and language in a canon that communicated monotheism coordinated with an attack on linguistic "idols," words that produced erroneous mental images and contributed to the belief in false gods. An example of this tradition was Friedrich Max Müller, who was himself a great iconoclast, an inheritor of the Hobbesian nominalist tradition who applied the critique of taking words for things to label myth a "disease of language" that contributed to idolatry and polytheism.[25] Müller's lifelong project to purify scriptures, including the Hindu *Vedas*, from this disease complemented his own proposal for a "missionary alphabet" that would allow the propagation of the Gospel in all languages and reverse the Curse of Babel.[26]

Iconoclasm is partly a solution to the problem of communication. But the insistence on the radical Otherness of the deity creates a further problem in this regard: How may we communicate with, or divine the intentions of, a God who is so far removed from our experience? Müller himself struggled with and clearly articulated this problem. He explained that the recognition of a "Beyond"—which achieved its most extreme formulation in Jewish iconoclasm—created a gulf between matter and spirit that had to be bridged in some way.[27] For Müller, the Christian Incarnation represented the most successful solution of this problem. He emphasized the title of Christ as *Logos* or the Word, illustrating his belief that, at bottom, the problem of religion was a problem of translation.

Iconoclasm is simultaneously a response to the deceptive power of images, and a bid to fix and delimit the relationship between human and divine, often in the service of a larger project to perfect communication. As an illustration of these points, we consider Jeremy Bentham's effort to rid language—including especially the language of law—of its false images, in order to guarantee the distortion-free communicability, translation, and enforcement of justice. Bentham's attack on "fictions" drew on Protestant iconoclasm, just as his complementary proposal for the codification of the law invoked Protestant scripturalism and notions of canon.

Statutes versus statues: Bentham's attack on the idols of language

A study of the English utilitarian philosopher and legal reformer Jeremy Bentham (1748–1832) allows us to explore the influence of Protestant literalism on the discourse of the scientific Enlightenment. Bentham's proposal for the "codification" of the law, a term he invented,[28] was closely connected with his critique of linguistic "fictions" that were to be expelled from the legal code, or even from language itself. His goal was to fix the meaning of terms and produce a language that was not only unambiguous, but also potentially devoid of synonyms. Not only must every word have a single meaning, but every idea should ideally be represented by one and only one word: "Identity of nomenclature is certificate of identity of nature: diversity of diversity:—how absurd, how inconsistent to make the certificate a false one!"[29] The same goal informed his ideal of a legal code, or "Pannomion," which was to contain the whole law and nothing but the law.[30] These proposals were heavily influenced by Protestant theology. During the Reformation, Protestants located religion increasingly in the literal interpretation of a canon of scripture, as opposed to the "idolatrous" customs of the Catholic Church. Bentham's proposal for the codification of the still largely customary English common law marked a similar relocation of the legal tradition. However, it was in his critique of fictions, including the common law itself, that the structural and historical connections with Protestant theology were most evident. Bentham labeled these illusions of language as forms of verbal "idolatry." Following in the footsteps of Bacon, Hobbes, and Locke, Bentham condemned the reification or personification of words in terms often borrowed from Christian tradition.

Positivists, who regard Bentham as one of their heroes, contend that law is separate from other domains of culture, including especially morals and religion.[31] The canon of the law is supposed to be self-contained. Whatever exists outside its margins, is not law. The authority of this canon consists, in significant part, of the impossibility of confusion or commingling with other, lesser norms. Already in its exclusiveness, however, law betrays a kinship with other domains of culture, especially religion, which shares a predilection for canon.[32] Jonathan Z. Smith argues that "the radical and arbitrary reduction represented by the notion of canon and the ingenuity represented by the rule-governed exegetical enterprise of applying the canon to every dimension of human life is that most characteristic, persistent, and obsessive religious activity."[33] Recognizing that the impulse toward canon is also distinctive of many legal traditions, Smith suggests that, in the future, "students of religion might find as their most congenial colleagues those concerned with . . . legal studies."[34] In modernity, the most common form of legal canon is the "code": the reduction of the law to a set of written statutes that is, ideally, complete, concise, and unambiguous. This poses a paradox: If law and religion coincide precisely at the point at which each claims to be most distinctive—namely, in its embodiment in a clearly delimited canon—then perhaps they are more alike than legal positivists care to admit?

Canon embodies the dream of a fully self-present discourse that is, impossibly, both complete and closed. Although Smith emphasizes the freedom enabled by the creative exegesis of a canon, the impulse toward canon can become virulently restrictive. Not only the words of the canon, but the permissible interpretations of these words may be limited in such a way as to exclude metaphorical or nonliteral meaning. By purging themselves of linguistic uncertainties, law and religion often aspire to be transparent and perfect languages. Modern law, like certain forms of religious fundamentalism, has established its authority as a form of literalism, in opposition to literature and other aesthetic discourses.[35] This strategic exclusion reinforces the status of law as not merely a language of command, but a metalanguage, a discourse that rules over other discourses.[36]

In seventeenth-century England, a number of codification proposals sought to replace common law with a simple code derived, in some cases, from the Bible.[37] Barbara Shapiro notes that such "radical" movements, prominent during the Revolution and Protectorate (1640–60), subsequently diminished.[38] Although, unlike some of these earlier reformers, Bentham did not propose to turn to religion as a source of law,[39] he depicted his codification project as an extension of the religious Reformation. The Protestant emphasis on a written canon of scripture to the exclusion of unwritten custom, combined with the translation of that canon into the vernacular and an emphasis on its literal meaning, had made religion more democratic. Bentham hoped to do the same for the law. Gerald Postema explains that Bentham "prided himself on being the 'Luther of Jurisprudence'

and it was precisely at this point that his jurisprudential Protestantism is
most pronounced. Just as access to God was not to be mediated by priests,
so too access to the law was not to be mediated by professional lawyers."[40]
Bentham was identified by the editor of his posthumous collected works, John
Hill Burton, with Moses, the lawgiver and smasher of idols.[41] For Bentham,
the remedy for both "Jurisprudential and Ecclesiastical Superstition[s]" was
to be found in codification, or "the forming a Digest of the Law," which
was "to Lawyers, what the making a translation of the Bible was to Church
men."[42] Such translations had put religion into the hands of individuals.
Similarly, Bentham hoped through codification to make "every man his
own lawyer."[43] Otherwise, the real legislator of the common law would be
the person who reduced its principles to a written compilation,[44] just as the
bookbinder might usurp the authorship of the Bible by adding to Jesus's own
words.[45] Of course, there were important differences between Bentham's
codification proposal and the Reformation idea of a scriptural canon, one
of the most obvious of which was that Protestants had attempted, albeit
unsuccessfully, to fix religion in a timeless and unalterable form ostensibly
dictated by God and subject to no amendments, whereas Bentham placed
great emphasis on the continual improvement of the law by the legislature.
His code was supposed to be comprehensive and authoritative, but not
eternal.[46] Although the codification of the law was most prominent in civil
law countries that were predominantly Catholic, Bentham's proposal for
codification carried distinctly Protestant connotations. The parallel between
Bentham's legal reforms and the earlier religious Reformation highlights
their common dependence on the growth of printing and literacy that came
with the technological innovation of movable type, a development explored
further in Chapter Five.[47]

At the time Bentham advocated his reforms, the common law was still
a disorganized and only partly written tradition couched in an arcane
terminology taken from Latin and Norman French. He proposed codification
as a remedy for the ills of the common law, including especially its
traditionalism, lack of system, uncertainty, secrecy, and unintelligibility:

> The case is this. A large portion of the body of the Law was, by the
> bigotry or artifice of lawyers, locked up in an illegible character, and in a
> foreign tongue. The statute [William Blackstone] mentions obliged them
> to give up their hieroglyphics, and to restore the native language to its
> rights. This was doing much; but it was not doing everything. Fiction,
> tautology, technicality, circuity, irregularity, inconsistency remain. But
> above all, the pestilential breath of Fiction poisons the sense of every
> instrument it comes near.[48]

This passage refers to a statute requiring the use of English as the language
of the law.[49] For Bentham, however, even the adoption of English did not
go far enough, as it left in place the reliance on custom and the use of

"fictions." Fictions were the disease for which codification would provide the cure.[50] "Fiction" had both narrower and broader meanings for Bentham: as applied to jurisprudence ("legal fictions" or "the fictions of lawyers"), and as applied to language in general ("fictions"). A "legal fiction" meant paying lip service to a rule of law while ignoring it in practice. Bentham's concept of legal fiction encompassed any case in which there was a gap between the reality and the language of the law. He included in this concept such devices as *pro forma* notice, judicial oaths (in which the swearers no longer believed), and laws that had become so badly outdated that they were respected in name only. John Hill Burton summed up Bentham's view that "a Fiction of Law may be defined in general as the saying something exists which does not exist, and acting as if it existed; or *vice versa*."[51]

For Bentham, the term "fiction" also had a broader meaning beyond jurisprudence. This meaning was elaborated in his writings on language and logic. He argued that all names were either "names of real entities" or "names of fictitious entities."[52] Bentham subscribed to a nominalist linguistic philosophy according to which words that were not fictions referred to individual existing things.[53] Abstract terms were derived from concrete ones, and class terms were fictions abstracted from individual members, as "Church" meant in reality only the members of the clergy.[54] "Genus" and "species," those terms favored by the Greek philosophers and their followers, were accordingly classified as fictions.[55] Bentham expressed "a contempt for ancient philosophy, or philosophy of words."[56] The English language was superior to inflected languages such as Greek and Latin, which promoted the belief in such fictions.[57] He argued that, in Aristotle's time, people were led by the patterns of grammar to believe that a name or noun substantive implied the existence of the thing it named.[58] Bentham allowed however that fictions were the consequence of a general human propensity to reify language: "so close a union has habit connected between words and things, that we take one for the other."[59] This error continued into the present:

> Wherever there is a word, there is a thing; so says the common notion— the result of the association of ideas. Wherever there is a word, there is a thing; hence the almost universal practice of confounding *fictitious* entities with *real* ones—corresponding names of fictitious entities with *real* ones. Hence, common law, mind, soul, virtue, vice.[60]

The use of fictions by "priests and lawyers" was especially pernicious, as it could deceive and control the unwary.[61] The antidote was to trace fictions back to their ultimate basis in reality, if such existed.[62]

In his attempt to classify and purify language, Bentham followed a British philosophical tradition, extending back to Bacon,[63] that was united by the effort to perfect language through the elimination of logical errors.[64] Bentham expressed his debt to Locke[65] and, for the idea of "fictitious beings," both the Frenchman Jean Le Rond D'Alembert (1717–83)[66] and John Horne Tooke.[67] Bentham embraced Locke's empiricism and argued that all words, as well as the ideas on which they were based, were ultimately derived from sense perception: "it is from corporeal ideas that all our mental ideas are derived . . . all words now employed in giving expression to incorporeal ideas, were originally employed in giving expression to corporeal ideas . . ."[68] Abstract or metaphysical terms, as well, were all derived from simple ideas; however, they could lead to abuse if their origin was forgotten. Echoing Hobbes, Locke, and Horne Tooke,[69] Bentham argued that the various terms for "spirits" were all derived from those for breath, air, or gas:[70] "that spirit means originally breath . . . is sufficiently notorious. In so far as any origin at all can be found for it, it is in a material import that the origin of the import of every word is to be found."[71]

To correct such errors, Bentham proposed first to analyze words into simple ideas, then to classify these ideas through a method of bifurcation or division modeled on Linnaean classification.[72] The first division of this classification was that which separated real entities from fictitious ones.[73] Real entities were further subdivided into perceptible and inferential. The former were known through empirical experience; the latter could not be. The class of real, inferential entities included God, the devil, and other subordinate spiritual beings, as well as the human soul.[74] For his proposition that God is an inferential entity, Bentham cited the New Testament statement that "no man hath seen God at any time."[75] The apparent orthodoxy of this conclusion thinly concealed a suggestion of atheism. Bentham allowed that, for those unwilling to infer God's existence, the necessary conclusion would be that God is a "non-entity."[76] What distinguished a "non-entity" from a "fictitious entity"? A non-entity is a concrete, individual being, of which real existence can be predicated. A fictitious entity, by contrast, is a creature entirely of language, something that is and must be spoken of as existing in order for communication to proceed. Examples include such abstract concepts as the human will, intentions, Justice, the Church, etc. No one would mistake these, upon serious reflection, for really existent beings; however, they are habitually spoken of as such in the course of conversation.

Despite the fact that fictions did not represent concrete beings, even of the nonexistent variety, Bentham likened their creation to a process of personification or prosopopoeia:

Beholding at a distance, in the dress of a man, sitting and playing upon an organ, an automaton figure, constructed for that purpose by the ingenuity of the mechanist, to take this creature of human art for a real man, is a sort of mistake which, at a certain distance, might happen for a time to be made by the most acute observer. In like manner, beholding a part of speech cast in the same mould with the name of a real entity, a really existing substance, no wonder if, on a variety of occasions, to the mental eye of a very acute observer, this fictitious entity thus accoutred should present itself in the character of, and be regarded and treated as if it were a real one.[77]

This was more to this than simply a critique of linguistic anthropomorphism. Like a number of his predecessors in the Baconian tradition, Bentham identified fictions as a form of verbal idolatry in a manner that coordinated with religious skepticism.[78] He frequently used the term "idol" to describe verbal fictions. He described Reason,[79] (Laws of) Nature,[80] Religion,[81] and Church[82] as words that denote "goddesses" or fictitious persons of the female gender. In his *Book of Fallacies*, Bentham categorized Law, like the Church, as an "allegorical idol."[83] Beginning already in the early *A Fragment on Government* (1776), Bentham suggested that William Blackstone's (1723–80) reverence for the common law depended on "a kind of *personification* . . . as if the Law were a living creature . . ."[84] On the contrary, only statute law is real, as it exists on the printed page.[85] In affirming the validity of *lex non scripta*, or unwritten laws, Blackstone had acknowledged the problem of how such laws are to be known and recognized as valid. His answer to this problem was that "the judges . . . are the depositaries of the laws; the living oracles, who must decide in all cases of doubt . . ."[86] Bentham now used Blackstone's analogy against him. The common law was an idol, although an invisible one that, by implication, did not exist. Lawyers disguised their self-serving proclamations as the oracles of this nonexistent deity.[87]

A letter dated 1817 included in Bentham's *Papers on Codification* shows the continuity of such ideas in his jurisprudence, as well as the extent of their connection with theological polemics:

> To be known, an object must have *existence*. But *not* to have existence—to be a mere non-entity—in this case, my friends, is a portion—nay, by far the largest portion—of that which is passed upon you for *law*. I speak of *common law*, as the phrase is: of the whole of common law. When men say to you, the *common law does this*—the *common law does that*—for whatsoever there is of reality, look not beyond the two *words* that are thus employed. In these words you have a name, pretended to be the name of a really existing object: look for any such existing object—look for it till doomsday, no such object will you find. *Great is Diana of the Ephesians*! cried the priests of the Ephesian temple, by whom Diana was passed upon the people as the name of a really existing goddess: Diana a goddess: and of that goddess, the statue, if not the very person, at any rate the express image. *Great is Minerva of the Athenians*! cried at that same time—you need not doubt of it—the priests of the Temple of Minerva at Athens: that Athens at which St. Paul made known, for the first time, the unknown God. The priests of Athens had their goddess of wisdom: it was this *Minerva*. The lawyers of the English School have her twin sister, their Goddess of Reason. *The law* (meaning the *common law*): "*The law*"

(says one of her chief priests, Blackstone) "*is the perfection of reason.*" By the author of the book on Ecclesiastical Polity, Hooker,—for between lawyercraft and priestcraft there has always been the closest alliance—the law had long before been discovered to be a supernatural person, and that person of the feminine gender. Yes: exactly as much of reality was there, and is there, corresponding to the word *Minerva*,—as there is, or ever has been, corresponding to the compound appellative *common law*. Would you wish to know what a law—a real law—is? Open the statute-book: in every statute you have a real law: behold in that the really existing object: the genuine object, of which the counterfeit, and pretended counterpart, is endeavoured to be put off upon you by a lawyer, as often as in any discourse of his the word *common law* is to be found.[88]

The line "Great is Diana of the Ephesians" and the reference to the Athenians worshipping an "unknown God" come from passages in Acts depicting Paul's preaching of the Gospel among idolaters.[89] Under the influence of empiricism, which insisted that all real entities were individuals, Bentham argued that the (singular) term "*a law*" had meaning only when applied to a statute law, which was discrete, existed on the printed page, and could be pointed to.[90] The "common law," a fictitious class term, could not be so discretely indicated. Although apparently empiricist, Bentham's argument actually highlights the absurdity of empiricism as applied to a code. The reality of such a code consists in the objects and actions, if any, in the physical world, to which its words refer, and not to the black-and-white images of such words on the printed page. To regard the code-book itself as the reality of the law is a form of bibliolatry.

Bentham's life ended on a bizarre note, one relevant to the question of whether his Utilitarianism was a form of secular religion. Against prevailing prejudices, he willed his body to medical science for dissection and the advancement of anatomical knowledge. This showed an absolute consistency to find practical usage for every last scrap of matter. However, his further instructions for the disposition of the corpse were less obviously rational. He directed that his body be preserved, then displayed in perpetuity in University College, London, where it stands to this day. (The original head was replaced with a wax one owing to the deleterious effects of the embalming process on the original's features.) He called this figure an "Auto-Icon," and authored a short satirical essay with that title that remained unpublished until a few years ago, although a few copies had been distributed after Bentham's death. Several themes in this essay are of interest. Bentham proposed that Auto-Icons become the standard treatment for the dead, and that they be displayed in churches attended by phrenologists in preference to priests. He explicitly invoked the theme of "every man his own lawyer," adding that "now may *every man* be *his own statue.*"[91] Henceforth stone statues could be dispensed with, as "What resemblance, what painting, what statue of a human being can be so like him, as, in the character of an Auto-Icon, he or she will be to himself or herself. Is not identity preferable to similitude?"[92] The same theory of representation or signification informing his concept of a code, namely that, so far as possible, there should be an identity between a thing and its verbal image, informed his argument for the Auto-Icon as an analogue of autobiography, or rather "auto-thanatography":[93] "Names may be invented—can be forged; and the existence of persons bearing them can be asserted . . . But Auto-Icons cannot be invented, cannot be forged."[94] There was also an element of illusion at play here. Bentham suggested that famous Auto-Icons be made to move and discourse in a theatrical tableau reminiscent of the later Hall of Presidents at Disneyland.

Like its verbal counterpart the code, the Auto-Icon was a critique of false images, and a mode of iconoclasm. Bentham's intention was, in part, to parody the religious practice of image-worship, as well as burial practices that, as he argued (echoing Puritan theologians[95]), were not sanctioned by any words of Jesus, but were designed solely for priestly enrichment.[96] Elsewhere, Bentham attributed such ceremonies to the idolatrous worship of the dead, embracing the common explanation of idolatry as having originated in ancestor worship.[97] Despite such reservations, or with tongue firmly in cheek, he proposed a ceremonial use for the Auto-Icons, a kind of secular replacement for religion: "On certain days the Auto-Icons might be exhibited, and their exhibition associated with religious observances."[98] He referred to the possibility that pilgrimages might be made to his own "*quasi* sacred Auto-Icon (if by the adverb, the attribute sacred may be rendered endurable) . . ."[99] This echoed a dream he once had, in which he saw himself as the "founder of a sect."[100]

How are we to understand such utterances? The Auto-Icon is surely a parody or satire of traditional religion, even though its recommendations were partly followed in the case of Bentham's corpse. This supports a more subversive reading of his other writings on religion. James Crimmins argues that Bentham was an atheist, whose ultimate intent was to undermine all religion.[101] As it was dangerous to criticize the Church directly, Bentham published his major writings on religion largely under pseudonyms, and he directed his arguments against various substitutes or straw men: the Catechism, the apostle Paul, and "natural religion."[102] Crimmins calls these arguments "devices" or "tactics,"[103] like "the Devil quoting scripture":[104] "Bentham knew his Bible well and rarely missed an opportunity to quote from it whenever it might embarrass the Church or contradict its teaching."[105] Yet Crimmins also acknowledges that "it is obvious that Bentham found it almost impossible to divorce his train of thought from the practices of conventional religion."[106] As Delos McKown argues, "Bentham read the Bible much as though he were an American fundamentalist; that is, he read it literally."[107] Although this style of reading was often a strategy to exploit the text's inconsistencies, this fact does not entirely invalidate the comparison.

Crimmins argues that Bentham's religion—his atheism—was integral to his thought. Philip Schofield has countered that Bentham's theory of logic and language was integral to his thought, whereas his religious views were not.[108] Consequently,

> [W]hether or not one concludes that Bentham was an atheist of some sort . . . Bentham's views in relation to the existence of God were derived from his theory of logic and language . . . Bentham did not have a theology because, according to his theory of logic and language, there was none to be had . . . Bentham was "secular" not in the sense that his starting point was a rejection of religious belief, but in that his starting point was independent of religious belief.[109]

I have to disagree with Schofield. The earlier analysis of Bentham's theory of fictions indicates that his views on language were deeply influenced by religious criticisms of idolatry, which were taken partly from scripture and theology, and partly from a philosophical tradition that condemned the personification of words. It appears increasingly anachronistic to call this philosophical tradition "secular" in the modern sense of the term, meaning "nonreligious." In fact, the long-standing engagement of this tradition with religion lends greater significance to Bentham's own appropriation of religious terminology. It is possible to argue that his use of theological idioms was a rhetorical device, designed to communicate and popularize covertly and essentially secular conceptions of language. However, it now appears more likely that religion contributed to the basic structure of Bentham's thought concerning language, and especially the language of the law. This fundamental structure borrowed from the opposition between canon and idolatry. Whereas other, nonreligious influences also informed Bentham's linguistic and jurisprudential theories, it is the religious influences that have been most neglected by scholarship. Ironically, this neglect was reinforced by Bentham's overt hostility to organized religion, despite the fact that this hostility itself now appears to have deep affinities with Reformation polemics.

Bentham's jurisprudence was religious in a fundamental and not a superficial sense. He may well have been, as Crimmins argues, an atheist, if by this we mean an opponent of traditional religion who believes that God is a fiction.[110] Yet Bentham's opposition to religion shared in several important characteristics of the religious Reformation: its devotion to the printed book, its democratizing tendencies, and its hostility to certain customs or habits of thought and language, regarded as idolatry. If "atheist" means someone who simply lacks religious belief, then a more accurate term for Bentham is "iconoclast." This places him in an historical line of development that led from religion to secularism. The disappearance of God began with the prohibition against idolatry in the Ten Commandments, and with God's refusal to let even Moses see him face-to-face: "you cannot see my face; for man shall not see me and live."[111] Such views led directly to the iconoclasm of the Reformation. For his proposition that God is an inferential entity, Bentham cited the New Testament statement that "no man hath seen God at any time."[112] Bentham was not the first person to build his canon on the foundation of iconoclasm. However, he may have taken iconoclasm to its logical endpoint, by banishing the face of God from both law and language.

The more important issue is not whether we should label Bentham "religious" or "secular," but what the history of religion contributes to our understanding of his jurisprudence and later developments in the law. Religious iconoclasm facilitated the construction of the law as an ostensibly purified, perfected, universal language. Bentham's case sharply illuminates the contributions of monotheism and the prohibition of idolatry to this linguistic project. The verbal analogue of monotheism is the monologue of a univocal language, one that fixes the relation between the word and the world. And the integrity of such a language depends on the exclusion of polyphony, ambiguity, and distortion, the verbal analogues of polytheism. As Bentham argued, "Identity of nomenclature is certificate of identity of nature: diversity of diversity:—how absurd, how inconsistent to make the certificate a false one!"[113] Or, as he elsewhere stated:

Eadem natura, eadem nomenclatura.

Whene'er the same nature,

The same nomenclature.[114]

Moreover, for absolute clarity and consistency in the code, "every draught [should] . . . be from beginning to end, if possible, the work of a single hand. *Hands not more than one.*"[115] This is, if you like, monotheism without God. Bentham represented an extreme or nodal point of this monologic, a point at which religion vanished into secularism.

Bentham's appropriation of such religious polemics was neither superficial nor haphazard. Instead, it shows the depth of influence of Protestant thinking on general culture. The same influences affected thinking on language well into the second half of the nineteenth century, as in the case of Friedrich Max Müller, if not beyond. Müller's "Science of Religion" labeled myth a "disease of language," a process of corruption by which language becomes reified and, ultimately, deified, in terms that recalled earlier religious attacks on idolatry: "[N]ames have a tendency to become things, *nomina* [names] grow into *numina* [spirits], *ideas* into *idols* . . ."[116] It is, therefore, not surprising that Lon Fuller, in his analysis of legal fictions, quoted Müller on the manner in which abstract terms are derived from concrete ones through a process of metaphorizing.[117] Fuller stated: "That original sin of human reasoning—hypostatization—is a failure to drop the fictions out of the final reckoning."[118] The condemnation of the "original sin" of idolatry links modern law with religion, or at least with Protestantism.

In Bentham's case, the structural analogy between law and religion suggested by their mutual dependence on canon turns out to signal a deeper, genealogical relation of law to religious iconoclasm. Moreover, his case was not idiosyncratic. Peter Goodrich has argued that the common law in sixteenth- and seventeenth-century England established its authority through an "antirrhetic," an attack on the power of images that borrowed from Reformation iconoclasm.[119] Polemics originally directed against Catholic ritual were applied to purify the language of the law. Law defined itself against an excluded, idolatrous Other. Costas Douzinas and Lynda Nead concur that "after the Reformation and the fusion of secular and ecclesiastical jurisdictions, iconophobic ideas became the explicit foundation upon which the common law was established."[120] The critique of idolatry was transposed to the domain of language and became an "internalization of iconoclasm to the text."[121] The law sealed itself off, both hermetically and hermeneutically, from other domains of culture, while paradoxically presenting itself as a universal language that had the power to translate every other discourse into its own idiom. The claim of law to constitute a perfect language was made possible by an exclusion or repression of verbal images.[122] To counteract such repression, Goodrich called for a genealogy "that is cognizant of a poetics repressed within institutional prose, of an affectivity harbored in its science, a power in its reason, an image in its logic, a justice in its law."[123] As applied to Bentham, such a genealogy reveals deeper connections between Protestant iconoclasm and the supposed "rationalism" of the secular Enlightenment, precisely at the convergence of their ideologies of representation.

Semiotics and the question of the secular

Bentham's case clearly illustrates the continuity between secular, indeed disenchanting tendencies within the Baconian tradition and earlier modes of religious thought. Such cases suggest that, whatever the "secular" might be, it is scarcely the opposite of "religion"—another highly fraught category—but might more accurately be described as a particular kind of religion.

The secularization thesis, or the standard historical account of how law and other institutions gradually disentangled themselves from religion in their onward progress toward modernity, has achieved the status of a charter myth, a monologue by and for our contemporary society. However, there are already visible cracks in this monolith, gaps that disclose the extent to which secularism is a development that occurred within religion itself, through an increasing restriction of the sphere of the Sacred. If we characterize the Secular simply as a movement critical of the Sacred, that is, of religion, then where in this bipolar or dichotomous classification do we locate the Reformation and the prohibition of idolatry? Criticism of religion is, as we have seen, not necessarily the opposite of religion. The Protestant attack on idolatry, which opposed "true" religion to "false," is a case in point. Throughout history, some of the most potent criticisms of religion have been developed by religion itself; and some of these remain, half-buried and mostly forgotten, within the text of secular law and other "scientific" discourses.

While contributing to a general skepticism concerning the nature and motives of the secular, and in particular its self-definition against religion (which too nearly parallels older definitions of Christianity as the true faith, as opposed to false religion, idolatry, or superstition), the account provided above focuses our attention on the extent to which both some secular and some Christian traditions have depended on semiotic distanciation—they have described a semiotic difference, sometimes real and sometimes imagined, from those other traditions of which they sought to purge themselves.

This demonstration reinforces one of the chief lessons of poststructuralism, namely, that such acts of distanciation or difference-making are always discursive constructs, creatures of language. The original postmodern philosopher *avant la lettre*, Friedrich Nietzsche, learned this lesson from studying the Platonic attack on rhetoric and poetry. His own account of the original disenchantment wrought by the Socratic tradition was deeply influenced by the Romantic idea that we have lost connection with the vital wellsprings of culture—mythology, poetry, and music—all of which semiotic forms were subordinated to, or even effaced by, the new *logos* of philosophy. In *The Birth of Tragedy*, Nietzsche quoted Plutarch's line, "Great Pan is dead," to express this ultimate tragedy of the West.[124] In so doing, he followed not only earlier Romantics but also, ironically, many Christians who gave Plutarch's account of the oracles' decline a different and more positive inflection, by attributing that event to Christ's redemptive sacrifice.[125] Bentham's own attack on Blackstone's common law judges as "oracles" echoed this Christian triumphalism, at some remove.

Nietzsche made the undoing of the semiotic difference between philosophy and poetry or myth one of the centerpieces of his philosophical project. Hence his increasing tendency, in later works, especially *Thus Spoke Zarathustra*, was to adopt a mythic mode of expression.[126] Such a move has also been made by many postmodern theorists, such as Jacques Derrida, often in deliberate imitation of Nietzsche, though never with his clarity and wit. Reading some of these theorists makes us sympathize with if not entirely endorse the Baconian tradition's opposite maneuver to purify language.

In *On the Genealogy of Morals*, Nietzsche made his boldest attempt to characterize Christianization as a discursive event.[127] He argued that the fundamental moral opposition between "good and evil" embraced by Judaism and Christianity represented a transformation and inversion of an earlier, very different Greek opposition between "good and bad" (in the sense of "noble and ignoble"). This seems to anticipate the structuralist discovery that all linguistic meaning or value is grounded in binary oppositions. And so Nietzsche's concept of genealogy has been linked or even entirely conflated with Saussurean linguistics by many poststructuralists. Bruce Lincoln's argument that the Platonic distinction between *logos* and *mythos* was just such an act of discursive opposition—creating meaning out of nothing, as it were—is a case in point.

This chapter has both supported and qualified such contentions. The secular does indeed appear to be a sign, to some extent an empty one, that requires for its own integrity or communicative power an "other" against which it defines itself. Part of the irony of this is that this very strategy of opposition is what reveals the affinity between secular and older, religious modes of discourse. As Nietzsche argued, opposites, especially of the metaphysical variety, are not truly opposite; they are bound together in a way that describes a deeper kinship.[128] The same certainly appears to be true of religion and the secular, as represented respectively by the discourses of the English Reformation and the Baconian Enlightenment. Nietzsche's etymological or genealogical method applies in this case to show that secular reason had antecedents in theological polemics against the sign: against the ambiguity and polyvalence of metaphor and myth, against the deceptive power of verbal images, against the fetishizing of poetic language.

Yet the discursive transformation that characterizes modernity—whether we take that to begin with the ancient Greeks or, more relevant for our situation, with the Reformation—is not merely the opposition of one, inherently meaningless term to another, but the replacement (albeit partial and gradual) of an entire semiotic ideology by another. Secularism is not merely a word, but a way of inhabiting the world through language, and especially a series of prohibitions and taboos established to police the use of discourse and its encroachments upon human (and divine) reason and autonomy. Thus, it cannot be the case that *mythos* simply meant "my opponent's speech." The real decline of poetic form in various genres, a topic explored more fully in the next chapter, shows some of the consequences of secularization for our habitation of a semiotic cosmos in which the powers of language have been sharply delimited.

All of this has implications for semiotic method, as well as for the study of culture in general, to the extent that this study adopts a structuralist or poststructuralist approach. It is scarcely sufficient to end the inquiry with the observation that "cultural differences are discursively constituted through verbal oppositions." This may leave the false impression that such differences are either "not real"—because merely an illusion of language, a rhetorical effect—or that they are always and everywhere the same. Not so. The difference in worldview under secularism, which describes a difference in semiotic ideologies, has had the most profound consequences for our experience of the world as a field for human action, for the encounter between human and divine, and for human autonomy under a regime of disenchantment that is reflected in the modern notion of the individual self as "buffered" (in Charles Taylor's term) from encroachments by images, magic, and spirits.[129] Given this, the recognition of the self-definition of modernity through the opposition to false verbal images can be only a beginning, an etymological point of departure for a deeper historical inquiry into the nature and genealogy of the secular.

CHAPTER FIVE

Transformations in poetic performance:

The coordination of Protestant literalism and print culture

The repudiation of ritual: attacks on ritual repetition and poetic performance

Bentham's critique of the rhetoric of law did not end with the problem of the reification of language. He also echoed Plato in condemning the power of poetry. In a footnote to his *Introduction to the Principles of Morals and Legislation* (1789), Bentham argued:

> Were the inquiry diligently made, it would be found that the goddess of harmony has exercised more influence, however latent, over the dispensations of Themis [the goddess of Justice], than her most diligent historiographers, or even her most passionate panegyrists, seem to have been aware of. Every one knows, how, by the ministry of Orpheus [the musician], it was she who first collected the sons of men beneath the shadow of the sceptre: yet, in the midst of continual experience, men seem yet to learn, with what successful diligence she has laboured to guide it in its course. Every one knows, that measured numbers were the language of the infancy of law: none seem to have observed, with what imperious sway they have governed her maturer age. In English jurisprudence in particular, the connexion betwixt law and music, however less perceived than in Spartan legislation, is not perhaps less real nor less close. . . . Search indictments, pleadings, proceedings in chancery, conveyances: whatever trespasses you may find against truth

or common sense, you will find none against the laws of harmony. The English Liturgy, justly as this quality has been extolled in that sacred office, possesses not a greater measure of it, than is commonly to be found in an English Act of Parliament. Dignity, simplicity, brevity, precision, intelligibility, possibility of being retained or so much as apprehended, every thing yields to Harmony. Volumes might be filled, shelves loaded, with the sacrifices that are made to this insatiate power. Expletives, her ministers in Grecian poetry are not less busy, though in different shape and bulk, in English legislation: in the former, they are monosyllables: in the latter they are whole lines.[1]

Bentham affirmed the enslavement of law to the bewitching power of harmony, music, or poetry.[2] The examples he gave, earlier in this note, of the rhetoric of law were the two Latin maxims *Delegatus non potest delegare* and *Servitus servitutis non datur*, which translate, roughly and respectively, as "A delegate may not delegate" and "A tenant may not grant a tenancy." He argued that, there being no reason that supported these rules, they were supported by rhetoric alone. Although Bentham contended that the poetry of law is most evident in the survival of such traditional rules, he also suggested that the poetry of English law, although less open or even hidden, was perhaps for that reason no less powerful.[3] Rhetoric that is concealed, by virtue of avoiding such obvious devices as rhyme or versification, is even more pernicious, as it operates subliminally, without raising suspicions. Although Bentham does not explain precisely what such hidden poetry looks like, nor how to differentiate it from prose, he may have in mind the case where a word is made to rhyme with itself, rather than with another word it merely resembles. (This is, indeed, not very different from the two Latin maxims he derides.) Thus, when a common law precedent occurs in the form of a "holding"—a verbal formulation of the decision of the case—and subsequent applications of this precedent repeat the holding while applying it to a new fact scenario, this amounts to rhyming one fact scenario with another, preexisting one, while claiming that it is in fact the same as the other one.[4] An example would be when we say, without further explanation, that deliberate and unprovoked killing is "murder," and killing in self-defense or wartime is "murder," and that these two actions should therefore be punished identically.

Bentham was not alone in criticizing the formalism of traditional law. In the early twentieth century, for example, the legal historian Frederick Pollock labeled the ritual and symbolic features of ancient law as a form of primitive or magical thinking that exaggerated the perennial lawyerly sin of formalism, meaning the rigid attachment to certain prescribed words or legal procedures. In contrast, modern society emphasizes the value of substantive law and of legal realism over formalism. Pollock recognized that in some cases formalism served the "rational" purpose of providing "a hard and fast rule."[5] However, the excessive formalism of ancient law stemmed from "the oldest form of superstition . . . the pre-historic belief in symbolic magic . . . [which] assumed that words have in themselves an operative virtue which is lost if any one word is substituted for any other." Pollock allowed the human instinct "to clothe . . . collective action in dramatic and rhythmical shapes . . . [which] are both impressive at the time and easily remembered." Yet he declined to follow any further the inquiry into "the aesthetic history of ritual."

Bentham and Pollock were not entirely wrong. The prevalence of poetic devices in early law is explored later in this chapter. My concern at present is to examine the origins and causes of the rise of such pejorative attitudes toward the poetry, formalism, and repetitiveness of ritual, as a means of accounting for the apparent decline of the types of rituals described in Chapter Two.

One source for such pejorative views of poetry may have been Protestant theology.[6] Matthew 6:7, in the King James Version, directs: "But when ye pray, use not vain repetitions, as the heathen: for they think that they shall be heard for their much speaking." A tradition that apparently originated with John Calvin's gloss of this verse condemned the use of "vain repetitions" in prayer as a form of rhetoric, magic, and idolatry.[7] This prohibition was directed against Catholics, with their incessant repetition of the Hail Mary and other prayers, especially in the Latin language that was incomprehensible to most people. The identification of such forms of prayer as rhetoric was straightforward enough; but what made such formulas so objectionable was that they were regarded as an attempt to influence God, as if He were a mortal man. They therefore violated biblical commands against magic and idolatry. This example of Protestant antiritualism illustrates the intersection of scriptural literalism with antiritualism and iconoclasm. The critique of vain repetitions also exemplifies the privileging of semantic content over form—especially poetic form—that marks a divide between modernity and its past. This shift in semiotic ideologies forbade certain forms of communication between human and divine: human beings could not reach up to heaven by means of language in order to pull God down to earth.

During the colonial period in India, many British of various stripes, including not only missionaries but also Orientalist scholars and government officials, echoed these earlier Puritan positions with their attacks against the unmeaning and superstitious repetition of Hindu Tantric mantras, Vedic chants, and similar formulas. (Buddhists and Muslims were not spared.) Such controversies—a variant of which, in the cultural encounter between Dutch Protestants and native Indonesians, has been described by Webb Keane—highlight certain distinctive features of the semiotic ideology of modernity, while suggesting that some of these features may find part of their genealogy in Protestantism. The British themselves drew the sharpest contrast between their own views of language and those of some native Hindus who believed in the consubstantiality of language with both nature and divinity, a belief that underwrote the further conviction in the ability of language to influence or even incarnate the gods. These polemical attitudes against certain types of poetic performance have carried over to the present day, as I have elsewhere shown.[8] Viewed against the background of Protestant attacks on repetitive prayers as the language of parrots and jackdaws,[9] Frits Staal's description of Vedic mantras and ritual as a form of "birdsong"—pattern and musicality devoid of semantic content—assumes a rather different aspect. Whether Staal here is reflecting specifically Protestant attitudes is hardly the question, as such attitudes have been disseminated so widely.

The critique of vain repetitions in prayer was part of a broader movement of antiritualism during the Reformation.[10] The "repudiation of ritual," if not its actual decline, has been posited as a distinctive feature of modernity by a number of scholars, including Peter Burke, Mary Douglas, Jonathan Z. Smith, and Catherine Bell.[11] Within the domain of religion itself, ritual was demoted in favor of an emphasis on a newly privileged category of "belief" or "doctrine." Even when ritual has been regarded favorably, this has generally been due to its reclassification as a mode of aesthetic expression together with artistic and other performances. This approach continues to privilege meaning or intention over behavior. The concept of "ritual" was constructed in the modern period, precisely as the negative image of some other, more valued category, such as "science," "rationality," or "utilitarian behavior."

These considerations direct us to reformulate the question of ritual away from positivistic inquiries into "what ritual is," as a possibly timeless human behavior, and toward the genealogical inquiry into transformations in the cultural location and valuation of ritual. This transformation has often been identified as a decline of ritual, for example by Max Weber, Keith Thomas, and Mircea Eliade. However, it may also represent a shift in attitudes, rather than in actual behaviors. Consequently, several scholars have concluded that we ought to abandon the idea of a "decline of ritual" or, at the very least, to separate polemics from reality. As Burke says, "if historians shift their ground from ritual acts to attitudes toward ritual, then they will have a story to tell which is just as dramatic as the old one [of disenchantment] told by Spencer and Weber, Gluckman and Shils."[12] Burke suggests that, instead of arguing that an actual decline of ritual occurred, we undertake the more manageable, and more circumspect, project of demonstrating the ascendance of negative attitudes toward ritual in the modern period. Similarly, Bell suggests that attacks on ritual may have contributed to a decline of ritual practices, but concludes that the actual evidence for such a decline is slim.[13] It should be pointed out that the two projects—documenting the rise of pejorative attitudes toward ritual, and demonstrating an actual "decline" of ritual, in some sense of that phrase— are by no means incompatible. Indeed, for one who maintains that there was a decline of ritual, or of some lesser included subset of ritual, such as magic, evidence of modern condemnations of ritual would constitute valuable, albeit circumstantial evidence for the thesis of decline. Polemics against ritual would demonstrate the existence of a motive for, or an important causal factor contributing to, the decline of ritual. This, indeed, was a major point of agreement that Keith Thomas identified between his and Hildred Geertz's differing interpretations of the "decline" of magic.[14]

In my view, however, the most strident rejections of both the concepts of ritual and its repudiation abdicate the responsibility to provide an account of the transformations in religious practice that have occurred in the modern era. The repetitiveness of ritual was not merely a projection, but is a common feature of many rituals, as described in Chapter Two. The best explanation of this feature is that repetition contributes to the function of ritual as a mode of communication, rhetoric, or performance. Disenchantment has witnessed a decline or denigration of such poetic performances, at least in certain genres of discourse. The neglect or pejorative evaluation of the poetic form of mantras and similar formulas, and of the contribution such devices make to the pragmatic function of ritual, evinces a general modern bias against formalism and poetry that must itself be accounted for.

Stanley Tambiah—pioneer of a "performative approach" to the repetition found in spells and other rituals—did attempt to account for the rise of skepticism regarding ritual repetition. He posited that changes in attitudes toward ritual arose from "ritual involution," meaning "a seeming overelaboration and overprolongation of ritual action" that reflected both "peasant inventiveness [and] peasant tedium."[15] Ritual involution describes the situation in which repetition is, as it were, overdone, and thus becomes counterproductive by bringing ritual to "the point of inventive exhaustion, aesthetic overstylization, and pecuniary bankruptcy"[16] as well as of "compulsive tedium."[17] Under ordinary conditions, the stylistic features of ritual, which, as we recall, include "formality (conventionality), stereotypy (rigidity), condensation (fusion), and redundancy (repetition)," contribute to a belief in its potency. One example Tambiah gave is the parallelisms found in the Hebrew Bible and in many traditional and oral cultures.[18] He affirmed the widespread belief that the longer, more elaborate, and more repetitive it is, "the more efficacious the ceremony is believed to be."[19] An example was Thai Buddhist monks' prayers for the dead: "This deliberately stereotyped and unvarying performance clearly signifies that the more times the monks chant the same sacred verses, . . . the more potent is the effect of making merit for the deceased."[20] This common belief in the power of ritual repetition posed a paradox that Tambiah acknowledged and attempted to account for, though not to his own satisfaction. The paradox is that the very same features that contribute to the efficacy of ritual as a mode of cultural performance can, when taken to an extreme, or under certain conditions that are not yet adequately understood, produce a sense of tedium and a loss of conviction in the efficacy of the ritual:

> Configurational patterning and meaning intensification, the positive features of redundancy in its creative aspects, are so dialectically bound with the processes of meaning condensation and fusion, that the more a

rite becomes formalized, conventionalized, and repeated the more it also seems vulnerable to the *rigor mortis* of meaning atrophy. . . . [O]ne must conclude that ritual oscillates in historical time between the poles of *ossification* and *revivalism*. All the substantive features which nourish the formalism of ritual also conspire to empty it of meaning over time. . . . One task, then, is to specify the conditions under which rituals . . . take opposite turnings: to the right when they begin to lose their semantic component and come to serve mainly the pragmatic interests of authority, privilege, and sheer conservatism; and to the left when committed believers, faced with a decline of referential meaning . . . strive to infuse purified meaning into traditional forms, as often happens during the effervescence of religious revival and reform. Such a dynamic view might make it possible to transcend the seeming dissonance between two perspectives: the approach which sees redundancy as contributing to pattern emergence, and the use of multiple media as resulting in message intensification; and the other approach, which, wearing the garb of realism, sees in formalism and redundancy a decline of semantic meaning, and the sovereign presence of power buttressing itself with ritual speech, and the exploitative strategies of priestly castes building castles out of esoteric knowledge.[21]

Tambiah ended by announcing, as an unfinished task, the framing of an explanation of the following paradox: How is it that the very same features that contribute to the function of ritual also precipitate its decline? How can devices that reinforce the power of ritual also undermine and weaken that power?

More recently, the cognitive anthropologist Harvey Whitehouse arrived at a similar impasse.[22] Whitehouse proposed a fundamental distinction between two "modes of religiosity" or types of religious transmission, the "imagistic" and the "doctrinal."[23] The imagistic mode, although it may involve the use of visual images, is characterized principally by its association with one-off, terrifying, or otherwise impressive ritual events, such as rites of initiation. The doctrinal mode is characterized by its dependence on the elaboration of a systematic body of doctrine that is transmitted verbally. In the absence of impressive images and harrowing experiences, the recall of such doctrine depends on a great deal of repetition. A key example would be the weekly sermon. Unlike the imagistic mode, therefore, the doctrinal mode supposedly produces tedium. These two modes of religious transmission coordinate with different forms of social organization. The imagistic mode is local, face-to-face, or in any case confined to small groups. The doctrinal mode allows larger and more centralized forms of political organization. Whitehouse suggests that the primary cause for the periodic decline of repetitive ritual is the "tedium effect." Robert McCauley and E. Thomas Lawson have also argued that, although repetition and "sensory pageantry" can serve to heighten the experience and promote the recollection of a ritual, they can also lead to fatigue and boredom.[24] Whitehouse has admitted the possibility that repetition may lead to "arousal" rather than tedium.[25] He has further acknowledged defects in his earlier "portrayal of the 'tedium effect' as a necessary outcome of routinization."[26] These admissions underscore the inability of the modes of religiosity theory to account for the conditions under which repetition will lead to tedium.

One question that a skeptic might immediately pose is: Whose tedium is in question here? What sort of subjectivity is it that we are inhabiting when we posit tedium as a natural reaction to ritual repetition? In many cultures, such as those of traditional India, the repetition of chants, or of dramatic performances in which the outcome is already known in advance, is not regarded as tedious. On the contrary, there may be a certain kind of satisfaction that comes from experiencing the expected, the anticipated, the fully predictable and endlessly reconsummated. Mantras and other elaborate and repetitive rituals are merely one example.[27] To modern Western tastes, the degree of foreshadowing in many traditional narratives may drain the stories of one of the primary qualities we have come to expect in our fictional literature, movies, and theatrical performances: a sense of novelty and dramatic tension. Yet, there is good reason to believe that our taste for spontaneity and suspense, like the modern concepts of individual authorship and originality, are of recent invention. These observations lead us into questions of the nature and genealogy of literature that cannot be addressed here. However, they already suggest that the sense of tedium that Tambiah, Whitehouse, and others identify as a natural reaction to repetitive rituals may be a projection of their own modern biases.

What is missing from the majority of these theories is a sense of how the historically bounded nature of permissible performances—of what is, and is not, allowable to ritual as a form of rhetorical discourse—depends upon the shifting norms that characterize different notions of performance in different cultures at different times. Also missing is a sense of how a convergence of norms has been imposed under the sign of modernity. The question of ritual involution, although until now it has been posed largely as a structural question regarding what the formal features of ritual "do" or "produce," resolves into a genealogical question: What is the meaning of the aversion to ritual repetition, viewed not as a natural reaction, but as one historically conditioned by the Reformation?

There is precedent for these contemporary scholars' attitudes toward both ritual repetition and ritual performance in Protestant theological polemics. These similarities may not be coincidental. Tambiah regarded the Reformation as a key moment of ritual involution, as is clear from his reference to periods of "religious reform" as a mode of "realism" that emphasizes "referential meaning" as opposed to the "exploitative strategies of priestly castes." These comments generalize the Protestant critique of Roman Catholicism by extending it to other cultural contexts. They follow an earlier article in which Tambiah had used the Latin mass as an example of ritual language that is stereotyped and drained of semantic content.[28] Similarly, Whitehouse appears to have based his modes of religiosity theory in part on the Reformation distinction between Protestant doctrine and Catholic icon.[29]

Despite certain continuities between Reformed theological and modern scholarly views of ritual, there are also important differences. Comparing Tambiah's and Whitehouse's descriptions of the aversion to ritual as "tedium" with the Protestant critique of vain repetitions, we can immediately perceive one discrepancy. The vehemence with which Protestants attacked such forms of ritual language, which, as a form of idolatrous corruption, threatened one's very soul, was not a sort of yawning boredom of the type that would induce one either to go to sleep or to walk away from the performance in a malaise. It was not tedium, but odium that Protestants directed against the superstitious and idolatrous belief in the magical efficacy of such formulas. Indeed, Protestants also sometimes depicted such ritual as a dull, monotonous activity, engaged in only under compulsion or with an eye toward some extrinsic benefit. Stories of Papists contracting out the performance of their repetitive prayers and other superstitious rituals projected this attitude onto the recitation of the Hail Mary. However, this attack on ritual tedium occurred in the context of a more basic attack on ritual as idolatry. The so-called "tedium effect" cannot, therefore, be regarded as a full explanation of the Protestant attack on vain repetitions in prayer and other modes of ritual.

This revaluation of modes of linguistic and ritual performance was also, at the same time, a change in the notion of performance itself, that is to say, in the notion of the "work" done by ritual. Jonathan Z. Smith has pointed to the fact that ritual is, above all, a form of work.[30] It can be time-consuming, tedious, and labor-intensive, but in this regard, it is revealed as an ordinary, rather than exceptional, form of behavior. Moreover, ritual is designed to "do" something, to "perform," and thus assumes a second, utilitarian characteristic of labor. Protestants acknowledged that ritual required effort. What they denied was that it had the power to accomplish anything, or to effect salvation. The "input" of such work, its laborious nature, was affirmed, while its "output" was called into question. Hence, Protestant criticisms of the doctrine of *ex opere operato*, the notion that, by virtue of the "work being performed," the ritual would be effective. This was reflected, above all, in the denial of magical efficacy of ritual devices and their reinterpretation as a mode of rhetorical performance.

Examination of the Puritan critique of vain repetitions suggests that this was associated with a radical transformation in the view of how ritual works. We must still explain this transformation, which Weber's account of the replacement of traditional Catholic sacramentalism by the Protestant work ethic helped us to understand. Why were some forms of traditional practice suddenly deemed unacceptable? Why was an ancient prohibition against "vain repetitions" resurrected, and reinterpreted, at just this moment in history? In addition to theological ideas promoting iconoclasm and literalism, another factor appears to have contributed to the attack on repetitive prayers in particular: the rise of a culture of the printed book, which altered the orientation toward language and contributed to the critique of poetic forms associated with oral performance. The remainder of this chapter explores the coordination between Protestant literalism and print culture, and in so doing, considers broader anthropological as well as historical explanations for the repudiation of ritual.

The literacy hypothesis

Before Printing, Old-Wives Tales were ingeniose: and since Printing came in fashion, till a little before the Civil-warres, the ordinary sort of People were not taught to read: now-a-dayes Bookes are common, and most of the poor people understand letters: and the many god Bookes, and variety of Turnes of Affaires, have put all the old Fables out of dores: and the divine art of Printing and Gunpowder have frighted away Robin-good-fellow and the Fayries.[31]

In this famous quote, John Aubrey, a folklorist and an early member of the Royal Society, attributed the disenchantment of the world to books. Around a century ago, Max Weber popularized the idea that the Protestant Reformation had brought about disenchantment. Both Aubrey and Weber may have had good reason, at least when it comes to the subject of poetic magic.

Scholars have long debated the connections of the Protestant Reformation with one of the major changes in media technology that gave birth to the modern age: the development and widespread application, beginning in fifteenth-century Europe, of movable type, and the culture of the printed book that grew up around the economies of information distribution that this technological innovation made possible. Print culture was associated with the rise not only of literacy, but also of fictional literature and literalism, as opposed modes of discourse. Among other things, print served as a vector for a culture of religiously inspired literalist prose.

Many of the verbal practices Protestants proscribed as idolatrous represented traditions that, though not exclusively oral, granted oral modes of performance a more prominent role in relation to writing. The coordination of printing with Protestantism is evident in the case of colonial India, where the British introduction of printing on a wide scale authorized textual traditions, both indigenous and foreign, while displacing oral custom. Although Indians had possessed writing for millennia, oral transmission preserved its prestige in a number of domains, and the introduction of printing brought about a different mode of relation even to those textual traditions that had previously existed in manuscript form. Significantly, a number of the ritual practices dismissed as vain repetitions, including Vedic recitation and the chanting of mantras, were intimately associated with the oral dimensions of South Asian culture.[32] In Bentham's case, as well, the emphasis on a printed code coordinated with an attack on oral, customary traditions and on poetry in legal language.

Consequently, we must reconsider the "literacy hypothesis," or the idea that writing, whether in manuscript or printed form, instituted a fundamental cultural divide. The classicist Eric Havelock and the anthropologist Jack Goody, among others, argued that the discovery of alphabetic writing in ancient Greece worked a profound transformation on culture.[33] Writing supposedly contributed to the decline of poetry and other oral genres, and the growth of skepticism and logic. Havelock and Goody both invoked this hypothesis to account for the origin of philosophy in ancient Greece, and especially Plato's attack on myth and poetry. Plato represented the ascendency of a more skeptical culture made possible by the advent of writing, which had been introduced into Greece within the preceding few centuries. The Sophists whom Plato attacked represented an older, primarily oral culture and system of pedagogy, which depended heavily on poetry for its transmission of knowledge. In this older culture, poetry had functioned as a storehouse of knowledge, or what Havelock referred to as the "Homeric encyclopedia." The repetitiveness of poetry contributed to the memorability of oral texts, as well as to their performance: "[Poetry] was selected for this role because, in the absence of the written record, its rhythms and formulas provided the sole mechanism of recall and of re-use."[34] Writing presented opportunities for recording, storing, and communicating ideas that rendered obsolete the mnemonic function of poetic devices in an oral culture.[35] The obsolescence of poetry coordinated with increasing skepticism concerning the manner in which it achieved its persuasive effects, as a mode of pedagogical training and oratorical performance.[36] Despite the pejorative comments in his *Phaedrus* regarding the deleterious effects of writing on memory,[37] Plato may exemplify the movement against an older oral culture.

Goody argued similarly that writing had important ramifications not only for culture, but also for human cognition. Literate cultures think differently from oral cultures. This difference was associated in some way with the development of logic and the critique of certain modes of thought, including magic, that anthropologists used to call "primitive." Goody emphasized that this development represented not some difference in cognitive capacities, but rather the superior opportunities for reflection made possible by writing. Writing enabled the comparison between oral and written modes, to the detriment of the former, as well as the accumulation of a certain critical mass of skepticism that would otherwise dissipate in the absence of its storage and dissemination through writing: "By making it possible to scan the communications of mankind over a much wider time span, literacy encouraged, at the very same time, criticism and commentary on the one hand and the orthodoxy of the book on the other."[38] Goody has examined also from a cross-cultural perspective the connections between literacy and the skepticism and iconoclasm directed against various cultural forms, including the pictorial, plastic, and dramatic arts.[39] Literacy is associated with a certain intolerance exemplified by the "religions of the book," and above all with Jewish and Christian iconoclasm:

> Intolerance is connected with universalism. Not all literate religions are necessarily universalistic, but they have tendencies in that direction, if only because their commandments tend to get phrased in somewhat decontextualized, that is, universalistic, ways. The establishment of the universal church necessarily excludes other views, for religion is no longer defined politically [by group membership] . . . but theologically, in fact scripturally, by writing. It can spread independently of political institutions, although political support, however temporary, often helps. And it emerges in opposition ("Thou shalt have no other gods but me"), hence giving birth to a boundary between Jew and Gentile, but more strongly between Christian and pagan.[40]

Goody refined the literacy hypothesis by rejecting any simplistic contentions that the birth of writing caused the death of poetry. He claimed that writing, in its earlier stages, actually increased the poetry of language, and may have been responsible for the formulaic epithets that have sometimes been cited as evidence for Homer's status as an oral poet.[41] Put crudely, Homer may have been one of the first written rather than the last oral Greek poets. Although oral cultures employ poetry as a mnemonic device, more rigid poetic formulas or structures of versification and the practice of verbatim repetition associated with these are often identified with written culture, which tends to fix texts in a particular form.[42] Writing may have contributed in some cases to an increase in formulaic rituals, including repeated prayers, as well as to the "orthodoxy of the book."[43]

Similarly, we observe that the use of poetry elsewhere is not confined to oral traditions. Even if a number of the poetic devices examined in Chapter Two of this book, such as the parallelism and chiasmus appearing in ancient Jewish and Hindu law, can be explained in part by their contribution to memorability in predominately oral genres of performance,[44] they evolved within increasingly specialized and literate legal traditions. It is unlikely that Leviticus 24:13–23 was an oral formula, as the text is too long, and the chiasmus too elaborate, being revealed only by backward scanning of the written text.[45] In such cases, we assume that poetic devices served primarily a rhetorical rather than a mnemonic function: they made punishment appear more just or fitting, as well as more impressive. Despite such qualifications, as noted by Bentham and further discussed below in this chapter, there does appear to have been a close association between the poetic form of many ancient laws and their function in an oral culture. Some of the more obviously poetic formulas in Dharmaśāstra, such as the invocations in the ordeals of the *Divyatattva* discussed in Chapter Two of this volume, occurred in instances of direct speech, and even of ritual "speech acts." Although prescribed in written texts, these formulas were meant to be spoken. As such, their poetry would have served to make them more impressive to an audience that must have consisted of literate and illiterate alike.

Goody's refinements of the literacy hypothesis are well-taken. Yet they highlight a fundamental problem involved in associating poetry with orality, and prose with literacy.[46] Writing has no necessary connection with any mode of discourse. It may be used to record poetry or prose, logic or laundry lists. The coexistence of written and oral genres, and the interaction of poetic and literal modes of discourse, are readily observable in a variety of types in different cultures, including our own.[47] If, in cultures with writing, poetry was no longer required as a mnemonic device, then why did it survive, or even increase, in certain genres or domains of culture, such as literature? And why did it decline or die out in others?

At this point, the hypothesis that poetry serves a mnemonic function ceases to be of much use. Why should a simple technological advance that permitted more efficient storage and dissemination of ideas and information have inspired criticism, skepticism, and polemics against poetry? All that this advance implies directly is the obsolescence and gradual replacement of oral transmission by writing. We must presume that poetry serves some function other than the mnemonic, such as persuasion, or aesthetic pleasure, in order to account for its continued use in certain genres, both oral and written. And, I suggest, the converse holds true: where poetry disappears, this cannot be presumed to be merely a consequence of the fact that there are other means of preserving cultural memory. In these cases as well, one must examine the functions assigned to discourse within the genre in question. These considerations suggest the importance of cultural factors, in addition to the material fact of print, in precipitating polemics against poetic language.

There is a significant analogy between the Greek and the Reformation cases. The Protestant attack on vain repetitions in prayer paralleled, in a number of respects, the rise of polemics against poetry that culminated in Plato's recommendation that we banish poets from the ideal Republic. Both Greek philosophy and Reformation theology identified certain forms or applications of poetry with rhetoric or sophistry, and with the irrational; and both of these movements have been attributed to changes in the dominant mode of cultural communication: in the case of Plato, the birth of alphabetic writing; in the case of the Reformation, the rise of a culture of the printed book. The Protestant critique of vain repetitions serves in many ways as an ideal test case for the literacy hypothesis, both because that critique represented a sustained attack on precisely those features of language that, according to this hypothesis, were the bone of contention between an oral culture and a culture of writing or printing, and because Goody and others have already extended the literacy hypothesis to the Reformation.

The inauguration of printing on a large scale prompted cultural changes that were arguably more pervasive and fundamental than the ones that came with alphabetic writing.[48] Even Ruth Finnegan, one of the most vocal critics of the thesis that literacy contributed to a "Great Divide" of cultures, allowed that "*printing* rather than writing in itself [was] the most important factor" in the emphasis on the primacy of the text in European cultures in recent centuries.[49] In the domain of religion, printing had the most direct consequences for the interpretation of scripture and the performance of the liturgy. It facilitated the dissemination of knowledge, prosecution of public debates, dislocation of authority from the Catholic Church, and relocation of that authority in a canon of scripture.[50] It also may have had more subtle and far-reaching effects on European mentalities. Walter Ong associated the Catholic sacraments with oral culture, and the Protestant critique of these sacraments with print culture and "the typographic state of mind, which takes the word to be quite different from things."[51] He claimed that "the well-known Protestant stress on literacy has deeper psychological roots than those allowed for when this stress is taken to be due simply to the desire to have as many as possible read the Bible for themselves."[52] Elizabeth Eisenstein contended that both Weber's account of the Protestant work ethic and Keith Thomas's account of the decline of magic were wrong to neglect the contribution of printing to these developments.[53] She argued that printing paved the way for

> a more thorough-going iconoclasm than any Christian church had ever known. . . . Printing made it possible to dispense with the use of images for mnemonic purposes and thus reinforced iconoclastic tendencies already present among many Christians. . . . [P]rinting fostered a movement "from image culture to word culture," a movement which was more compatible with Protestant bibliolatry and pamphleteering than with the Baroque statues and paintings sponsored by the post-Tridentine Catholic Church.[54]

Similarly, Hildred Geertz suggested during her debate with Keith Thomas that literacy may have been a factor in the rise of skepticism toward those practices retrospectively described as "magical."[55] Peter Burke also implied the role that changes in media technology may have played in the repudiation of ritual in early modern Europe when he suggested that, more recently, "new media, television in particular, have been able to remystify authority."[56] Peter Goodrich has advanced the thesis that "The discourse against images, technically the antirrhetic . . . became in the aftermath of print culture a discourse against textual figures, painted words, and imaginary signs."[57]

As with invocations of the literacy hypothesis to explain the "Greek miracle," or assertions of a "Great Divide" between cultures with and those without writing, it is easy to be skeptical of these claims concerning the changes effected by printing during and after the Reformation.[58] The doubts raised above concerning Goody's and Havelock's accounts of Plato's attack on poetry apply to the case of print culture as well. The idea that printing alone effected such profound changes seems to ignore the role played by culture. As Richard Bauman and Charles Briggs emphasize, the thesis that printing "mark[s] the threshold between past and present" is itself part of the ideology of modernity, an autobiographical narrative that already figured in Aubrey's connection of printing with disenchantment and in Bacon's account of the discoveries that serve to divide the "moderns" from the "ancients."[59] Bauman and Briggs argue that

> What is missing from the scholarly project devoted to the constructional history of print culture and the authorization of print discourse . . . is the focused investigation of concomitant processes by which print and its attendant discursive formations are constructed in *symbolic and ideological opposition* to other technologies of communication and modes of discourse.[60]

Bauman and Briggs accordingly join with the effort "to provide a critical corrective to conceptions of the printed word that view its purported capacities for social transformation as inherent in the medium itself."[61] Indeed, the Reformation brought more than a printing press. However, as Eisenstein's nuanced account already showed, it is difficult to ignore the pervasive connections among printing, on the one hand, and the rise of Protestant iconoclasm and attitudes toward language, on the other.[62]

In addition to the colonial Indian case, some other cases of ethnographic encounter suggest a similar bias of modern print cultures against modes of oral performance.[63] Poetic parallelisms were lost in the course of being written down. Ethnographic records sometimes deliberately omitted such poetic forms as redundant or irrelevant, a distraction from the message being recorded. In the context of arguing for the literary function of poetic parallelisms, Viktor Shklovsky complained against the practice on the part of some Russian folklorists of deleting such devices or viewing them derisively as "tautologically musical parallelism."[64] Bauman and Briggs recount a similar case in North America, that of Henry Rowe Schoolcraft, whose contempt for the Ojibwe tendency toward "tautology," "repetition and redundancy"[*sic!*], and other modes of verbal excess led him to trim such forms out of his written records of their folklore.[65] What is noteworthy is that writing, in these cases, clearly coordinated with pejorative attitudes toward repetitive oral discourse. To a less extreme extent than in Protestantism, perhaps, the emphasis on the semantic content of language, at the expense of its poetic form, was at least associated with, if not directly inspired by, a mentality oriented toward the printed word.

These connections may be illustrated by the disappearance of poetic parallelisms from English legal formulas, one instance of which is observable in the codification of the marriage oath in the *Book of Common Prayer*. Consideration of this example strongly suggests that the Puritan critique of vain repetitions coordinated with print culture in bringing about not only a fundamental shift in attitudes toward ritual, but also, in certain areas or genres of culture, an actual decline in particular modes of ritual repetition.

"To have and to hold"

The newly printed liturgy of the Church of England, the *Book of Common Prayer* (hereinafter "*BCP*") authored by Archbishop Thomas Cranmer in 1549, replaced and effaced older, oral traditions. The enactment of a uniform, authoritative liturgy was a necessary development in the construction of a single, authoritative Protestant Church of England.[66] This, in turn, coordinated with the well-known Protestant dictum of "scripture alone" as the exclusive authority on matters religious. Over time, the Bible and other authoritative texts were translated into the vernacular, so that in theory anyone, or at least anyone who could read, could look and see for him- or herself what was written there.[67] With the emphasis on a textual canon replacing the authority of the customs and traditions of the Roman Catholic Church, it was natural for this emphasis to manifest itself also in a uniform book of liturgy. Like the Bible, the *BCP* established an apparently solid, textual basis for religion. Although the Quakers rejected any prescribed form of liturgy, Cranmer's *BCP* was more conservative. Latin passages were translated into the vernacular, to reflect the new emphasis on comprehension, rather than mere performance, of the liturgy. Cumbersome ritual sequences were streamlined, and the number of prayers reduced.

In the Preface to the *BCP*, Cranmer explained that, with the passage of time, the purity of the ancient rites had been corrupted by "uncertain Stories, and Legends, with multitude of Responds, Verses, vain Repetitions, Commemorations, and Synodals," with the result that insufficient time and attention had been given to communicating the entire Bible, and its meaning, to the people. Moreover, the use of Latin in the old liturgy meant that people "have heard with their ears only." Accordingly, the *BCP*'s translation of the liturgy into the vernacular was accompanied by a streamlining or reduction that eliminated things, whereof some are untrue, some uncertain, some vain and superstitious; and nothing is ordained to be read, but the very pure Word of God, the holy Scriptures, or that which is agreeable to the same; and that in a language and order as is most plain for the understanding both of the readers and hearers . . . And whereas heretofore there hath been great diversity in saying and singing in Churches within this Realm; some following Salisbury Use, some Hereford Use, and some the Use of Bangor, some of York, some of Lincoln; now from henceforth all the whole Realm shall have but one Use.

The "Uses" to which Cranmer referred were local ritual forms contained in manuscripts and administered within particular Bishoprics, including those of Sarum (Salisbury) and York. These were eliminated and replaced by a standardized, uniform printed liturgy. In the view of many Puritans, the *BCP* did not go far enough to eliminate the idolatrous ceremonies of the Papists. However, the compromise was enforced. An edict was passed banning other liturgical practices. Edward VI's *An Act for the Abolishing and Putting Away of Divers Books and Images* (1549) proscribed these physical manifestations of the Sarum and York rites, and even called for them to be "deface[d]" to prevent their further use. The conflation between idolatry and older modes of verbal worship was complete. Cranmer echoed the association between idolatry and various abuses of language, including rhetorical and magical uses.[68] His liturgical reform embraced the ideals of Protestant literalism, and of ritual simplicity, combined in the attack on vain repetitions.

Cranmer's linguistic biases may have influenced his reform of the marriage vow contained in the *BCP*, which replaced almost all of the alliterative, poetic parallelisms attested in manuscripts. These manuscripts recorded those local "uses" or forms of ritual that, as we have seen, were proscribed as idolatrous, but Cranmer's oath derived from these earlier liturgical uses. The full formula of this oath, which has become so much a part of our common culture, runs (in the bride's version; the version for the groom omits the oath of obedience):

> I N. take thee N. to my wedded husband, to have and to hold from this day forward, for better for worse, for richer for poorer, in sickness and in health, to love, cherish, and to obey, till death us do part, according to God's holy ordinance; and thereto I give thee my troth.

"To have and to hold" was an ancient legal performative that predated even the separation of English and German cultures. Numerous versions of this phrase appear in ancient German law.[69] Versions of this phrase can be found in such tenth- to eleventh-century Old English texts as *Beowulf*, the *Battle of Maldon*, the *Blickling Homilies*, and the *Lacnunga*, which contains the so-called Anglo-Saxon charms; an example ("and have those kine and hold those kine") was analyzed in Chapter Two.[70] Accordingly, Francis Palgrave rightly noted Cranmer's marriage vow as an echo or vestige of poetic parallelisms otherwise common in early English law.[71] He pointed to the disappearance from that vow of several, more poetic local variants in use at the time of institution of the *BCP*.[72] In some varying older versions of the marriage rite, the phrase "for fairer for fouler" had appeared in the first part of the oath.[73] The wife's promise, in Cranmer's version, "to love, cherish, and to obey" replaced an earlier promise, in some versions, "to be bonour and buxom at bed and at board."[74] Although these more alliterative oaths may not have been much older than the fourteenth or fifteenth century,[75] they obviously reflected very ancient patterns, and some of their precise phrasings were ancient. The *BCP* replaced some of the most obvious poetic parallelisms in the marriage oath with their literal "translations" into more modern English. The meaning or content of the promise was retained, while the form was changed in a direction that reduced its poetry, or at least its alliteration, to a minimum. Catholics retained older formulas of the marriage oath, while with the establishment of the Church of England and the *BCP* as the solely authorized liturgy of that Church, the marriage oath was made official in the form previously described.

Why did Cranmer institute such changes in the marriage vow? One explanation for why Cranmer abandoned other alliterative forms while retaining "to have and to hold" is that this formula constituted the heart of the oath, the declaration of ownership and possession known as the "habendum et tenendum," which means simply "have and hold" in Latin.[76] Another explanation that has been advanced is that Cranmer sought to exclude a formula like "bonour and buxom," which had, or was on the point of acquiring, sexual connotations.[77]

It is tempting to suggest a connection between Cranmer's liturgical reforms and the theological attack on vain repetitions. However, several caveats are necessary. First, the marriage vow was not, strictly speaking, a prayer. The complaint against vain repetitions had not been levelled directly against the earlier versions of this vow.[78] Indeed, the source and meaning of Cranmer's use of the phrase "vain repetitions" are uncertain. The *BCP* predated by 11 years the 1560 Geneva Bible, which was the first English Bible to use the phrase "vain repetitions" to translate Matthew 6:7. In his own translation of that biblical verse, Cranmer used "babling." It is possible that, in using the phrase "vain repetitions" in the *BCP*, Cranmer was drawing on a nascent theological tradition that referred to Matthew 6:7. He may have taken the phrase directly from Calvin's Latin gloss of this verse.[79] One of the other early uses of the phrase "vayne repetitions" in English literature appeared in Thomas Wilson's *The Arte of Rhetorique* (1553),[80] along with an attack on alliteration: "Some use overmuche repeticion of some one letter, as 'pitiful povertie praieth for a peny . . .'"[81] Interestingly, Wilson associated such linguistic forms with Papist liturgy.[82] Alliteration was the very figure Cranmer excised from the marriage vow. Of course, Cranmer's version of the marriage vow possessed its own sort of poetry,[83] just as the later King James Bible did. Yet his vow differed from the profuse alliteration of former Anglo-Saxon versions.

Whatever the source of Cranmer's complaint against vain repetitions, it distilled a new ideal of literalism in which the combined emphases on translation into vernacular prose, on the goal of understanding the liturgy, and on uniformity contributed to the disappearance of much of the poetry of the marriage oath. It appears significant that these developments were associated with an increasing institutionalization of print culture. The poetic forms of the older versions of the marriage vow suggest their function as mnemotechnics, survivals from an earlier, oral stage of culture. With the fixing of such texts in printed form, there was no longer any need for poetic forms as a mnemonic device or aide-mémoire. The "translation" of such poetic forms into plain prose in order to render their literal meaning more clearly was a corollary of an emphasis on the vernacular, and on the importance of understanding the liturgy. However, it was not only the obsolescence of such poetic devices as mnemotechnics, but the perception of them as "idolatrous," that contributed to their displacement from the liturgy. As Ramie Targoff explains:

> Th[e] earlier imposition of learning [the liturgy] was simplified . . . by the use of English verse, which was mnemonically accessible to the unlearned in ways that both Latin and English prose were not. . . . [P]oetic form served a practical, not an aesthetic imperative: the more accessible the rhyme, the more likely the prayer was remembered. When the Protestant Reformation introduced a vernacular Prayer Book into the Church of England, the mutually dependent relationship between poetic and devotional production was permanently unsettled. Once the public liturgy consisted only of comprehensible, English texts, the lay population no longer required easily digestible translations in order to learn their own prayers. These new vernacular texts were written entirely in prose and not verse, a decision that no doubt reflected both the practical exigencies of individual [poetic] limitations . . . and more abstract prejudices against rhyme as symptomatic of an idolatrous relationship to language.[84]

Austin's account of "performative utterances" which, as mentioned previously, ignored the contribution of poetic repetition to verbal performance, reflected, if only indirectly, the influence of these earlier biases against poetry. Austin's prime example of a performative utterance was the statement "I do" [sic: the actual words are "I will"] occurring in the course of the marriage vow, as it appears in the BCP. The full version of Cranmer's oath contained semantic parallelisms (e.g. "for richer for poorer") omitted by Austin. Yet Cranmer's version, as we have seen, already represented a suppression of earlier, more alliterative formulas. Austin's further reduction of the form of the oath to a two-word declarative merely completed a process of suppression of the contribution of poetry to verbal performance.[85] Despite his efforts to recover for philosophy a sense of "how to do things with words," Austin perpetuated a division between poetic and philosophical language long established in modern Britain.

Apart from attempting to divine Cranmer's intentions in framing the *BCP*, another approach to understanding the disappearance of these poetic formulas is to consider them in a broader context. As indicated previously, the poetic parallelism of the marriage oath reflected a long tradition. In early Anglo-Saxon and German cultures, as in many others, various metrical devices, including especially parallelisms based on rhyme or alliteration, contributed to the memorability and binding force of many vows, oaths, and declarations. The German linguist and folklorist Jacob Grimm (1785–1863), in his essay "On Poetry in Law" (*Von der Poesie im Recht*, 1816), catalogued numerous such forms in early German law. I have tried to preserve in translation the poetry of some of his examples:

Gut oder gelt	Goods or gold
Haut und haar	Hide and hair
Lesset und leihet	Lease and lend
Schuld und schaden	Debt and damages
Bus und besserung	Penalty and payment

Grimm speculated that this poetry had an internal need to "complete" itself through parallelism.[86] According to him, such formulas reflected an oral stage of society in which poets, bards, and singers served as the repositories of tradition. The law was essentially backward-looking, in the sense of remembering and giving voice to tradition; not forward-looking, as is our current system of continual relegislation.[87] This agrees with Rudolph Hübner's opinion that such alliterative formulas served to stamp law on the memory,[88] a function that became obsolete with the growth of literacy, for "writing is the sworn enemy of all [other] sensuous representation."[89] Esther Cohen noted a similar use of rhyming parallelisms, such as *tenir et garder, pouvoir et devoir, estans et manans*, in medieval French law. She suggested that such devices served a mnemonic function, yet also claimed that they are common in modern and written law as well.[90] However, most obvious forms of poetry, including especially alliteration and rhyme, have all but disappeared from contemporary law. Legal language is now the epitome of dry prose, famous for its dullness; and it is hardly written in verse, although it still contains many tautologies (e.g. "give, bequeathe, and devise") in its boilerplate, devices that reflect not only a certain formalism but also the desire to enumerate and plan for all possible contingencies.[91] Many other scholars, even before Bentham, have contended either that similar poetic formulas in different legal systems reflected an oral stage of culture in which such formulas served a primarily mnemonic function, or that it was the advent of writing or printing that precipitated the decline of such formulas.[92] When its function of recording and preserving was replaced by writing, the poetry of law disappeared. This was the opinion of the eminent scholar of Anglo-Saxon culture, Francis Palgrave:

> When they first settled in England, their [the Anglo-Saxons'] law . . . was entirely oral and traditionary. It was a common law, existing as the common law of England still exists, in customs . . . [A]n aid to the recollection was often afforded . . . by poetry, or by the condensation of the maxim or principle in proverbial or antithetical sentences. . . . The marked alliteration of the Anglo-Saxon laws is to be referred to this cause . . .[93]

These analyses lend support to Goody's and Havelock's contentions that writing may have inspired skepticism toward poetry, and suggest that the decline of poetic forms, at least in certain genres, may have been an effect of the rise of either writing, increasing literacy, or print culture.

The literacy hypothesis revisited

None of what I have said above should be mistaken as an unqualified endorsement of the literacy hypothesis. Rather, these explorations of the complex relationship between the advent of print culture and the rise of pejorative attitudes toward certain forms of language more closely associated with oral performance have tended to confirm the opinion of Bauman and Briggs that the opposition between printing (or writing) and orality is a cultural, not a natural distinction. Moreover, it is important to emphasize that pejorative attitudes toward modes of oral performance in some cases, such as that of the Protestant critique of vain repetitions in prayer, appear to have focused their ire on the persuasive or performative aspects of language, rather than on the mnemonic functions of language or on orality per se. This distinction is not made clearly by some existing versions of the literacy hypothesis.

There are good reasons for skepticism regarding the literary hypothesis as an explanation for attacks on certain forms of poetic language. We have returned to a version of the same problem described earlier. Obsolescence, due to the lack of a continuing necessity for such poetic devices in a culture where writing now obviates their mnemonic function, is supposed to account for the decline of poetry. Yet things are not quite so straightforward. For one thing, the explanation is too general, as it applies to all types of language and every area of culture, and therefore fails to explain why, in particular, prayers, vows, oaths, and legally binding declarations employed such poetic devices? After all, in an oral culture, every datum of information would require the same versification or risk being forgotten. Certainly we may appreciate why sacred texts such as the *Vedas* were metricalized. The proponent of the literacy hypothesis will say that legal rituals such as oaths—like the brilliant deeds of the Achaeans at Troy—were of more than ordinary importance, and were metricalized so as to rescue them from the oblivion that might otherwise befall them. Less significant scraps of information could stand to be lost; and the mundane is also the quotidian, which is supported well enough by short-term memory and rote experience. In response, one might say that the truly significant events are less likely to be forgotten: we all know the saying "If it's important, you'll remember it." In any case, it would be more effective simply to have more witnesses on hand. This would reduce the risk that everyone will forget, and alone would seem sufficient for this purpose. Poetry may help an individual remember a private vow, but if no one else in the community knew that such a vow had been made, it would be vain to ask the community to enforce it. The claim that the same devices that make a vow more memorable for an individual, make it more memorable for each member of a group, confounds those who repeat the vow with those in the audience who merely hear it.

Moreover, what sort of memory is it, precisely, that we are talking about here? Is it memory of the traditional form of the vow, so that this may be followed as closely as possible on all occasions on which such a vow is taken? Or is it memory that a vow was taken on a particular occasion, so that the fact of its having been taken may be invoked at some later date? Or is it memory of each and every provision in a vow, so that these are more likely to be observed? Or is it some combination of these? The literacy hypothesis commonly confounds such types of memory, although they are arguably quite different. The failure of the literacy hypothesis to address such distinctions is a serious omission.

However, the most important criticism of the literacy hypothesis may be that it emphasizes the mnemonic function of poetry at the expense of its persuasive function. Poetry is impressive not only on the memory, but also in the moment. The most obvious explanation for the use of poetry in mantras, early English oaths and other speech acts or performative utterances is that poetry contributed in some way to the binding force of such formulas. Their association with poetry was not merely adventitious, but went to the heart of their function as a form of effective speech or ritual performance. Several of the legal formulas of the type Grimm catalogues appeared in the Anglo-Saxon charms,[94] and, in general, they shared with magical formulas their poetic form, their pragmatic function, and the requirement that they be repeated precisely in order to be effective.[95] They were, as Palgrave said, "words of power," with "binding force" and "efficacy in themselves."[96] Harold Berman has also pointed to the ceremonial function of poetry, which "was more appropriate than prosaic and literal language, especially on solemn occasions involving the law."[97]

One of the most widespread religious phenomena cross-culturally is the use of poetic devices in spells, incantations, and prayers, as described in Chapter Two. Such devices, as I have argued, contribute to the rhetorical force of ritual language. Our intuition that rhythmic form subjectively reinforces the strength of spells is supported by several observations. The first is that this converges with the folk explanation in some traditions, such as Hindu Tantra, that poetic repetition makes such spells more powerful. The second is the continuing role of such devices in contemporary culture, where magic has declined but analogous uses of rhythmic language for rhetorical purposes are ubiquitous in advertising jingles and political slogans. The third is that the contribution of such devices to persuasion or illusion made repetitive ritual language the target of Reformation polemics, and may have contributed to the historical decline of such language.

Other examples may be found closer to home. Consider the political slogan analyzed by Roman Jakobson: "I Like Ike."[98] Is the primary function of such a phrase to be memorable, or to persuade? Actually, both functions are perfectly consonant. The formula works on us the more it is called to mind. But clearly, when placed in its proper (pragmatic) context, the goal of the formula is not simple self-propagation. The goal is to persuade someone to vote for Ike. The mnemonic function of the formula is ancillary or subordinate to its rhetorical function. One is encouraged to associate Ike with positive feelings ("like"). One is encouraged to repeat, or really to ventriloquate, a phrase that indexes one's allegiance to Ike. Another, everyday example of how repetition contributes to the pragmatic force of discourse is: "Do it, John! Do it now!" When I repeat myself in this way, am I trying to get John to remember what he is supposed to do, or am I, quite simply, reinforcing the message that, whatever it is, *it must be done quickly*?

What some theorists have interpreted as the function of rhythm or repetition in ritual, namely its contribution to memorability, does not account for the prominence of such devices in ritual language. Such devices, considered merely as mnemotechnics, may serve to promote the memorability of *any* cultural form. Why, then, should they be especially prevalent in effective rituals, such as magic? The answer appears to be that such devices contribute not only to memorability, but also to the persuasiveness of rhetoric, the illusionism of spells, and the binding force of oaths and other performative utterances. This reinforces the proposition advanced earlier: poetry is precisely coextensive with neither oral culture nor the mnemonic function. We still have to ask why, in any particular case, poetry disappeared. In the case of the Protestant critique of vain repetitions, the performative and rhetorical dimensions of certain forms of ritual poetry seem to have marked them as candidates for suppression.

The Protestant critique of vain repetitions underscores the importance of cultural factors in polemics against ritual poetry, and the inadequacy of any explanation that attempts to derive the impetus for such polemics from the medium of communication alone. Following the introduction of printing, both Protestants and Catholics, Anglicans and Dissenters could disseminate more easily their views concerning the propriety of different forms of devotion. Prayers of all types, repetitive as well as minimalist, could be and still are printed, reflecting a wide variety of religious orientations. In the South Asian context, mantras that were formerly transmitted orally and in secret could be printed and distributed to a wider audience, a practice that continues to this day. Moreover, the Protestant critique of vain repetitions was limited largely to prayers and prayer-like uses of language. Types of rhetoric prohibited in prayer might be perfectly acceptable in other genres, or for other applications. This critique depended on a set of assumptions regarding the nature of the divinity and its interactions with the human world. The association between vain repetitions and idolatry, in particular, suggests the degree to which the attack on repetitive prayers reflected concepts distinctive to Protestant Christianity, at least in its origins, despite its subsequent dissemination to India and other places. Finally, the critique of vain repetitions further highlights a central weakness of the literacy hypothesis previously mentioned: Why should the mere obsolescence of poetry as a mnemotechnic have exposed it to such attacks? Should we not have expected that such poetic forms would die a natural death, as they were gradually replaced by more efficient, written forms, rather than meeting an untimely end at the hands of hostile critics? The Protestant critique of vain repetitions demonstrates that the nature of the complaint against certain poetic forms of prayer was not that these were less efficient than writing, and therefore no longer needed. It was instead a violent assault on the rhetorical and magical dimensions of such language. At stake was precisely the efficacy of poetic ritual language, its status as a mode of performance. Above all, it is the neglect of the performative dimensions of ritual that undermines the literacy hypothesis as an explanation for the decline of ritual repetition. A survey of the polemics against repetitive prayers shows that what was at stake was precisely their rhetorical function. Reformation polemics against poetic ritual language emphasized the persuasion-producing rather than the memory-inducing function of such language.

There is a further analogy to the case of polemics against poetry in ancient Greece. The "debate" between Plato and Gorgias, described in Chapter One, illustrates the crux of the controversy as arising from the convergence between poetry and magical or rhetorical performance. The literacy hypothesis does not appear to explain this controversy fully. The difference of styles between Gorgias and Plato is not reducible to that between orality and literacy, as both men were writing, albeit in a mode that either suggests or mimics orality: for Gorgias, the forensic argument; for Plato, the dialogue. Moreover, it was not the mnemonic but rather the persuasive function of poetry that Plato attacked; indeed, in his *Phaedrus* he criticized the deleterious effects of writing on memory. As a form of both rhetoric and magic, poetry threatened the new regime of literalism represented by philosophy. At least some of the polemics against poetry in ancient Greece appear to share with the later Protestant attack on vain repetitions a similar distrust of the rhetorical and magical dimensions of poetic discourse. This indicates once again that the literacy hypothesis on its own may be unable to account for such polemics against poetry.

The Protestant critique of vain repetitions suggests, more strongly than the analogous Greek case, that the contrast between orality and a new form of writing, namely, the printed book, may have played some role in inspiring a heightened critical awareness or "semiotic recognition" of the rhetorical dimensions of repetitive ritual language. The forms of language against which this critique was directed were strongly associated with oral performance, even if they coexisted with manuscript writing, as they did in both medieval Britain and precolonial South Asia. Indeed, the Protestant polemic against vain repetitions appeared in these two different contexts in close proximity to the introduction of printing. Although the change of linguistic medium alone does not fully explain the appearance of these polemics against poetic performance, it does appear that, in some cases at least, these polemics were associated with the rise of print culture.[99]

One possible way of understanding these developments may be to recognize that poetry may serve both a mnemonic and a persuasive function, neither of which can be sharply distinguished from the other. Whereas the mnemonic function of poetry becomes partly obsolete in a culture of writing or printing, its persuasive (or aesthetic, or more broadly rhetorical) function remains useful. Most of the overt criticisms of poetic performance we have observed focus precisely on this second, persuasive function. The birth and growth of writing, or of printing, may have shifted the balance between these two functions of poetry, in such a way as to highlight the rhetorical function, and thereby expose it to deeper critique. However, the other conditions that contribute to just such a heightening of awareness regarding the rhetorical dimensions of poetic discourse are far from clear.

Modern commercial advertising is one example of a domain where the continued use of poetic parallelisms serves both a mnemonic and a persuasive function. Although such uses are allowed in contemporary culture, they are understood by everyone (one hopes) as a palpable attempt to impress a product or service on the minds of listeners, and to persuade them of the value of such goods. This is a further indication of the close association between such uses of rhetoric and orality, because the arena where such devices are deployed are primarily radio and television, modes of communication where the written word is less dominant. Perhaps this affords another point of connection between rhetoric and ritual for, as Peter Burke stated, despite the repudiation of ritual in the early modern period, modern electronic media have been able in some cases to "remystify" authority.[100]

CHAPTER SIX

Arbitrariness, anomaly, and agency:

A critique of Mary Douglas's structuralist idea of the Holy

Throughout this book, we have considered the manner in which semiotic processes confront the fact of the arbitrariness of the sign as a problem. From one perspective, this appears to confirm the structuralist insistence on the recognition of the arbitrariness of the sign as the precondition of a science of culture. A proper understanding of the form and function of signs requires an emergence from a naïve attachment to the belief that signs have a direct connection with the natural order. Given the absence of such a connection, we must not take signs one-by-one, considering them only in relation to their individual referents, but must instead consider signs as part of a system in which their relationship to other signs establishes their meaning or value.

The importance of this realization has been demonstrated again and again in the preceding chapters. The belief in a natural language is misguided, a ruse of culture motivated by a particular anxiety over the ability of signs to communicate, in the broadest sense: between word and thing, but also between ritual and reality, and between human and divine. The rise of an awareness of the arbitrary nature of the sign during the Reformation and Enlightenment contributed an impetus for various proposals to guarantee the communicative power of language in the face of this awareness. Even in the absence of such an awareness in many traditional cultures, the most adequate explanation for a number of devices commonly found in magic spells and other rituals was that these were attempts to bridge the gap between sign and referent, so as to produce a result in the here-and-now.

Repetition, verbal and physical forms of pointing or indexing, and the exhaustive catalogues of protection spells all attempt to overcome the distortion that stands in the way of the ritual's message. This distortion includes not only practical challenges but also existential threats and even the riddle of salvation itself. Arbitrariness is evidently much more than simply the technical problem of how to make words meaningful; it is implicated in some of the most fundamental human problems at the divide between nature and culture.

The present chapter revisits the concept of the arbitrariness of the sign in connection with a key issue in religion—the nature of the Holy—and provides a critique of some well-known structuralist approaches to that issue. The empirical focus of the chapter is the interpretation of the dietary prohibitions in the Hebrew Bible by Mary Douglas, Jean Soler, and other scholars. However, the primary goal of this chapter is not to introduce a new theory of the dietary prohibitions, much less of the Holy—which is beyond the scope of the present work—but rather to demonstrate that the structuralist view of the arbitrariness of the sign has introduced certain biases into our understanding of the Holy. By projecting a negative view of arbitrariness or "anomaly" onto the Hebrew Bible, structuralists such as Mary Douglas have arguably both misread the text, and misunderstood the nature of the sign.

The Jewish dietary laws commonly known as the kosher laws, which go back to Mosaic tradition (Leviticus 11 and Deuteronomy 14), contain a number of prohibitions such as that against eating pork or fish without scales and fins (e.g. shellfish). Among the numerous interpretations that have been given of these and related ritual laws are the following:[1]

- They are purely arbitrary commands, designed to signify submission or obedience to divine will, according to many Jewish traditionalists who upheld these laws and also many English Deists, who on this basis condemned these rituals as violations of natural law.[2]

- They are hygienic: the animals designated "impure" for ritual purposes are actually unhealthy to eat, as carriers of disease, etc., according to some traditional and some more contemporary rationalizing interpretations.[3]

- They express ethical considerations, as a restriction of meat-eating and the violence associated with this, according to Jacob Milgrom.[4]

- They are symbols, in that the classification of animals as pure or impure is motivated with respect to a coded cosmology, according to some traditional Jewish and Christian allegorical interpretations and Mary Douglas's structuralist account (addressed below).[5]

- They are, according to traditional Christian modes of typological interpretation, a foreshadowing of events and institutes in the Gospel, to which the Mosaic laws bear a metaphorical relation: as the animal sacrifices associated with the dietary laws in Leviticus foreshadowed Christ's final, redemptive sacrifice, following which neither animal sacrifices nor the dietary laws themselves were necessary.[6]

- They establish a social separation between the Jews and their neighbors: either they are marks of distinction, or they make it difficult (or impossible) to mingle with other social groups, like the prohibition on intermarriage, by outlawing common food combinations or prohibiting commensality.[7]

- They are concessions to the Jews' supposed propensity to idolatry (exemplified by the worship of the Golden Calf in Exodus 32), which required special barriers as a prophylaxis against recidivism. The Jews' infantile nature required weaning them off of superstitious rites gradually. Thus, the Mosaic laws were designed to resemble the rites of the idolaters, but with sufficient differences that the Jews would be kept apart from actual idolatry.[8]

- They are opposed to specific practices of the Jews' idolatrous neighbors, that is, they prescribe the inverse of out-group practices. This explanation overlaps to some extent with the one just preceding, except that it emphasizes the difference of Mosaic ritual from idolatry.[9]

We shall not be considering each of these explanations in detail; they are set forth here to provide some orientation to the argument that follows. The focus is on Mary Douglas's *Purity and Danger*, which retains a special authority among anthropologists and students of comparative religion on the issues of the meaning of Holiness and the interpretation of the dietary prohibitions of Leviticus and similar taboos. Building from the work of William Robertson Smith and Franz Steiner, as well as from structuralist semiotics, Douglas suggested a rationale for the "abominations of Leviticus" that remains compelling on many fronts. The creatures that may not be eaten, such as the pig, or fish without scales, or things that slither and "swarm," are those that do not conform to the normal characteristics of the class of animals to which they belong or have been assigned. The pig is anomalous because, although like cattle it has a cloven hoof, unlike cattle it is not an ungulant. Overall, such creatures are "abominations" because they are aberrant in terms of the cosmology that Douglas deciphers in the lists of animals that may and may not be consumed. Her conclusion is that lawfulness—meaning here the legality of a particular food—is synonymous with orderliness. Thus, the famous quotations: ". . . dirt is essentially disorder";[10] ". . . ideas about separating, purifying, demarcating and punishing transgressions have as their main function to impose system on an inherently untidy experience";[11] and perhaps the most famous:

> [H]oliness is exemplified by completeness. Holiness requires that individuals shall conform to the class to which they belong. And holiness requires that different classes of things shall not be confused.[12]

There is little doubt that Douglas has succeeded in illuminating a number of the provisions in Leviticus, particularly those where what is being prohibited is a "mixing" of different categories, such as meat and milk (Exodus 34:26, Deuteronomy 14:21), or linen and wool (Leviticus 19:19). The understanding that something holy (Hebrew *qadosh*) is set apart from the ordinary appears to coincide with the structuralist discovery that meaning depends on the creation of distinctions.

Douglas emphasizes the efforts made in traditional cultures to ward off the dangers presented by disorder and anomaly. Her premise is that ". . . we find in any culture worthy of the name various provisions for dealing with ambiguous or anomalous events."[13] In keeping with this point of view, it is a foregone conclusion that the Levitical laws must have some meaning, even if one that we have not been able to divine. She insists upon this, against the prevailing tendencies to explain these laws as either arbitrary commands or moral allegories: "All the interpretations given so far fall into one of two groups: either the rules are meaningless, arbitrary because their intent is disciplinary and not doctrinal, or they are allegories."[14] Douglas also rejects rationalizing interpretations that these rules are medically beneficial.[15]

In keeping with her commitment to structuralism, Douglas's own mode of interpretation is a form of allegory—understood not in its restricted, traditional Christian sense but more broadly as a mode of symbolic displacement that requires a decoding of the message of ritual. Structuralism acknowledges arbitrariness only to defuse this by focusing on the construction of symbolic value through the creation of a web of oppositions and homologies; ultimately, structuralism proposes a solution to the problem of arbitrariness. This is not the same thing as a positive embrace of arbitrariness; not, in any case, the kind of valuation of arbitrariness that we find in some traditional interpretations, described below, that associate that quality with the Holy.

Douglas's interpretation recovers or discovers a concept of natural law or, more broadly, a cosmology at the basis of the kosher laws.[16] Her approach appears to be contained within a horizon in which arbitrariness has become problematic. This explains the urgency of her effort to salvage a meaning for the Levitical laws, against those who posit their lack of reason. Ignoring the historical contingency of her own concept of the Holy, Douglas affirms that her definition of this category as "order" "involves us in no clear-cut distinction between sacred and secular" and "involves no special distinction between primitives and moderns."[17] She suggests that the only difference between "primitives and moderns" is that "in primitive culture the rule of patterning works with greater force and more total comprehensiveness."[18] In other words, the boundaries of the Holy are enforced by more rigorous distinctions.

Douglas's view that the concept of Holiness, at least as expressed in the Hebrew Bible, views things that are anomalous as "abominations," has been tremendously influential, both as a specific interpretation of the dietary prohibitions of Leviticus and as a general account of the Sacred in Durkheimian perspective.[19] Her explanation of Leviticus is considered further below. What concerns me now is her conflation of the Holy with the structuralist theory of the sign. Supposedly, the Holy, like any language, communicates through a series of binary distinctions, in this case, Sacred and Profane, or edible and inedible. And those things that confuse or confound this distinction—"anomalies"—are especially anathema. In Douglas's interpretation, then, arbitrariness is a problem analogous to the problem of profanity. Both are to be eliminated in order for there to be a distortion-free communication of the Holy. As Walter Houston describes Douglas's theory, "the opposition of clean and unclean" underwrites the function of each of these categories as "a pure sign in the Saussurian [*sic*] sense."[20]

A similar conflation between the semiotics of the Holy and the axioms of structuralism occurs in Jean Soler's account of the dietary laws, which is more rigidly structuralist than Douglas's.[21] Like Douglas, Soler argues that the "unclean animals . . . show an anomaly in their relation to the element that has 'brought them forth' or to the organs characteristic of life, and especially locomotion, in that element. If they do not fit into any class, or if they fit into two classes at once, they are unclean . . . because they are unthinkable."[22] For Soler, not only the dietary laws but also other provisions of the Mosaic law function exactly as should be predicted according to structuralist principles. Circumcision and the Sabbath day of rest also serve to create a "cut" or distinction in the order of things that is the fundamental condition of meaning: "The cut is at the origin of differentiation, and differentiation is the prerequisite of signification."[23] And such differences communicate meaning only in terms of the system of signs of which they constitute a part. The answer to why certain food items, such as the pig, were prohibited "must not be sought in the nature of the food item, any more than the sense of a word can be sought in the word itself. . . . A social sign—in this case a dietary prohibition—cannot be understood in isolation. It must be placed into the context of signs in the same area of life, together with which it constitutes a system."[24]

Although one of Douglas's fundamental goals is the salutary one to rescue the Jewish dietary laws from the charge of meaninglessness that has plagued them especially in modern times, ultimately she presents us with an image of the primitive that is almost as condescending. The ritual distinctions of the Hebrew Bible ostensibly exemplify both a universal human propensity and a peculiarly primitive obsession with the exclusion of the anomaly.[25] Traditional cultures supposedly exhibit a deeper anxiety over the boundary between Sacred and Profane, order and disorder, similar to the tension between nature and culture revealed in Lévi-Strauss's analysis of myth. Douglas's suggestion that the dietary prohibitions of Leviticus reflect a heightened concern for order echoes, however faintly, older Christian polemics against Judaism as excessively legalistic and obsessed with minute details.

A number of other interpreters less enamored of structuralist principles have nevertheless endorsed Douglas's view that the key to understanding the dietary prohibitions of Leviticus lies in appreciating the systematic nature of these rules, particularly in relation to a cosmology or conception of natural order. Robert Alter presents some trenchant criticisms of Douglas's and especially Soler's accounts, but embraces the general analogy between the dietary laws and the structuralist view of the systematic nature of language,[26] and ultimately endorses the idea that the Hebrew Bible exhibited an allergy to "whatever had the look of indeterminacy or amorphousness . . . in sum, everything in the zoological realm that seemed in any way dissonant with the principle of ordered, shaped creation, everything that aroused dim uneasy recollections of the primordial chaos and void out of which God called the world into being."[27]

Jacob Milgrom criticizes many of Douglas's central arguments— including the notion that the pig was especially abominable to the authors of Leviticus. He nevertheless states that her theory at least "meets the canons of scientific method," meaning that, unlike most symbolic interpretations, it is falsifiable,[28] and that, with its emphasis on distinction or differentiation as the basis of the symbolic function of the dietary prohibitions as a system of signs, it reinforces the correct view that the "most important factor" of these laws is

> the determination to set apart the Israelites from the idolatrous practices of their neighbors. That this fact can be isolated and identified is thanks to the perfection of the scientific discipline of comparative linguistics as applied to biblical research.[29]

Milgrom's own approach converges with Douglas's in confronting "the problem posed by the seeming arbitrariness of the specific food prohibitions" by rejecting the notion that these laws are, in the end, arbitrary. He agrees with Douglas that they have a basis in earlier cosmological accounts and, more generally, in the idea of an ordered cosmos: "Thus, the Priestly distinction between pure and impure is not an arbitrary divine fiat but a rational decision that is derived from the laws of nature."[30] There is, moreover, an ethical dimension to these rules, which restrict meat-eating and restrain the human impulse toward killing: "the real contribution of this Priestly theology is that it manifests the beginning of an ecological doctrine."[31]

These views are designed to oppose the view of the dietary laws as merely arbitrary commands or "divine fiat," a view that had been endorsed not only by critics of these laws, but also by many supporters among traditional Jewish thinkers. Thus, Milgrom notes "The traditionalist view that the list of prohibited animals is simply arbitrary, the unalterable and inscrutable will of God," that must be followed simply because it is God's command and not for any other, extraneous reason.[32] Jiří Moskala refers to this as the "Arbitrary Command Explanation":

> The Mosaic dietary laws were classified as irrational laws [on this view], because no reason can be found for their existence. They were given as a demonstration of God's authority. Jewish scholarship has traditionally assigned these laws to a special type designated by the term *hukkim* because "their explanation is known only to God."[33]

Both Douglas's and Milgrom's explanations are designed to counter this current of traditionalist opinion. Yet there are others who adhere to the traditionalist view. Isaac Heinemann discussed the positions of various Jewish thinkers over the centuries concerning whether the commands (*mitzvot*) are rational or irrational and arbitrary: a distinction he framed in terms of Kant's distinction between heteronomy, or laws given by an outside authority, and autonomy, or laws given by and to one's self.[34] Heinemann argued that, upon a fair reading, and as acknowledged to varying degrees by most major Jewish thinkers, certain of the commands, especially the statutes (*hukkim*) such as the kosher laws, are indeed either without reason, or without one accessible to human understanding and in any case must be obeyed whether or not one comprehends their reason.[35] Indeed, a number of major Jewish thinkers expressed the opinion that it was more virtuous to obey a command for which one can perceive no reason, out of simple obedience to God.[36] This is a direct contradiction of the Kantian understanding of moral duty. Heinemann concluded that "the appreciation of obedience and heteronomy contradicts, if not 'the spirit of modern times,' at least the spirit of liberalism, with which Judaism is to be identified, according to the view of some of our friends and all of our enemies!"[37]

Given the difference of opinion that obtains among different experts, we are justified in asking whether it is really the case, as Douglas claims, that the anomaly is anathema to the primitive, or that signification requires precisely the exclusion of the anomaly, understood, in this context, as a synonym of the arbitrary? Actually, neither of these questions can be answered unambiguously in the affirmative. To the contrary, I will argue that Douglas's understanding of the sign contributes to a distortion in her characterization of the Holy. First, I will dispute the notion that it is fundamental to the notion of the sign that it be considered in relation, as part of a system of signs, and suggest instead that the proper context for considering the dietary laws as signs may instead be the notion of the miracle, as a singular event that is established as a sign precisely through its opposition rather than conformity to the laws of nature. As divine revelation, the dietary prohibitions and other provisions of the Mosaic law suggest an understanding of the sign that is in conflict with Douglas's view. Second, I will trace the genealogy of the exclusion of this older view of the sign in Deist and other Protestant polemics against Mosaic law and revelation. Deist attacks on the "arbitrary" nature of these laws exemplify the rise of a modern view of the sign that anticipated Douglas's own. Although she adopts a more positive view of Mosaic law, Douglas nevertheless shares with these older views a conviction that the arbitrariness of the sign is a problem to be confronted and eliminated. Third, I will suggest an alternative account of the sign-function of some of these provisions of the Mosaic law. Finally, I will argue that part of what is at stake in the change in attitude toward arbitrariness is a shift in the view of the appropriate relationship of human agency to divine sovereignty. This shift is arguably characteristic of the modern era and fundamental to what has been described as the disenchantment of the world.

Deist semiotics and the attack on revelation

It is one of the axioms of structuralism that signs have meaning only in relation. A single word has no meaning in itself; it is only as part of a system of oppositions in which that word is minutely distinguished from and related to other words, as antonyms, synonyms, etc. This system of relations is the "structure" from which Structuralism derives its name.[38]

While illuminating for many purposes, it is nevertheless the case that this view of the sign is, in many respects, highly counterintuitive, both because of the instinctive view that signs directly reflect nature and derive their meaning not from their relations to other words, but from a deeper connection to reality; and because the traditional meaning of a "sign" includes something singular, exceptional, or unusual. A "sign" can also mean an omen or a miracle. Thus Paul Tillich noted that "The New Testament often uses the Greek word *semeion*, 'sign,' pointing to the religious meaning of the miracles."[39] A miracle, as Tillich defined it, is "a happening that contradicts the laws of nature":[40] its signifying power depends upon this supernatural status.

This older view of the sign, which was hardly peculiar to the New Testament, is well-illustrated by the biblical episode of Korah's rebellion against Moses's authority (Numbers 16):

Then Moses said, "This is how you will know that the Lord sent me to do all these things and that it was not of my own will: If these men die naturally as all people would, and suffer the fate of all, then the Lord has not sent me. But if the Lord brings about something unprecedented, and the ground opens its mouth and swallows them along with all that belongs to them so that they go down alive into Sheol, then you will know that these men have despised the Lord. Just as he finished speaking all these words, the ground beneath them split open.[41]

Divine intervention is known precisely through an interruption in the natural course of events. Absent such an interruption, there is no evidence—no sign or *semeion*—of God's will. Something unprecedented, that is utterly new and singular, is required to communicate this will.

Now, I think, we can begin to see a crack in Douglas's view of the Mosaic law. There are actually two senses in which her concept of the sign does not fit the traditional view. The first concerns her insistence on the structuralist axiom that signs have meaning only in relation, and that single signs are, by definition, meaningless. Actually, just the opposite view appears to be expressed by the episode of Korah's rebellion. It is precisely the singularity or uniqueness of the sign that enables us to recognize it as such. If this is meaning-in-relation, it is a strange kind of relation, and not the one contemplated by structuralist analysis. Second, Douglas ultimately converts the Levitical laws into the sign of an ordered cosmology. The separation of the creatures into clean and unclean, edible and inedible comports with God's original ordering of the world in Genesis 1. This is to subordinate the divine will to natural law: something that, as we have just seen, is out of step with other portions of the Hebrew Bible. If God has the power to violate the natural order on one occasion, why may not his ritual commands, a number of which appear to violate human nature and instinct, do so on other occasions as well?

There is precedent for Douglas's rejection of the notion that the Mosaic laws are arbitrary commands, and for her subordination of divine fiat to natural law, in earlier theological debates that called into question the authority of miracles and revelation, including the revealed Mosaic laws, as potentially arbitrary commands. By revisiting these debates, we can better appreciate the influence they have had on contemporary interpretations of the Jewish dietary laws, including Douglas's.

The traditional Christian interpretation that the Mosaic ritual laws had a symbolic function, as a foreshadowing of the Gospel, preserved these laws and, indeed, the entire Old Testament by subordinating it to the New. In 1748, Moses Lowman presented an orthodox defense of the Mosaic laws against Deist attacks: *A Rational of the Ritual of the Hebrew Worship; in which the Wise Designs and Usefulness of that Ritual are Explain'd, and Vindicated from Objections*. Lowman anticipated many of the contemporary explanations for the Mosaic laws, including the dietary prohibitions. For example, he argued variously that these laws separated the Jews from their idolatrous neighbors;[42] were designed in some cases to oppose the specific details of the rituals of idolators; or served as aides-mémoires: in the case of the Sabbath, of the history of God's creation;[43] in the case of circumcision, of God's covenant with Abraham.[44] Lowman even anticipated contemporary scholarly arguments that the ancient Israelite classification of animals permitted to be eaten was modeled on the animals commonly raised in that agricultural and pastoral society: "the gentler Sort of Creatures, and of most common Use, such as were bred about their Houses, and in their Fields, and were, in a Sort, domestick."[45] But Lowman cautioned that it would be a mistake "to look for the Reason of every Rite in one Design only."[46]

Lowman also upheld the traditional Christian view that the Mosaic law was a type or symbol of the Gospel: "the Law of Moses is the Gospel of the *Messiah*, in Hieroglyphick, or Figure."[47] This was necessary as a concession to the Israelites' predilection for "a figurative Instruction by Symbols."[48] Thus, circumcision is a "Sign or Mark,"[49] "a visible Mark in the Flesh, as was very fit to be a Sign to all the Seed of *Abraham*, that they were to account themselves an holy Nation."[50] Lowman embraced a semiotic interpretation of ritual: "the Law of Moses was designed to be a Figure of good Things to come, it was therefore necessary it should be a Ritual."[51]

By Lowman's time, certain forms of Protestant literalism had already called into question this traditional solution of the problem of the relationship between the Old and New Testaments. Although many Protestants adhered to older modes of Christian typological interpretation, others, inspired by the idea that the Gospel represented the triumph of "plain speech" over the veils and shadows of Mosaic law, further denigrated the symbolic dimensions they perceived in the Old Testament and, in some cases, rejected the value of that text even as precedent for the Gospel. This tendency culminated in the movement we call "Deism."[52]

Deists were, like other Protestants, a diverse group, with a variety of opinions. Indeed, it is often difficult to draw the line between Deist and non-Deist British Protestants, and Deist views were widely influential long after the debates they inspired had quieted down. Among the central themes of Deism were the belief in a natural religion (a term often used synonymously with natural law[53]) that was knowable by the exercise of human reason, and therefore did not require any revelation; and the identification of this natural religion with a plain and simple form of worship liberated from most ritual as well as the other subtleties of "priestcraft." Deists directed much of their vitriol against the rituals, miracles, and other superstitions they perceived in the Old Testament. Yahweh, the God of the Jews, exemplified the kind of arbitrary, despotic authority that Deists detested in matters of religion. Exhibit A was the bloody sacrifices, superstitious ceremonies, and senseless slaughters He commanded of the Israelites.

Many of these themes are well known, although the significance of the Deist critique of ancient Judaism for what we call secularization has yet to be properly investigated.[54] What I should like to focus on here is the semiotic ideology of Deism, and the parallel between the Deist critique of the arbitrariness of Jewish law and some contemporary structuralist theories, which have also puzzled over the Mosaic tradition.

According to Deists, natural law is timeless and unchanging. The Gospel represented, in the words of one of the most important Deists, Matthew Tindal, author of *Christianity as Old as Creation* (1730), merely a "republication" of the religion of nature.[55] That this should have been necessary was a result of the corruption of religion under the Mosaic dispensation. Both Jewish particularism and the historically contingent, and apparently irrational, ceremonial laws promulgated by Moses typified the very opposite of natural religion. The Deists' constant refrain is that the ritual laws of the Jews are merely "positive" and "arbitrary," and can have no further part in the divine economy, if they ever did.[56]

The Deists' attack on Mosaic law reflected the rise of awareness of the arbitrariness—meaning historical contingency and particularity—of the sign toward the end of the seventeenth century in England. Two works published within a few years of each other serve to mark the rise of this consciousness. One, John Locke's *Essay concerning Human Understanding* (1690), firmly established the arbitrariness of linguistic and other signs.[57] The other, John Spencer's massive work on Hebrew ritual, *De legibus hebraeorum* (1685), attempted to provide a rational explanation for the Mosaic ceremonial laws in the face of arguments that these were merely arbitrary.[58] Spencer argued that these ritual laws were prescribed by the Deity either as an inversion of practices followed by the Jews' idolatrous neighbors such as the Egyptians, or as an accommodation of and concession to idolatrous tendencies on the part of the Jews themselves.[59] Spencer's interpretation was a logical outgrowth of both Protestant examinations of the biblical text and a deepening knowledge of philology and comparative ethnology. Increasing recognition of cultural diversity tended to call into question the authority of revelation. Although Spencer himself largely refrained from so doing—indeed, his explanations of the Mosaic law were also invoked by Lowman in defence of an orthodox interpretation—this was done in short order by Deists who adopted many of Spencer's arguments.

Spencer's explanation of the Mosaic laws as a symbolic inversion of pagan practices was a kind of structuralism *avant la lettre*. The meaning of these laws was to be found in the construction of an opposition or the assertion of difference. And this explanation was a means of refuting the charge that these laws were merely arbitrary. In this explanation, Spencer relied on a distinguished predecessor—the twelfth-century Jewish philosopher Maimonides—who had similarly endeavored to give reasons for the Jewish commands to defend against the charge that these were arbitrary. As John Edwards recounted in 1699,

This *Maimonides* was indeed the first that opposed and confuted the opinion of some *Jewish* doctors, that there was no *Reason* to be given of the *Ritual Law*, but that it was wholly from the Soveraign Will and Pleasure of God. He on the contrary proves that these *Mosaick Rites* have *Reason* to vouch them, and that they were not given as the Arbitrary Commands of an Absolute Empire over mankind. . . . He largely insists on this Proposition, that most of the Jewish Rites were instituted to oppose the Superstitions of those *Zabii* [Sabaeans], an antient sort of Idolaters in the *East*.[60]

The resemblance between these older accounts and contemporary structuralism has been implicitly acknowledged, for example by Milgrom, who, as we saw earlier, attributed to "the scientific discipline of comparative linguistics" (i.e. structuralism) the discovery of the "most important factor . . . the determination to set apart the Israelites from the idolatrous practices of their neighbors." This is what had solved "the problem posed by the seeming arbitrariness of the specific food prohibitions." Granting the differences between Douglas's application of structuralism and Spencer's earlier application of the principle of symbolic opposition, it appears that Milgrom should have given some of the credit to Spencer and Maimonides for the discovery that, in Jean Soler's words, "differentiation is the prerequisite of signification."[61]

When I say that there was a rise of consciousness of arbitrariness at the end of the seventeenth century, I mean that many became aware of arbitrariness as a problem that required a specific solution or adaptation. The solution to linguistic arbitrariness proposed by Locke and others was the empirical study of nature, the bringing of our language into accordance with the discoveries of science, and the elimination of metaphysical verbiage that corresponded to nothing in reality. As described in Chapter Three, the various proposals for a perfect, universal language that began to appear in the seventeenth century were one response to arbitrariness that sought to overcome this problem either by finding a language that perfectly accorded with nature or, more commonly and circumspectly, by ordaining a universal language by convention. Hobbes responded to the problem of arbitrariness by affirming the authority of the sovereign to determine both the laws and their interpretation; this extended also to the interpretation of scripture. Whatever the favoured response, arbitrariness was seen as a problem that had to be confronted and eliminated.

Matthew Tindal responded to the problem of arbitrariness by championing "the Law of Nature . . . A Law, which does not depend on the uncertain Meaning of Words and Phrases in dead Languages, much less on Types, Metaphors, Allegories, Parables, or on the Skill and Honesty of weak or designing Transcribers."[62] According to Tindal, the Jews and other Asiatic peoples had been particularly prone to "affect[] hyperbolical, parabolical, mystical, allegorical, and typical ways of expressing themselves."[63] For

Tindal, our understanding of what is required for salvation can no more depend on diverse and changing interpretations of scripture than it can depend on the performance of arbitrary ceremonies, whether instituted by Moses or by the present Church. Thus "the placing Religion in any indifferent Thing, is inconsistent with the Nature of Christianity; 'tis introducing Judaism."[64]

Tindal accordingly ridiculed the symbolic interpretation of divine law.[65] In response to the claim "that some Things may be requir'd by God as Governour of the Universe, which are merely positive; nay, that *Rites*, and *Ceremonies, Signs,* or *Symbols* might be arbitrarily enjoin'd," he answered that "was there an instituted Religion which differs from That of Nature, its Precepts must be arbitrary, as not founded on the Nature and Reason of Things, but depending on meer Will and Pleasure."[66] One of the key Deist complaints against such revealed traditions, as against miracles, was: How can one know that they are valid revelations, if they are not in accord with natural law and reason?[67] A revelation that deviates from reason is false, while a revelation that agrees with reason is redundant and unnecessary. Many opponents of Deism clearly recognized that such arguments would undermine the notion of revelation altogether.

Tindal fully endorsed Locke's view that words are "but arbitrary Signs."[68] Tindal alluded to the idea of a universal language or character as a means for unifying religion and reversing the curse of Babel, although he discounted the possibility of such a scheme.[69] He expressed concern "Were Men not to be govern'd by Things, but Words,"[70] given the vagaries of communication and the perils of translation. In short, he participated in the semeiophobia of his age, an age in which Protestant literalism and scientific empiricism conspired to attack symbolic discourses such as that exemplified for many Christians by the Old Testament.

This semiotic ideology had profoundly negative implications for the argument that the Mosaic laws had continuing value as a symbolic foreshadowing of the Gospel. Deists utterly condemned the idea that our knowledge of natural religion could depend upon our ability to decipher such enigmatic messages as those many Christians had thought to find in the Hebrew Bible. Instead, every sign must carry its own conviction, must be plain speaking and transparent. The very fact that the Old Testament required a typological interpretation—a libretto—demonstrated its epistemological deficiency as a fully self-communicating sign. As Tindal argued:

> If you must have recourse to Words, to explain the Signification of such Symbols, are they not arbitrary Marks, whose Meaning cannot be known, but from Words; and, not being capable of expressing things more fully than Words, wholly needless as to that purpose? Nay Words themselves being such arbitrary Signs, to multiply such Signs needlessly would be very absurd.[71]

The same logic that rendered revelation redundant if not in accord with natural reason rendered the symbol redundant if it required a gloss: indeed, worse than redundant, because it was an inefficient form of communication. In this case, Christian supersession merged with a profound skepticism concerning the value of symbolic discourses in general and the Old Testament in particular. As we have seen, John Toland argued that, as the Gospel had made plain and replaced the "mysteries" of the Hebrew Bible, especially its "figurative words and rites," such obscure discourses no longer had a purpose.[72]

Thus, there is precedent for a number of contemporary views that to conclude that the Jewish dietary laws are "arbitrary" would be intensely problematic. Many of the solutions presented to avoid this conclusion find antecedents in older interpretations, particularly in Maimonides's rationalizing efforts.[73] During the Reformation, the Deists led the charge against the representation of the divine will as arbitrary, and as evidenced primarily through an interruption of the natural order. The difference was that, rather than defending the Mosaic law, the Deists made it the chief representation of an idea of the Holy that was completely out of accord with natural law and reason.

The Deist polemic against everything singular and exceptional—against miracles, revelation, and sacrifice—and against everything culturally particular and historically contingent—as exemplified by Jewish tradition—revealed a horror of the "anomaly" beyond anything that Douglas identified in the Hebrew Bible. Indeed, it was those very anomalies that some have identified as characteristic expressions of the Holy in the Hebrew Bible[74] that Deists most especially objected to. While echoing some traditional Jewish explanations that the Mosaic laws are arbitrary precisely because they are expressions of divine sovereignty—only God can command against human instinct and reason, as well as against the laws of nature—the Deists found in the image of such a God nothing they could embrace. The Deist moment, as Carl Schmitt noted, represented an assertion of lawfulness against the arbitrariness of divine sovereignty.[75]

A number of contemporary interpretations of the Mosaic laws, including Douglas's, appear to operate within a set of assumptions that has been influenced by these earlier theological debates. Like Tindal, Douglas abhors the idea of an arbitrary ritual; like Lowman, she seeks to preserve the Mosaic laws from this charge by finding for them a symbolic rationale. Being secular rather than orthodox, she does not advance the standard Christian typological interpretation. However, there are striking parallels between structuralist interpretations of myth and Christian typological interpretations of scripture, both of which claim to discover, through decryption, a "message" that is hidden within the text. Lévi-Straussian analysis, like orthodox Christian typology, asserts a parallel between two events or episodes that are temporally separated within the narrative sequence, an isomorphy or metaphorical resemblance such that one must be read in light of the other, and provides the interpretation for the other. A crucial distinction is that structuralism collapses this metaphorical relation into a single, timeless structure, which may be equally evident at any point of the myth, whereas Christian typology asserts a progressive evolution or unfolding of the sign culminating in the revelation of the Gospel.

It is not only Douglas who argues that Holiness is an expression of an orderly cosmology that was laid down at the Creation, and that excludes the "anomaly." The leading scholar of Leviticus, Jacob Milgrom, also contends that "the Priestly distinction between pure and impure is not an arbitrary divine fiat but a rational decision that is derived from the laws of nature."[76] Both of these scholars are as committed as were the Deists before them to excluding the possibility of arbitrariness—meaning the senselessness of divine command, as the merely positive institution of God's will. The difference is that Douglas and Milgrom find ways to conclude that the kosher laws are not arbitrary.

The historical context for contemporary debates over the nature of the Holy, as expressed in these interpretations of the Levitical dietary prohibitions, suggests that somehow the nature of arbitrariness has been rendered increasingly problematic in modernity. In place of Douglas's diagnosis of the Holy as an aversion to the anomaly, we find our own aversion to arbitrariness, meaning to an antinomian idea of the Holy such as is expressed in the Hebrew Bible according to Deists, some traditional Jewish thinkers, and some contemporary scholars such as Rudolf Otto. The question of the Holy then becomes a question about ourselves, and about the genealogy of modernity in theological opposition to another, and arguably older, notion of the Holy as, in Otto's phrase, "wholly Other," constrained by neither moral nor natural law.[77] Have we simply remade the Holy in our own image?

In broader perspective, it should come as no surprise that it is precisely the older, more positive evaluation of the arbitrariness of divine command that has been called into question in modernity. This evaluation was expressed in the Jewish notion of *hukkim*, which asserted that the reason for certain commandments was not rational. Irrationality could even be a sign of special Holiness, as in Tertullian's doctrine of "I believe it because it is impossible" (*credo quia absurdum*).[78] What would faith represent if it asked nothing more of us than to follow the dictates of the senses, as interpreted in light of our own reason? Modernity has rejected such views in the name of freedom, meaning the autonomy of human reason. The possibility of divine fiat undermines this, which is why the miracle and other violations of natural law had to be prohibited. This is not a value judgment, but a historical conclusion.

The dietary laws revisited

None of this is to suggest that all of the various interpretations of the dietary laws and other provisions of the Mosaic code that have been advanced are wrong. On the contrary, some of them are quite persuasive. My intention has been to demonstrate a bias in certain contemporary approaches to the dietary laws, above all Douglas's, in order to call into question her semiotics of the Holy. But it will be worthwhile to return to an examination of the dietary laws with any eye toward describing better their semiotic function.

Convincing interpretations of certain of these rules have been advanced. Various scholars have pointed out that the classificatory scheme according to which edible animals must both part the hoof and chew the cud does not create, *pace* Douglas, a special class of "abominations" that are anomalous as a result of straddling the boundary of pure and impure, by possessing one but not both characteristics.[79] The enumeration of the two criteria was done simply in order to make it absolutely clear which animals are, and are not, edible: this is the true semiotic function of the "abominations of Leviticus." Like any good law, Leviticus seeks to draw a bright line between what is permitted, and what is prohibited, in order to communicate the decision rule as clearly as possible. As Seth Kunin argues,

> The primary element of the system is that the categories are clearly defined and impermeable. If an animal is in one category it will never be in the other and there is no possible movement between categories. Where animals appear to bridge this structure, they are removed by either [*sic*] being specifically mentioned and if they are commonly used for food they are negatively valenced.[80]

Further, what the establishment of these taxonomic markers serves to do (as Lowman suggested a quarter millennium ago) is to codify as pure and edible those creatures that were the common food species among the peoples at the time. Cattle, sheep, and goats were not only the most readily available sources of meat, but also, not surprisingly, the animals most commonly used for sacrifice, by both the Israelites and neighboring tribes. Edwin Firmage has made this argument most clearly:

> [F]rom long before the Israelite priesthood came on the scene, a handful of domestic species had provided the bulk of the ordinary man's diet, as well as virtually all the animals sacrificed to local deities. . . . That domestic cattle were clean was therefore a given in the considerations that eventually gave rise to the biblical dietary law. The first and most important criteria of this law (Lev. xi 3) were perforce derived from these few domestic species because they constituted *de facto* the category of

clean food. . . . [This] transformed a limited dietary preference into an all encompassing classification scheme of singular significance. . . . The criteria for the selection of clean quadrupeds are therefore a précis of the paradigm constituted by the cattle, sheep and goats.[81]

In other words, what we have here is simply the elevation of what is "normal" to a legal "norm." Innumerable examples of this phenomenon can be found within the history of culture, from the religious sanction provided to heterosexuality and the condemnation of homosexual liaisons, to the demonization of the left hand, as reflected in the negative connotations that have attached to the word "sinister," which originally meant merely "left-wards."[82] The addition of a supernatural sanction to what is otherwise ordinary practice provides a level of conviction and certainty that has been described previously in this essay as the "naturalizing of the arbitrary," meaning the designation of what is merely culturally contingent as being in the nature of things or even divine and holy. Accordingly, Walter Houston appears to be correct in concluding, against Douglas and Milgrom, that the classificatory rules followed and ratified rather than preceded practice;[83] although, once codified, these rules of course became a guide to future practice.

All of this may appear obvious in retrospect. Yet it does not entirely settle the issue. I should like to emphasize in particular that while the dietary prohibitions themselves are rendered perfectly clear—fully established as signs—the meaning for these prohibitions is not so clearly elucidated. This has been the fundamental precondition for the possibility of diversity of interpretations of this meaning, a diversity which continues to this day. As Houston points out, "the Torah itself is remarkably sparing in explanation of its rules of ritual; . . . the accounts given by Jews of the rules that they observe . . . tend to be no less diverse than those given by outsiders."[84] Partly in recognition of this fact, William Robertson Smith, in his *Lectures on the Religion of the Semites*, already granted primacy to the social dimensions of ritual practice over its theological explanations: the performance of the ritual is more constant and in any case more primary than the manifold interpretations that have been given to it.[85] Heinemann noted a traditional practice that "The sages of the Land of Israel did not publicize the reasons for their decrees until after twelve months had passed, in case someone might not agree with the reason and thus disparage the decree."[86] In this case, the rule was literally prior to the reason.

If there has been such disagreement over the meaning of the dietary laws, such that many even within the Jewish tradition have declared them to be arbitrary, then in what sense can Douglas or any other cryptologist ever be correct in concluding that the true meaning of these rules is to be found in a coded cosmology? Even were we to grant that such a cosmology was known to the composers of the Priestly Code (the part of Leviticus that contains these provisions), would this serve as an explanation of the meaning of these laws to the vast majority of those who have followed them down the long centuries?

On the contrary, we would be completely justified in concluding that the very indeterminacy of meaning of these laws is part of their function; that their semantic content is subordinated to their pragmatic function in providing a bright line rule; and that our unwillingness to perceive this has been conditioned by a modern revolt against the idea of arbitrary rules. In a parallel case, one looks in vain for any clear account in the Hindu *Laws of Manu* of many of the dietary rules prescribed there for Brahmins and others. A nascent movement in favor of vegetarianism is clearly part of their rationale, as is the function of social separation (in this case among castes, rather than among tribes). Yet the fact remains that one is not given a reason, in most cases, for the lists of prohibited foods.

The impulse to look for meaning behind these rules is, I would suggest, part of a general modern bias against the rule considered as an arbitrary command. And this coordinates with a bias against the pragmatic function of ritual, as opposed to its semantic function. Although the search for a symbolic meaning of the biblical dietary prohibitions began already in ancient times, it has been further encouraged by the Protestant privileging of the content of belief or the inward intention of the believer over ritual form. This contrast can be illustrated by another example. The Akedah or binding of Isaac (Genesis 22), as Eric Auerbach noted, gives almost no insight into the inner life of Abraham as he prepares to sacrifice his son.[87] Nor does God provide any reason for issuing his abominable command. Auerbach sees in this a contrast between Jewish and Greek modes of narrative: unlike the Homeric epics, the Hebrew Bible leaves out many details, including psychological states, which are merely implied in a way that may serve to increase the suspense of the narrative. In any case, the minimalism of the Akedah episode most forcefully confronts us with the fact of the apparent arbitrariness of divine command, and the horror of its violation of human instinct and feeling. Søren Kierkegaard singled out this episode as an illustration of the fear and trembling precipitated by the awefulness of the Holy.[88] Kierkegaard constructed his own series of meditations in order to fill in the missing details and especially human, emotional dimensions of the story. Ironically, this very project served to highlight the difference between his own Protestant inwardness and the emphasis of the biblical story on the brute facts of command and obedience.

Such commands resemble a host of other provisions that fall under the heading of "asceticism." They are restrictions on natural human behavior comparable to fasts, sacrifices, and other deprivations. As Milgrom points out, "The choice of animal foods is severely limited."[89] These restraints, by defying freedom and instinct, signal a special type of agency.

In his essay "Sacred Persistence," Jonathan Z. Smith emphasizes the role of agency in ascetic practices.[90] He focuses on the tendency of certain cultures to organize behaviors in accordance with a traditional "canon." His chief example is the dietary prohibitions observed by many cultures, though perhaps most familiar to his audience from Jewish tradition. Following an initial restriction of permitted edibles by excluding some from among the universe of potential foodstuffs, there is formed a canon of foods which may then be recombined and manipulated to create an almost infinite variety of recipes. Tradition therefore combines with innovation, in a manner that demonstrates human agency and autonomy. This interpretation coordinates with a perennial theme of Smith's work, which is to recover an understanding of the role of human beings in constructing, performing, and adapting religious tradition, as against the various articulations of the Sacred (especially Eliade's) that understand this as a revelation from without which is passively experienced by humans. Implicit also in Smith's account, I will suggest, is an attempt to defend the legitimacy of Judaism or, rather, a particular conception of that tradition against some Christian critics, who have condemned that tradition precisely for its supposed legalism. Smith's reasoning is compelling, although one has to point out that he has chosen to emphasize the human agency and ingenuity that operates within such a set of constraints, rather than the initial command (which is, in the case of the kosher laws, a full revelation) that establishes the canon.[91] Unlike Douglas—whose interpretation of the kosher laws Smith inexplicably leaves out of account—he assumes that the initial selection of permitted and prohibited foods is indeed "arbitrary."[92]

The dietary provisions of Leviticus were originally articulated within the context of a book devoted to the prescription of sacrifice, and, as various scholars have noted, are intended in the first instance to detail the practices that render one pure for purposes of approaching the sacrificial altar. As such, the dietary prohibitions bear a close relationship to a host of other restrictions or deprivations, including refraining from work on the Sabbath, abandoning cultivation during the Sabbatical and Jubilee years (Leviticus 25), and refraining from sexual intercourse during a woman's menstrual period (Leviticus 18:19). What is the "message" of such restrictions, which are paralleled in other cultures, including many with very different cosmologies?

Timothy Lubin suggests a partial answer to this question:

Ascetical systems everywhere are, among other things, methods for asserting control over those aspects of bodily experience to which most people are inclined to succumb: the urge to eat, to sleep, and to have sex. These urges, of course, are essentially endemic (even if non-conforming individuals might be found). . . . In Peircean terms, if eating and sleeping are taken to indicate helplessness and mortality, fasting and vigil contrariwise indicate fortitude and independence—perhaps even immortality.[93]

Or, one might add, Holiness. What provides part of the motive force of such provisions is that they defy instinct and represent an interruption of nature, in a way that indexes the intervention of some countervailing agency: either the divine, or culture, or the willpower of the individual ascetic.[94] Louis Dumont already emphasized how the individual ascetic in ancient India, by defying both bodily instinct and caste prohibitions, signified "liberation" and a kind of autonomy,[95] if not precisely that contemplated by post-Kantian Enlightenment. I think this brings us a bit closer to appreciating how such restrictions can signify even in the absence of a mythological, cosmological, or doctrinal libretto. They represent agency or what Bataille called "sovereignty," the clearest manifestation of which is sacrifice,[96] which violates economic instinct in the same way that the miracle violates natural law.

Such a notion of sovereignty is precisely what troubled the Deists. Their critique of the Mosaic law, including the dietary prohibitions, centered on the problematic view of divine sovereignty that appeared to be communicated by such "merely positive and arbitrary" commands. In their view, such a representation of the divine threatened human autonomy and agency, by leaving us perpetually open to ruptures in the natural and moral orders and calling into question the capacity of human reason to know and perform natural law. I want to suggest that it is precisely such a fear of divine arbitrariness that underlies part of the modern allergy to such ritual prohibitions as the dietary laws of Leviticus. Despite Douglas's claim that traditional cultures, such as that represented in the Hebrew Bible, are more concerned than our own with maintaining order, a genealogical study has suggested the irony that it is instead modernity itself that has inherited, from such earlier theologies as that represented by the Deist concept of natural law, a bias against the supra-legal or disorderly dimensions of the Holy. Rather than the Holy expressing a fear of the anomaly, then, it is our own fear of arbitrariness that has called the Holy into question.

Conclusion

Given the vast amount of terrain covered—as well as the many important topics omitted due to limitations of space and this author's competence—it might appear presumptuous to attempt to sum up the semiotic approach presented in the preceding pages. Nevertheless, it is important to review some of the findings, to outline trajectories that have emerged over the course of the several case studies that have been presented, and to indicate some themes of broader importance for understanding the nature of both signs and religion, as well as their intersection. This will afford an opportunity also to gesture to some areas in the semiotics of religion that have not received sufficient attention in this book, but which might benefit from further inquiry along the lines delineated here.

Religion and communication

The analysis of the form and function of rituals undertaken above has reinforced the conviction announced at the beginning of this work: namely, that many rituals and other modes of religious expression are best understood as attempts to communicate, attempts that resemble and are in some cases parasitic upon ordinary modes of human social intercourse. Magic spells deploy poetic repetition to an extent beyond that found in most other forms of discourse, in order to lend efficacy to the ritual performance and enable it to cross over the gap between sign and referent. The accumulation of imperatives, deictics, and other "pointers" highlights the pragmatic function of ritual as a mode of rhetorical performance. At the same time, this stratagem reveals that certain rituals, although they may be culturally effective, also represent a type of wish-fulfillment, the dream of a perfect form of communication in which human language would be adequate to achieve both salvation and more mundane goals. A vestige of this dream remains even in many of those semiotic ideologies that reject the possibility that symbolic magic can influence the world. In this case, the goal is to purify our discourse so that it reflects an undistorted image of nature, the human mind, or even the divine plan.

As we have seen, some of the greatest debates in the history of religions concerned the communicative power of rituals such as symbolic magic, prayers, and sacrifices. Christians rejected most consistently those portions of the Mosaic tradition that prescribed sacrifice; the ritual provisions of Leviticus were the core of the "ceremonial law" that had been abrogated and superseded by the Gospel. Despite this, Christians substituted their own sacrifice or communal meal that depended equally on a translation between the human and divine realms. In the Catholic interpretation, the Eucharistic host was transubstantiated into the divine flesh and blood. Many Protestants rejected this interpretation. The denial of the power of ceremonial to influence God, as evidenced also by the theology underlying the Puritan critique of vain repetitions in prayer, closed off certain channels of communication between human and divine. Sacraments came to have a memorial rather than a magical function. A similar logic, as we have seen, also underlay iconoclasm or the critique of the image. Puritan iconoclasm coordinated with an insistence on divine omnipotence and transcendence. Deists took matters a step further, converting this transcendent God into one who was withdrawn or absent, having left His creation to proceed in accordance with the regular operation of natural law. The subordination of divine omnipotence to natural law foreclosed another channel of religious communication, namely revelation and miracles. One turning point came when the Reformation humanized prayer by making it an individual expression of plain and sincere words. Another came when, pursuant to Vatican II, the Roman Catholic Church embraced vernacularization and also had the priest while saying Mass turn toward the congregation, rather than face outward as before, along with the congregation, toward the heavenly Father. This suggests that the Mass has now become more like a colloquy among human beings and less like a converse with the infinite.

A semiotic approach highlights equally both the communicative dimensions of many religious performances, and the control of communication as central to questions of cosmology, theology, and salvation.

Arbitrariness and certainty

The examples considered in previous chapters have afforded a different perspective on the fundamental problem, emphasized especially by structuralists, of the arbitrariness of the sign, and on the manner in which the sign responds to this problem. Despite the differences among these traditions in terms of their assumptions and the methods they apply, the massive proliferation of poetic devices in some premodern magical traditions, the Baconian and Protestant efforts to purify and police language, and even the miracle in the Hebrew Bible are all attempts to produce certainty in the face of uncertainty or arbitrariness, understood in a broader sense. There are, of course, other functions of the sign: for example, to convey information; to bring two or more minds into a single train of thought or conduct; to influence, dissimulate, and command; to heighten emotion and promote memorability; to record something for posterity; to communicate more efficiently by using abbreviations or shorthand; and so on. In many cases, however, the production of certainty is a precondition for these other functions.

The use of motivated signs such as icons and indexes in magic is designed to reinforce the association between a ritual and the goal it signifies and points to, as a means of producing subjective certainty in the achievement of this goal. The exhaustive repetition of synonyms, taxonomies, and different contingencies in both spells and legal formulas highlighted the convergence in function between these cultural forms, each of which serves as a kind of insurance policy. With the rejection in the Baconian and other modern semiotic ideologies of the efficacy of magic, and the embrace of something approaching the modern doctrine of the arbitrariness of the sign, the anxiety over the ability of signs to communicate was arguably heightened. This anxiety had to be alleviated in a different way, by the nominalist purging of false metaphysical verbiage and the establishing of a secure relationship between language and reality through empirical adequation and political fiat. This was the heart of Bentham's codification proposal.

As such examples illustrate, the arbitrariness of the sign is much more than the problem of how to ground the meaning of language so as to permit communication among the members of a group. "Arbitrariness" refers also to such life-or-death matters as the harvest, illness, and death, each of which may be the signified of the ritual signifier. "Arbitrariness" also defines the less tangible but no less important existential problem of salvation. Protestants associated the misuse of language with false religion or idolatry, and the perfection of a universal language with the reverse of the Curse of Babel or even, in the case of John Bulwer, with the redemption from original sin. The closeness of the relation between salvation and communication is shown by the association of the Gospel with the advent of "plain speech" and the overcoming of pagan oracles and Jewish ceremonial.

Paradoxically, sometimes arbitrariness can be the precondition of signification. The recognition of the miracle as a sign or *semeion* depends precisely upon its violation of natural law. In this case, as in the case of many trials by ordeal, the certainty of such events as signs depends upon their ability to signal, through the establishment of sheer difference from the norm, the intervention of a supernatural force. There is an analogy here to a tenet of modern communication theory, which defines "information" as based in part on the "statistical rarity" of a sign.[1] From this perspective, the miracle, as a pure expression of divine will, communicates precisely because it is arbitrary or, rather, singular. The Deists, however, rejected this view by condemning evidence of a deity that did not accord with natural law as arbitrary in a different sense, namely nonverifiable and meaningless.

Given the importance of certainty as a cardinal function of the sign, it is bizarre how fashionable it has become to conclude, based on the structuralist idea of the arbitrariness of the sign, that all forms of communication are ultimately uncertain—a matter of perspective and subjective preference—and that interpretation, whether of texts or other expressions, is limitless.[2] These propositions, although not entirely mistaken, are combined with the claim that the Western metaphysical tradition has enforced a false divide between logic and myth, and with this a hierarchy between truth and error that is ultimately unsupportable. Such a claim is problematic, both because it attributes to Western tradition a unique obsession with guaranteeing the certainty of the sign, when as we have seen this preoccupation is entirely universal; and because it mischaracterizes the specific semiotic contours of modernity. The quest for certainty in communication is not merely a habit of post-Homeric or post-Reformation Europeans: as we have seen, the authors of the Hindu *Tantras* also arranged the syllables of their mantras precisely so as to exclude the possibility of doubt in their communicative efficacy. It is true that, as described above in Chapters Four through Six, post-Reformation Europeans have pursued with particular vehemence a critique of poetic and figurative language, motivated in part by a deepened awareness of the arbitrary nature of the sign. This was done out of a recognition that the dangers posed by rhetoric are real. We live in a post-Lockean age and, for the most part, are all good nominalists now. There is no question of going back to a magical view of language.

Moreover, as we are aware from our own experience, communication happens every day—along with miscommunication, although we know the difference! As Peirce recognized, it is more productive to focus on pragmatics—on what works in a given situation—rather than on repeating *a priori* theories of the fallibility of language which, if taken to an extreme, allow for no distinction in value and efficacy among different modes of discourse. Rather than repeating truisms concerning the uncertainty of communication, semiotics should attend to the specificities of rhetorical performance and the historical dimensions and causes of transformations in attitudes toward performance.

From pragmatics to semantics, and back again

J. L. Austin, speaking from within the tradition of analytical philosophy, pointed out that not all statements are declarative: not all are descriptions of some state of affairs that can be labeled "true" or "false." He focused attention on the class of performative utterances and related uses of language. In so doing, he was also highlighting a history of exclusion of the pragmatic dimensions of language from our theoretical cognizance. This book has gone some distance toward recuperating, for theory, modes of rhetorical performance that Austin himself did not describe. It has also sketched part of the history of the repression of rhetoric and, in the process, demonstrated the extent of the shift away from certain magical conceptions of language to the Enlightenment emphasis on meaning and the transparency of language to thought. It was this earlier shift, which can be described roughly as one from pragmatics to semantics, which necessitated, by way of compensation, contemporary efforts to recuperate the pragmatic dimensions of language. Protestant literalism emphasized the semantic content of language over its form, as indicated by the move to render scripture in the vernacular, to condemn the Latin liturgy and ceremonial formalism, and to promote spontaneity and sincerity in prayer. As we have seen, this promotion of the semantic also coordinated with a severe truncation of the pragmatic dimensions of ritual that eventually extended beyond the liturgy to scientific and ostensibly secular modes of discourse. The effort to strip away all rhetoric must, of course, remain utopian; and people have never stopped "doing things with words." Yet the ideological shift against rhetoric and pragmatics in favor of semantics nevertheless has had long-term consequences, not least for our inability to appreciate the intimate connection between poetry and performance.

This book participates in a broader movement in semiotics, inspired by structuralists from Saussure and Vladimir Propp to Lévi-Strauss, from content to form, and with this, away from pure semantics. As the importance of such a shift has still not been absorbed within religious studies, it bears emphasizing again here. Much historical and ethnographic work in the study of religion remains stuck at the level of describing the cosmologies and ritual behaviors of particular traditions, and the meaning attached by particular groups to their symbols, that is, cultural semantics. This is obviously the first level of engagement, without which no further progress in understanding other cultures may be made. However, if we remain at this level, it is impossible to compare and contrast other cultures effectively through a systematic redescription, so as to recognize in the data the evidence for a general theory of the human or a true anthropology. We are left to repeat endlessly that "This is what the Bororo, etc., believe," where any cultural form must always be referred to some substratum of belief that may be reexpressed in propositional form. It is, however, a mistake to suppose that, by confining oneself to the level of description, one may provide an accurate account even of what is going on in one particular culture. The rhetorical devices found in rituals often function at a subliminal or unconscious level, like the structures in myths or ordinary forms of language. We cannot expect to find a fully worked-out indigenous theory that accounts for this function. However, we should not be surprised when, as for example with the Hindu Tantric procedures for making mantras "effective" (*siddha*), we discover some convergence between indigenous perspectives on performance and our own theories. I hope that some of the general principles announced above may help to illuminate features of the data collected by other explorers in the human sciences.

Reason, autonomy, and the critique of the sign

The shift from a focus on semantics to one on pragmatics can be difficult to absorb because it threatens a certain concept of human autonomy, or the idea that humans choose, in every particular, the meanings that they attribute to the world. The recognition that certain kinds of devices—whether binary oppositions, as analyzed by Lévi-Strauss, or poetic repetition, as analyzed by Gorgias and Jakobson, and in the present work—have a special ability to communicate and persuade, which explains their deployment and proliferation in certain contexts of use, contradicts the idea that meaning is fully conscious. It suggests that we are subject to a power beyond our control. Keane has emphasized how the circumscription or even proscription of certain pragmatic uses of language, together with the compartmentalization of such uses in particular genres, coordinated with another important trajectory toward Enlightenment and modernity: the ascendancy of a particular concept of the autonomy of the individual, and of the self-sufficiency of reason.

Plato's attack on sophistry anticipated more recent polemics against poetry and rhetoric as threats to human autonomy. Gorgias's defence of Helen amounted, in the end, to a series of contentions that human beings are not free to choose their own actions; Helen was absolved of responsibility for her adultery by being deprived of her agency. If we accept his argument for the power of rhetoric—and by all evidence (see Chapter Two) it appears that we must accept it to some extent—then our own autonomy appears to be at risk.

A number of Protestant polemics against ritual appear to have been motivated by similar concerns. The Puritan critique of vain repetitions objected to the idea that God could be coerced by prayer: an idea that threatened divine autonomy. The relocation of the nexus of religion toward the inward contrition and purity of faith of a sincere heart, and away from the performance of external ceremonies (and from the control of a church hierarchy), promoted the autonomy of the individual worshipper. The Deist revolt against the Mosaic laws, as arbitrary commands that reinforce the notion of divine sovereignty, arguably completed this cycle. Subsequently, the failure of various efforts, including Douglas's, to reduce the function of the Mosaic laws to the expression of a cosmology—that is, to a particular symbolic or semantic content—merely underscores the extent of the gap between our own semiotic ideology and that of the ancient Israelites and other premodern ritual traditions. The point is not that the modern emphasis on autonomy is wrong—how could we disavow this?—but rather that it has contributed to certain distortions in our ability to understand other cultures. So, our contemporary understanding of human agency and autonomy should not be applied uncritically to other cultures where a different understanding may be prevalent.

Last words

In conclusion, let me reaffirm my conviction that semiotics as a methodological approach, a mode of textual analysis, a set of conceptual tools, and a philosophical problematic emerging from the communicative dimensions of the human situation, has a great deal to contribute to our understanding of both traditional religions and secular modernity. There are, as we have seen, semiotic dimensions to many behaviors as well as to the cosmologies, soteriologies, and notions of identity that inform these behaviors. Despite the view of many that semiotics has nothing left to offer the study of religion—that structuralism has exhausted itself—even ancient texts can disclose new vistas when viewed from a perspective attuned to the nexus between structure and communicative function. But this is not a one-way street. Semiotics also needs to engage with the data of religion, and with the theoretical concerns of those who study religion, as a means of challenging itself to grow and develop. Recognition of the need to study different semiotic ideologies, and to appreciate the divide between other traditions and our own over even some of the most basic questions of representation and communication, constitutes an advance beyond the legacy of structuralism and poststructuralism, which it has been the purpose of this book to achieve.

NOTES

Acknowledgments

1 Robert A. Yelle, "The Rhetoric of Gesture in Cross-Cultural Perspective," in Paul Bouissac, ed., "Gesture, Ritual and Memory," special issue of *Gesture* 6, no. 2 (2006): 223–40.

2 Robert A. Yelle, *Explaining Mantras: Ritual, Rhetoric, and the Dream of a Natural Language in Hindu Tantra* (London and New York: Routledge, 2003).

3 Robert A. Yelle, "Bentham's Fictions: Canon and Idolatry in the Genealogy of Law," *Yale Journal of Law & the Humanities* 17 (2005): 151–79.

4 Robert A. Yelle, "Moses' Veil: Secularization as Christian Myth," in Winnifred F. Sullivan, Robert A. Yelle, and Mateo Taussig-Rubbo, eds, *After Secular Law* (Stanford: Stanford University Press, 2011), 23–42; Robert A. Yelle, "The Hindu Moses: Christian Polemics against Jewish Ritual and the Secularization of Hindu Law under Colonialism," *History of Religions* 49 (2009): 141–71.

CHAPTER ONE

1 This does not of course rule out other functions served by these ritual forms. Edmund Leach argued that many cultural phenomena can be viewed from a dual perspective, as either communication or exchange. Leach, *Culture and Communication: The Logic by which Symbols are Connected* (Cambridge: Cambridge University Press, 1976), 5–6. Claude Lévi-Strauss's analogy between kinship exchange and language is an illustration of this point. Lévi-Strauss, *The Elementary Structures of Kinship* (Boston: Beacon, 1969), 492–7. The same could also be said of sacrifice. As has frequently been pointed out, many sacrifices depend on the idea of exchange or reciprocity: in the Latin formula, *do ut des*, I (the sacrificer) give so that you (the god) may give in return. Joseph Henninger, "Sacrifice," in Lindsay Jones, ed., *Encyclopedia of Religion*, 2nd edn (New York: Macmillan Reference USA, 2005), 7997–8008 at 8002, attributes this theory to E. B. Tylor. Sacrifice, like other modes of gift exchange, and particularly when it includes a communal meal, encourages reciprocity and sociality. Cf. Marcel Mauss, *The Gift: The Form and Reason for Exchange in Archaic Societies*, trans. W. D. Halls (New York: W. W. Norton and Co., 2000). As such, sacrifice has both communicative and economic dimensions.

2 Edmund Leach, "Ritualization in Man," *Philosophical Transactions of the Royal Society*, Series B, No. 772, 251 (1966): 403–8 at 403. Leach claims that many anthropologists distinguish among three types of behavior: "rational technical," "communicative," and "magical." He then argues for collapsing the second and third of these into a single category, "ritual." While recognizing the affinities among communicative and magical behaviors, for the reasons given in Chapter Two I nevertheless regard it as useful to retain "magic" as a distinct category.

3 Viktor Shklovsky, *Theory of Prose*, trans. Benjamin Sher (Elmwood Park, IL: Dalkey Archive Press, 1990), 1–14.

4 See Robert A. Yelle, *The Language of Disenchantment: Protestant Literalism and Colonial Discourse in British India* (New York: Oxford University Press, 2013), especially chapter 1, "Orientalism and the Language of Disenchantment," and chapter 6, "The Hindu Moses: Christian Polemics against Jewish Ritual and the Secularization of Hindu Law under Colonialism"; Yelle, "The Trouble with Transcendence: Carl Schmitt's 'Exception' as a Challenge for Religious Studies," *Method & Theory in the Study of Religion* 22 (2010): 189–206; Yelle, "Moses' Veil."

5 The term "linguistic ideology" or "language ideology" has become popular in linguistic anthropology and sociolinguistics to denote theories of the nature and functions of language held within particular cultures. See Bambi B. Schieffelin, Kathryn Ann Woolard, and Paul V. Kroskrity, *Language Ideologies: Practice and Theory* (New York: Oxford University Press, 1998); Paul V. Kroskrity, *Regimes of Language: Ideologies, Polities, and Identities* (Sante Fe, NM: School of American Research Press, 2000). Webb Keane, *Christian Moderns: Freedom and Fetish in the Mission Encounter* (Berkeley and Los Angeles: University of California Press, 2007), 2, 16–18, uses the terms "semiotic ideology" and "language ideology." For a discussion of Keane's work, see pages 19 and 97 in this volume.

6 Volney P. Gay and Daniel Patte, "Religious Studies," in Thomas Sebeok, ed., *Encyclopedic Dictionary of Semiotics*, 3 vols (Berlin: Mouton de Gruyter, 1986), 2: 797–807 at 798.

7 Cf. 2 Corinthians 3:12–13 (KJV). See discussion below.

8 Yelle, *Language of Disenchantment*, chapter 1; Yelle, "The Trouble with Transcendence."

9 Jonathan Z. Smith, *Imagining Religion: From Babylon to Jonestown* (Chicago: University of Chicago Press, 1982); Talal Asad, *Genealogies of Religion* (Baltimore: Johns Hopkins University Press, 1993); Asad, *Formations of the Secular: Christianity, Islam, Modernity* (Stanford: Stanford University Press, 2003); Tomoko Masuzawa, *The Invention of World Religions, or, How European Universalism Was Preserved in the Language of Pluralism* (Chicago: University of Chicago Press, 2005).

10 See also Yelle, *Explaining Mantras*, esp. 13–17, 24–27, 75–87.

11 Roman Jakobson, "Two Aspects of Language and Two Types of Aphasic Disturbances," in Stephen Rudy, ed., *Roman Jakobson: Selected Writings*, 8 vols (Berlin: Mouton de Gruyter, 1962–88), 2: 239–59.

12 See Chapter Two and Table 2.1 in this volume for a description of this typology and references.

13 Roman Jakobson, "Closing Statement: Linguistics and Poetics," in Thomas Sebeok, ed., *Style in Language* (Cambridge, MA: MIT Press, 1960), 350–77 at 356, 358.

14 See Michael Silverstein, "Metapragmatic Discourse and Metapragmatic Function," in John A. Lucy, ed., *Reflexive Language: Reported Speech and Metapragmatics* (Cambridge: Cambridge University Press, 1993), 33–58; Silverstein, "The Improvisational Performance of Culture in Realtime Discursive Practice," in R. Keith Sawyer, ed., *Creativity in Performance* (Greenwich, CT: Ablex Publishing Corp., 1998), 265–311; Michael Silverstein and Greg Urban, eds, *Natural Histories of Discourse* (Chicago: University of Chicago Press, 1996).

15 Keane, *Christian Moderns*; Keane, "From Fetishism to Sincerity: Agency, the Speaking Subject, and their Historicity in the Context of Religious Conversion," *Comparative Studies in Society and History* 39 (1997): 674–93; Keane, "Religious Language," *Annual Review of Anthropology* 26 (1997): 47–71; Keane, "Sincerity, Modernity, and the Protestants," *Cultural Anthropology* 17 (2002): 65–92.

16 Thomas Sebeok, *Signs: An Introduction to Semiotics* (Toronto: University of Toronto Press, 1994); Sebeok, ed., *Encyclopedic Dictionary of Semiotics*; Winfried Nöth, *Handbook of Semiotics* (Bloomington: Indiana University Press, 1990); Paul Bouissac, ed., *Encyclopedia of Semiotics* (New York: Oxford University Press, 1998).

17 As trenchantly argued in a number of Paul Bouissac's editorial comments on the SemiotiX website, www.semioticon.com/semiotix.

18 For example, Claude Lévi-Strauss, *Structural Anthropology*, trans. Claire Jacobson and Brooke Grundfest Schoepf (New York: Basic Books, 1963); Leach, *Culture and Communication*; Victor Turner, *The Ritual Process: Structure and Anti-Structure* (Ithaca: Cornell University Press, 1977); Mary Douglas, *Purity and Danger: An Analysis of Concepts of Pollution and Taboo* (London: Routledge and Kegan Paul, 1966).

19 In addition to Michael Silverstein and Webb Keane, other examples include Richard Bauman, Richard Parmentier, Steven Caton, and Joel Robbins. Jens Kreinath, "Semiotics," in Jens Kreinath, Jan Snoek, and Michael Stausberg, eds, *Theorizing Rituals: Issues, Topics, Approaches, Concepts* (Leiden: Brill, 2006), 429–70, adopts an approach to the semiotics of ritual that is informed by an engagement with anthropological literature.

20 For example, Seth D. Kunin, *We Think What We Eat: Neo-Structuralist Analysis of Israelite Food Rules and Other Cultural and Textual Practices* (London: T & T Clark, 2004). Wendy Doniger has produced a formidable body of work in this area, beginning with Wendy Doniger O'Flaherty, *Śiva: The Erotic Ascetic* (New York: Oxford University Press, 1981).

21 For example, Massimo Leone has written about the historical semiotics of sainthood and conversion in Roman Catholic tradition. See his *Religious Conversion and Identity: The Semiotic Analysis of Texts* (London and

New York: Routledge, 2004); Leone, *Saints and Signs: A Semiotic Reading of Conversion in Early Modern Catholicism* (Berlin and New York: Walter de Gruyter, 2010). Fabio Rambelli has contributed to the cultural semiotics of Japanese esoteric Buddhism: for example, "An Introduction to Buddhist Semiotics," http://projects.chass.utoronto.ca/semiotics/cyber/ramout.html; Rambelli, *Buddhist Theory of Semiotics* (London: Bloomsbury, forthcoming).

22 For example, Umberto Eco, *The Search for the Perfect Language*, trans. James Fentress (Oxford: Blackwell, 1995); Gérard Genette, *Mimologics*, trans. Thaïs Morgan (Lincoln: University of Nebraska Press, 1995); Vivian Salmon, "Language-Planning in Seventeenth-Century England; its Context and Aims," in *The Study of Language in Seventeenth-Century England*, 2nd edn (Amsterdam: John Benjamins, 1988), 129–56; Rhodri Lewis, *Language, Mind and Nature: Artificial Languages in England from Bacon to Locke* (Cambridge: Cambridge University Press, 2007).

23 Peter Harrison, *Religion and the Religions in the English Enlightenment* (Cambridge: Cambridge University Press, 1990); Harrison, *The Bible, Protestantism, and the Rise of Natural Science* (Cambridge: Cambridge University Press, 1998).

24 Keane, *Christian Moderns*; Yelle, *Language of Disenchantment*.

25 For example, Jesper Sørensen and Harvey Whitehouse. Sørensen, *A Cognitive Theory of Magic* (Lanham, MD: Rowman and Littlefield, 2006), 44–5, 56–9, deploys Peircean categories to explain magic. For a discussion of such theories, see Robert A. Yelle, "To Perform or Not to Perform?: A Theory of Ritual Performance versus Cognitive Theories of Religious Transmission," *Method & Theory in the Study of Religion* 18 (2006): 372–91; and Yelle, Review of *A Cognitive Theory of Magic*, by Jesper Sørensen, in *Journal of the American Academy of Religion* 76 (2008): 527–31. For a discussion of religious transmission in connection with the literacy hypothesis, see Chapter Five in this volume.

26 Alfred M. Johnson, Jr, *A Bibliography of Semiological and Structural Studies of Religion*, in Dikran Y. Hadidian, *Bibliographia Tripotamopolitana*, Number XI (Pittsburgh: The Clifford E. Barbour Library, Pittsburgh Theological Seminary, 1979).

27 The second edition of the *Encyclopedia of Religion*, which was published in 2005, had, like the 1987 edition, no article on "Semiotics," although it did have a new article on "Symbol and Symbolism" and an article on "Structuralism [Further Considerations]" that updated Edmund Leach's entry on "Structuralism" from the first edition. Both of these new articles referenced semiotics—as distinguished from structuralism—but only briefly. Jones, *Encyclopedia of Religion*.

28 For example, Tim Murphy, *Representing Religion: Essays in History, Theory, and Crisis* (Sheffield, UK: Equinox, 2007).

29 See the discussion of Mary Douglas, et al. in Chapter Six.

30 See Chapter Three for some exceptions to this trend of ignoring iconicity.

31 Claude Lévi-Strauss, *The Savage Mind* (Chicago: University of Chicago Press, 1966), 233–4.

32 Bruce Lincoln, *Theorizing Myth: Narrative, Ideology, and Scholarship* (Chicago: University of Chicago Press, 1999), 3–43.

33 Friedrich Nietzsche, "On the Genealogy of Morals," in Walter Kaufmann, ed., *Basic Writings of Nietzsche* (New York: Random House, 1968), 439–599, esp. "First Essay," 460–92.

34 Friedrich Nietzsche, "On Truth and Lying in an Extra-Moral Sense," in Sander Gilman, Carole Blair, and David Parent, eds, *Friedrich Nietzsche on Rhetoric and Language* (New York: Oxford University Press, 1989), 246–57.

35 For a good summary, see Gary Gutting, "Michel Foucault," in Edward N. Zalta, ed., *The Stanford Encyclopedia of Philosophy (Fall 2011 Edition)*, http://plato.stanford.edu/archives/fall2011/entries/foucault.

36 Bruce Lincoln, "The Tyranny of Taxonomies," in *Discourse and the Construction of Society* (New York: Oxford University Press, 1989), 131–41; see discussion in Yelle, *Explaining Mantras*, 93–4.

37 A similar inability to acknowledge the contribution of formal features to rhetorical persuasion is reflected in Lincoln's anti-definition of authoritative discourse: "I take the effect [of discursive authority] to be the result of the conjuncture of the right speaker, the right speech and delivery, the right staging and props, the right time and place, and an audience whose historically conditioned expectations establish the parameters of what is judged 'right' in all these instances." Bruce Lincoln, *Authority: Construction and Corrosion* (Chicago: University of Chicago Press, 1995), 11. This is to reject the very possibility of a systematic poetics or rhetoric; it reflects the anti-formalism of contemporary scholarship. How, then, do we explain the convergences across different cultures regarding the types of formal features that make discourse persuasive?

38 Jonathan Z. Smith, *Map Is Not Territory* (Chicago: University of Chicago Press, 1993), 252–53; see discussion in Yelle, "Rhetorics of Law and Ritual: A Semiotic Comparison of the Law of Talion and Sympathetic Magic," *Journal of the American Academy of Religion* 69 (2001): 627–47 at 634, 640.

39 Jakobson, "Closing Statement," 356.

40 The term is from Peter Goodrich, *Oedipus Lex: Psychoanalysis, History, Law* (Berkeley and Los Angeles: University of California Press, 1995), 44–56.

41 See, for example, Benjamin I. Schwartz, ed., "Wisdom, Revelation, and Doubt: Perspectives on the First Millennium B.C.," *Daedalus* 104, No. 2 (Spring 1975); S. N. Eisenstadt, *The Origins and Diversity of Axial Age Civilizations* (Albany: SUNY Press, 1986); and more recently, Charles Taylor, "The Future of the Religious Past," in Hent de Vries, *Religion: Beyond a Concept* (New York: Fordham University Press, 2008), 178–244; Robert Bellah, *Religion in Human Evolution* (Cambridge, MA: Harvard University Press, 2011), 265–566.

42 Gorgias, *Helen*, trans. George Kennedy, in Patricia P. Matsen, Philip Rollinson, and Marion Sousa, eds, *Readings from Classical Rhetoric* (Carbondale: Southern Illinois University Press, 1990), 34–6. On this text, and Gorgias more generally, see Robert Wardy, *The Birth of Rhetoric: Plato, Gorgias, and Their Successors* (London: Routledge, 1996).

43 Jacqueline de Romilly, *Magic and Rhetoric in Ancient Greece* (Cambridge, MA: Harvard University Press, 1975).

44 Plato, *Republic*, 601; Aristotle, *Poetics*, chap. 1 (1447a–b). All references to Plato are to Edith Hamilton and Huntington Cairns, eds, *The Collected Dialogues of Plato* (Princeton: Princeton University Press, 1961). All references to Aristotle are to Richard McKeon, ed., *The Basic Works of Aristotle* (New York: Random House, 1941).

45 Plato, *Gorgias*, 502c.

46 Aristotle, *Rhetoric*, Book 3.

47 Plato, *Republic*, 598d, 601b, 602d, 607c, 608a.

48 Michael Foucault, "The Order of Discourse," in Robert Young, ed., *Untying the Text: A Post-Structuralist Reader* (London: Routledge and Kegan Paul, 1981), 48–78 at 70.

49 Plato, *Apology*.

50 Lincoln, *Theorizing Myth*, 33–34, discusses Gorgias's *Helen* but avoids the issues I am raising here.

51 Certain theorists, such as Eric Havelock and Jack Goody, argue that this rise of semiotic awareness was precipitated in part by the advent of alphabetic writing. The coordination of printing with Protestant polemics against poetic language is described in Chapter Five.

52 Similarly, Lincoln, *Theorizing Myth*, 209, states that "If myth is ideology in narrative form, then scholarship is myth with footnotes." Yet he would never omit such references from his own academic work product. Lincoln's works are always copiously annotated, and his statements well-documented. What such contradictions evidence is the bad conscience of the Enlightenment turning against itself.

53 See Chapters Four through Six and Yelle, *Language of Disenchantment*.

54 Mircea Eliade, *The Sacred and the Profane: The Nature of Religion*, trans. Willard R. Trask (New York: Harcourt Brace and Company, 1959), 11–12.

55 Mircea Eliade, *The Myth of the Eternal Return: Or, Cosmos and History*, trans. Willard R. Trask (Princeton: Princeton University Press, 1974), 3–34.

56 Ibid. at 110–11, 137, 159–62.

57 On the Christian typological interpretation of the bible in general, see Eric Auerbach, "Figura," in *Scenes from the Drama of European Literature* (Minneapolis: University of Minnesota Press, 1959), 11–78; Friedrich Ohly, "Typology as Historical Thought," in *Sensus Spiritualis: Studies in Medieval Significs and the Philology of Culture* (Chicago: University of Chicago Press, 2005), 31–67; Sacvan Bercovitch, *Typology and Early American Literature* (Amherst: University of Massachusetts Press, 1972); Paul Korshin, *Typologies in England 1650–1820* (Princeton: Princeton University Press, 1982).

58 Dante Alighieri, "The Letter to Can Grande," in Robert Haller, trans., *Literary Criticism of Dante Alighieri* (Lincoln: University of Nebraska Press, 1973), 95–111.

59 See the discussion of John Toland at the beginning of Chapter Four of this volume.

60 Keane, *Christian Moderns*, 6–7. See also the discussion of Keane in Yelle, *Language of Disenchantment*, 27–8, 29, 133.

CHAPTER TWO

1 Robert N. McCauley and E. Thomas Lawson, *Bringing Ritual to Mind: Psychological Foundations of Cultural Forms* (Cambridge: Cambridge University Press, 2002), 7, 114, 123.

2 Sigmund Freud, "Obsessive Acts and Religious Practices," in James Strachey, ed., *The Standard Edition of the Complete Psychological Works of Sigmund Freud* (London: Hogarth Press, 1953–74), 9: 117–27.

3 Eliade, *Eternal Return*, 5, 10, 17–21.

4 Frits Staal, *Ritual and Mantras: Rules without Meaning* (Delhi: Motilal Banarsidass, 1996), 253–93.

5 See discussion and references at pages 69–70 below.

6 Catherine Bell, *Ritual: Perspectives and Dimensions* (New York: Oxford University Press, 1997), 81; cf. Bell, *Ritual Theory, Ritual Practice* (New York: Oxford University Press, 1992), 7–8, 74, 90, 140–1.

7 Bronislaw Malinowski, *Coral Gardens and Their Magic* (New York: American Book Company, 1935), 2: 218–23.

8 For an overview of the concept of ritual as performance, see Catherine Bell, "Performance," in Mark C. Taylor, ed., *Critical Terms for Religious Studies* (Chicago: University of Chicago Press, 1998), 205–24.

9 Victor Turner, *Dramas, Fields, and Metaphors: Symbolic Action in Human Society* (Ithaca: Cornell University Press, 1974); Turner, *The Anthropology of Performance* (New York: Performing Arts Journal Publications, 1987); Richard Schechner, *Essays in Performance Theory, 1970–1976* (New York: Drama Book Specialists, 1977); Schechner, *The Future of Ritual: Writings on Culture and Performance* (London: Routledge, 1993).

10 J. L. Austin, *How to Do Things with Words* (Cambridge, MA: Harvard University Press, 1975); John Searle, *Speech Acts: An Essay in the Philosophy of Language* (Cambridge: Cambridge University Press, 1969). See additional references and discussion in Yelle, *Explaining Mantras*, 18, n.62.

11 For a critique of this omission in Austin's theory, see Chapter Five and also Yelle, *Explaining Mantras*, 87–90.

12 See the discussion in Chapter Five.

13 Stanley Tambiah, "A Performative Approach to Ritual," in *Culture, Thought and Social Action* (Cambridge, MA: Harvard University Press, 1985), 123–66 at 128.

14 Ibid. at 156. See below in this chapter for a discussion of Michael Silverstein's concept of the "indexical icon."

15 Ibid. at 72, 77.

16 Ibid. at 36.

17 Leach, "Ritualization in Man," 404; Smith, *Imagining Religion*, 54.

18 McCauley and Lawson, *Bringing Ritual to Mind*, 52.

19 See discussion in Chapter Five of this volume.

20 Ibid.

21 E. B. Tylor, *Primitive Culture*, 2 vols, reprint edn (New York: Gordon Press, 1974 [1871]), 1: 104; James George Frazer, *The Golden Bough: A Study in Magic and Religion*, abridged edn (New York: Macmillan, 1951), 12–52.

22 Jerome Rothenberg, *Technicians of the Sacred* (Berkeley and Los Angeles: University of California Press, 1985), 71. Frazer, *Golden Bough*, 17–18, gives a charm against jaundice from the "ancient Hindoos"; this may be the same as *Atharva Veda* 1.22: "Into the parrots do we put your yellowness and into the yellow-green ropanaka-birds. Similarly into the yellow turmeric do we deposit your yellowness." Translated in Ainslie T. Embree, ed., *Sources of Indian Tradition*, vol. 1, 2nd edn (New York: Columbia University Press, 1988), 21–2.

23 Fritz Graf, "Historiola," in Hubert Cancik and Helmuth Schneider, eds, *Brill's New Pauly* (Brill Online, 2012), http://referenceworks.brillonline.com/entries/brill-s-new-pauly/historiola-e515850. Cf. Paul Allan Mirecki, Iain Gardner, and Anthony Alcock, "Magical Spell, Manichaean Letter," in Paul Allan Mirecki and Jason BeDuhn, eds, *Emerging from Darkness: Studies in the Recovery of Manichaean Sources* (Leiden: Brill, 1997), 1–32 at 21, defining historiola as "an abbreviated narrative that is incorporated into a magical spell."

24 Mircea Eliade, *Patterns in Comparative Religion*, trans. Rosemary Sheed (Lincoln: University of Nebraska Press, 1996), 296. Another example is from John George Hohman, *Pow-Wows; or Long-Lost Friend: A Collection of Mysterious and Invaluable Arts and Remedies for Man as Well as Animals*, reprint edn (Pomeroy, WA: Health Research, 1971), 43. Originally published in German in 1820 by a Pennsylvania Dutchman, this collection is interesting for its apparent connections to older Christian magic as well as for its apparent familiarity with some ancient magic (e.g. there is a SATOR magic square in Latin at p. 48). The spell in question is titled "A Direction for a Gypsy Sentence, to be Carried about the Person as a Protection under All Circumstances": "Like unto the prophet Jonas, as a type of Christ, who was guarded for three days and three nights in the belly of a whale, thus shall the Almighty God, as a Father, guard and protect me from all evil. J. J. J." The end of the spell is an instruction to repeat Jesus's name thrice.

25 Rothenberg, *Technicians*, 118.

26 Thomas Sebeok, *Contributions to the Doctrine of Signs* (Bloomington: Indiana University Press, 1976), 31–2, 76–7, 131–2. Tambiah also identified Frazer's types of magic with the Peircean categories, while Jakobson identified them with his own categories of metaphor and metonymy. See Tambiah, *Culture*, 35; Roman Jakobson and Morris Halle, *Fundamentals of Language* (Hague: Mouton and Co., 1956), 81.

27 Adapted from Yelle, "Semiotics," in Michael Stausberg and Steven Engler, eds, *Handbook of Research Methods in Religious Studies* (London and New York: Routledge, 2011), 355–65 at 357.

28 See the discussion of sound symbolism in Chapter Three.

29 Adapted from Yelle, *Explaining Mantras*, 76.

30 Example from Frazer, *Golden Bough*, 15.

31 Ibid. at 17–18.

32 See ibid. at 47–9 for related examples. The seventeenth-century Englishman Kenelm Digby, an early member of the Royal Society, tried to create a weapon salve or powder of sympathy which, when applied to the offending implement, despite the passage of time and the physical separation from the victim, had the power to cause the wound to heal. See Keith Thomas, *Religion and the Decline of Magic* (New York: Charles Scribner's Sons, 1971), 225.

33 See Nöth, "Arbitrariness and Motivation: The Language Sign," in *Handbook of Semiotics*, 240–6.

34 Leach, *Culture and Communication*, 29, 31.

35 See references above and discussion in Yelle, *Explaining Mantras*, 71–3.

36 Silverstein and Urban, *Natural Histories*, 1–4.

37 Example from Nöth, 189.

38 "How to Cure a Burn," in Hohman, *Pow-Wows*, 23.

39 "Another Remedy for Burns," in ibid., 48.

40 Jakobson, "Closing Statement," 367–8; Thomas Sebeok, "The Structure and Content of Cheremis Charms," in Dell Hymes, ed., *Language in Culture and Society* (New York: Harper and Row, 1964), 356–71 at 363–4.

41 Jakobson, "Closing Statement," 367–8. See discussion in Yelle, *Explaining Mantras*, 69–70, 81–3.

42 Yelle, *Explaining Mantras*, 11–21, 23–47.

43 Adapted from Yelle, *Explaining Mantras*, 38.

44 For a discussion of the *haṃsa* mantra, see the section on "Chiasmus and communication" later in this chapter.

45 Adapted from Yelle, *Explaining Mantras*, 47.

46 Umberto Eco, *A Theory of Semiotics* (Bloomington: Indiana University Press, 1976), 6–7.

47 Nietzsche, "On Truth and Lying."

48 Bellah, *Religion in Human Evolution*, 109–16, explores the relationship or resemblance between play and religion or ritual.

49 See *PGM* IV.970–4, in Hans Dieter Betz, ed., *The Greek Magical Papyri in Translation*, 2nd edn, vol. 1 (Chicago: University of Chicago Press, 1992), 57.

50 "A Good Remedy for Consumption," in Hohman, *Pow-Wows*, 21.

51 On counting-out rhymes, see David Rubin, *Memory in Oral Tradition: The Cognitive Psychology of Epic, Ballads, and Counting-Out Rhymes* (New York: Oxford University Press, 1995), 227–56.

52 Hohman gives a charm "To Stop Bleeding," in *Pow-Wows*, 18, that instructs to count down from 50 to 3, at which point the bleeding is supposed to cease.

53 See Yelle, *Explaining Mantras*, 84–5.

54 Joseph Frank Payne, *English Medicine in the Anglo-Saxon Times* (Oxford: Clarendon, 1904), 136. I have divided the lines of this charm differently so as to make the countdown structure more visible.

55 See discussion in Yelle, *Explaining Mantras*, 81–4. Hohman has an example that uses colors: "A good Remedy for Worms, to be used for men as well as for Cattle,"

in *Pow-Wows*, 11: "Mary, God's Mother, traversed the land, / Holding three worms close in her hand; / One was white, the other was black, the third was red."

56 Tambiah, *Culture*, 36, 41.

57 Gunter Senft, "Trobriand Islanders' Forms of Ritual Communication," in Gunter Senft and Ellen B. Basso, eds, *Ritual Communication* (Oxford: Berg, 2009), 81–102 at 88.

58 Francis Palgrave, *The Rise and Progress of the English Commonwealth: Anglo-Saxon Period* (London: J. Murray, 1832), pt. 2: 187; cf. Felix Grendon, "The Anglo-Saxon Charms," *Journal of American Folklore* 22 (1909): 105–237 at 181. For additional examples, see Palgrave, *Rise*, pt. 2: 185–8; pt. 1: 10, 34. Palgrave is apparently the source of the examples quoted by Harold Berman, *Faith and Order: The Reconciliation of Law and Religion* (Atlanta: Scholars Press, 1993), 48; Berman, *Law and Revolution: The Formation of the Western Legal Tradition* (Cambridge, MA: Harvard University Press, 1983), 58–9.

59 Grendon, "The Anglo-Saxon Charms," 180–1.

60 "A Charm against Shooting, Cutting or Thrusting," in Hohman, *Pow-Wows*, 53–4.

61 Bronislaw Malinowski, *Magic, Science and Religion and Other Essays* (Boston: Beacon Press, 1948), 13–14.

62 A well-known version of this law is found in Exodus 21:22–5 (RSV): "When men strive together, and hurt a woman with child so that there is a miscarriage, and yet no harm follows, the one who hurt her shall be fined, according as the woman's husband shall lay upon him; and he shall pay as the judges determine. If any harm follows, then you shall give life for life, eye for eye, tooth for tooth, hand for hand, foot for foot, burn for burn, wound for wound, stripe for stripe." Cf. *Code of Hammurabi*, secs. 196–7, in G. R. Driver and John C. Miles, *The Babylonian Laws*, vol. 2 (Oxford: Clarendon Press, 1955). There are also provisions in the Hebrew Bible (e.g. Deuteronomy 19:18–21) according to which one is made to undergo the punishment assigned to the crime of which he falsely accuses another. Plato offers examples of talionic rebirths, possibly from the Orphic or Pythagorean tradition: "If any man have slain his father, there shall come a time when he shall have to suffer the same violent end at the hands of a child; if his mother, his certain doom in later days is to be born himself a female creature and, in the end, to have his life taken by those whom he has borne. When pollution has been brought on the common blood, there is no other way of purification but this; the stain refuses to be effaced until the guilty soul have paid life for life, like for like . . ." (Plato, *Laws*, 9.872e). In Hinduism and Buddhism, karma is frequently depicted as analogical or talionic. *Laws of Manu* 12.8–9 articulates a general rule: "A man experiences the good and bad results of mental actions in his mind alone; those of verbal actions in his speech; and those of bodily actions, in his body alone." Patrick Olivelle, trans., *Manu's Code of Law* (New York: Oxford University Press, 1995) (hereinafter "*Manu*"). For many more examples of talionic and analogical punishments, see Yelle, "Rhetorics of Law and Ritual."

63 *Manu* 8.279. Trans. Olivelle.

64 Ibid. at 11.104.

65 Ibid. at 9.237.

66 Ibid.

67 Trans. Olivelle. See the discussion of *Manu* 5.55 below.

68 Mieczysław Wallis, *Arts and Signs* (Bloomington: Indiana University Press, 1975), 17; Esther Cohen, *The Crossroads of Justice: Law and Culture in Late Medieval France* (Leiden: Brill, 1993), 165.

69 Frazer, *Golden Bough*, 50.

70 Jeremy Bentham, *The Works of Jeremy Bentham*, ed. John Bowring, 11 vols (Edinburgh: William Tait, 1843), 1: 92.

71 Ibid. at 1: 403–4, 408, 409–11.

72 Ibid. at 1: 92.

73 Ibid. at 1: 404.

74 Ibid. at 1: 407.

75 Ibid. at 1: 407–8.

76 Ibid. at 1: 408.

77 *Manu* 8.270–1. Trans. Olivelle.

78 Bentham, *Works*, 1: 398–9.

79 Ibid. at 1: 404.

80 Ibid. at 1: 408.

81 Ibid. at 1: 398.

82 Ibid. at 1: 405, 411–13.

83 Ibid. at 1: 94.

84 Ibid. at 1: 412.

85 Cf. ibid. at 1: 94, note.

86 Ibid. at 1: 88–90, 401–2.

87 See Jeremy Bentham and George Grote [Philip Beauchamp, pseud.], *An Analysis of the Influence of Natural Religion on the Temporal Happiness of Mankind* (London: R. Carlile, 1822).

88 See, for example, Friedrich Creuzer, *Symbolik und Mythologie der alten Völker, besonders der Griechen*, 3rd edn, 4 vols (Leipzig and Darmstadt, Carl Wilhelm Leske, 1837–42), 2: 599–601; Johann Jakob Bachofen, *Johann Jakob Bachofens Gesammelte Werke*, ed. Karl Meuli, vol. 4, *Versuch über die Gräbersymbolik der Alten* (Basel: Benno Schwabe and Co., 1954 [1859]), 18, 61–3. For a discussion, see Robert A. Yelle, "The Rebirth of Myth?: Nietzsche's Eternal Recurrence and its Romantic Antecedents," *Numen* 47 (2000): 175–202 at 193.

89 Stanley Fish, *Is There a Text in This Class?: The Authority of Interpretive Communities* (Cambridge, MA: Harvard University Press, 1982), is a good example of this point of view. See Umberto Eco, *The Limits of Interpretation* (Bloomington: Indiana University Press, 1991), for a critique of the "limitless semiosis" endorsed by deconstructionists.

90 See Yelle, "Poetic Justice"; Yelle, "Hindu Law as Performance."

91   Richard Lariviere, *The Divyatattva of Raghunandana Bhaṭṭācārya: Ordeals in Classical Hindu Law* (New Delhi: Manohar, 1981) (hereinafter "*Divyatattva*").

92   *Divyatattva*, sec. 209.

93   Ibid., sec. 219.

94   Ibid., sec. 213.

95   Ibid., sec. 214.

96   Ibid., sec. 284.

97   Ibid., sec. 287. Similar forms of repetition were found also in the Anglo-Saxon ordeals. The accused had to fast and attend mass on each of the three days prior to the ordeal. Then, following another mass and invocation to the trial element of iron or water, the ordeal was carried out. In the case of the ordeal by hot iron, the accused had to carry the iron nine steps, which were divided into three groups of three steps each. After three days, the hand of the accused was examined for burns. See F. L. Attenborough, *The Laws of the Earliest English Kings* (Cambridge: Cambridge University Press, 1922), 188. The structuring of the ordeal by threes, which in the Christian context was probably a reference to the Holy Trinity, produced a symmetry resembling that found in the Hindu ordeal by hot iron.

98   *Divyatattva*, sec. 214.

99   Ibid., sec. 330.

100 Ibid., sec. 168. This is a quote from *Mahābhārata* 1.74.16.

101 Ibid., sec. 301.

102 Ibid., sec. 216.

103 Ibid., secs. 169–70. I have modified Lariviere's translation, which does not sufficiently communicate the etymological form of these lines.

104 As in the ordeals of taking the oath (*Divyatattva*, secs. 332–50) or drinking holy water (ibid., secs. 283–4), each of which was followed by a prescribed waiting period following which, if no calamity befell the accused, he was pronounced innocent.

105 See the discussion of the sign-function of miracles in Chapter Six.

106 E. E. Evans-Pritchard, *Witchcraft, Oracles, and Magic among the Azande* (New York: Oxford University Press, 1976 [1937]).

107 For example, S. N. Pendse, *Oaths and Ordeals in Dharmaśāstra* (Vadodara: University of Baroda Press, 1985), 93.

108 Rebecca Colman, "Reason and Unreason in Early Medieval Law," *Journal of Interdisciplinary History* 4 (1974): 571–91 at 588–9.

109 *Divyatattva*, secs. 214–20.

110 Ibid., secs. 248–50.

111 Ibid., secs. 285–9.

112 J. Duncan M. Derrett, "Ancient Indian 'Nonsense' Vindicated," *Journal of the American Oriental Society* 98 (1978): 100–6.

113   *Divyatattva*, secs. 265–8.

114   Ibid., secs. 330–1.

115   Trans. Olivelle.

116   On the chiastic structure of this passage, see Thomas Boys, *Key to the Book of Psalms* (London: L. B. Seeley, 1825), 41; Bernard Jackson, *Studies in the Semiotics of Biblical Law* (Sheffield, UK: Sheffield Academic Press, 2000), 291–2; Jacob Milgrom, *Leviticus: A Book of Ritual and Ethics* (Minneapolis: Fortress Press, 2004), 295–6.

117   Leviticus 24:13–23 (RSV).

118   John W. Welch, "Criteria for Identifying and Evaluating the Presence of Chiasmus," in John W. Welch and Daniel B. McKinlay, eds, *Chiasmus Bibliography* (Provo, UT: Research Press, 1999), 157–74 at 162, 165.

119   Mary Douglas, *Leviticus as Literature* (Oxford: Oxford University Press, 1999), 27.

120   Steven Caton, "*Salaam Tahiya*: Greetings from the Highlands of Yemen," *American Ethnologist* 13 (1986): 290–308 at 297.

121   Yelle, *Explaining Mantras*, 50–1.

122   *PGM* I.15–20, in Betz, ed., *The Greek Magical Papyri*, 3.

123   Adding fuel to this speculation is the mysterious command at *PGM* IV.2320ff. (Betz, *The Greek Magical Papyri*, 80): "[T]o escape the fate of my words is impossible: happen it must. Don't force yourself to hear the symbols forward and then in reverse again." Cf. *PGM* XIII.560 (ibid. at 186): "[W]hen written forwards and backwards this is great and marvelous." It appears that there was at least some conscious reflection on the pragmatic force of such devices within the Greco-Egyptian tradition, although the fact that we have mainly only recipes for spells makes it hard to be certain.

124   Bernard Jackson, "An Eye for an I?: The Semiotics of Lex Talionis in the Bible," in William Pencak and J. Ralph Lindgren, eds, *New Approaches to Semiotics and the Human Sciences: Essays in Honor of Roberta Kevelson* (New York: Peter Lang, 1997), 127–49 at 133.

125   Michael Caesar, ed., *Dante: The Critical Heritage 1314(?)–1870* (London: Routledge, 1989), 423.

126   Dante declares that the number of these structural levels is three: "The form of the treatise is threefold, according to its three kinds of divisions. The first is that which divides the whole work into three canticles [the *Inferno, Purgatory,* and *Paradise*]. The second is that which divides each canticle into cantos. The third, that which divides the cantos into rhymed units [the rhymed tercets (*terza rima*)]." Dante Alighieri, "Letter to Can Grande," 9, in Haller, trans., *Literary Criticism.*

127   Dante Alighieri, *The Divine Comedy*, trans. Mark Musa, 3 vols (New York: Penguin, 1986), 1: 43. All references to the *Inferno, Purgatory,* and *Paradise* are to this translation.

128   *Inferno*, 12.

129   Ibid., 33.

130   Ibid., 23.

131 Ibid., 28.

132 Caesar, *Dante*, 424.

133 See discussion in Yelle, *Language of Disenchantment*, 13–18.

134 Evans-Pritchard, *Witchcraft, Oracles, and Magic*.

135 See, for example, Randall Styers, *Making Magic* (New York: Oxford University Press, 2004).

136 Leach, *Culture and Communication*, 29–32; Keith Thomas, "An Anthropology of Religion and Magic, II," *Journal of Interdisciplinary History* 6 (1975): 91–109.

137 Ram Kumar Rai, ed., *Śāktānandataraṅgiṇī* (Benares: Prachya Prakashan, 1993), 9.

138 Jonathan Z. Smith, "Sacred Persistence: Toward a Redescription of Canon," in *Imagining Religion*, 36–52; Smith, "The Bare Facts of Ritual," in ibid. at 53–65.

139 Yelle, *Explaining Mantras*, 12.

140 Eliade, *Eternal Return*, 3, 5, 34–5.

141 See the discussion in Chapter Five of Jakobson's analysis of the political slogan "I like Ike."

142 Stanley Tambiah, "Form and Meaning of Magical Acts," in *Culture*, 60–86, esp. 77–84.

143 Cf. Jonathan Z. Smith, *To Take Place* (Chicago: University of Chicago Press, 1992), 103.

144 Godfrey Lienhardt, *Divinity and Experience: The Religion of the Dinka* (Oxford: Oxford University Press, 1961), 280. Cf. Mary Douglas, *Natural Symbols* (London: Barrie and Jenkins, 1973), 35–6, discussing Robin Horton's critique of Lienhardt on this point.

145 G. Brewer and C. A. Hendrie, "Evidence to Suggest that Copulatory Vocalizations in Women Are Not a Reflexive Consequence of Orgasm," *Archives of Sexual Behavior* (May 18, 2010).

CHAPTER THREE

1 Plato, *Cratylus*.

2 Ferdinand de Saussure, *Course in General Linguistics*, trans. Wade Baskin (New York: McGraw-Hill, 1966), 67–8. However, Jean Starobinski's investigations into Saussure's work on anagrams or hidden relationships in Latin poems revealed that he was also interested in the study of motivated language. Starobinski, *Words upon Words: The Anagrams of Ferdinand de Saussure*, trans. Olivia Emmet (New Haven: Yale University Press, 1979).

3 Lévi-Strauss, *Elementary Structures of Kinship*, 492–7.

4 Lévi-Strauss, "The Structural Study of Myth," in *Structural Anthropology*, 206–31; cf. Leach, *Culture and Communication*, 72–5.

5 Leach, "Ritualization in Man," 404.

6 Sigmund Freud, *The Interpretation of Dreams*, trans. James Strachey (New York: Avon Books, 1965), 588–9.

7 Roman Jakobson and Linda Waugh, "The Spell of Speech Sounds," in Stephen Rudy, ed., *Roman Jakobson: Selected Writings*, 8 vols (Berlin: Mouton de Gruyter, 1962–88), 8: 181–234.

8 For example, by Eco, *Theory of Semiotics*, 191–217; cf. Thomas Sebeok, *The Sign and Its Masters* (Austin: University of Texas Press, 1979), 112–13, 115.

9 See, for example, Jakobson and Waugh, "The Spell of Speech Sounds"; Leanne Hinton, Johanna Nichols, and John J. Ohala, eds, *Sound Symbolism* (Cambridge: Cambridge University Press, 1994); Costantino Maeder, Olga Fischer, and William J. Herlofsky, eds, *Outside-in–Inside-out: Iconicity in Language and Literature 4* (Amsterdam and Philadelphia: John Benjamins, 2005).

10 Yelle, *Explaining Mantras*, 75.

11 Maeder, et al., *Outside-in–Inside-out*, 4.

12 Ernst Cassirer, *Language and Myth* (New York: Dover, 1953), 49.

13 Friedrich Max Müller, *Lectures on the Science of Language*, 2 vols (London: Longmans, Green and Co., 1877), 2: 572–4.

14 Brian Vickers, "Analogy Versus Identity: The Rejection of Occult Symbolism, 1580–1680," in *Occult and Scientific Mentalities in the Renaissance* (Cambridge: Cambridge University Press, 1984), 95–163, esp. 95.

15 See discussion and references in Chapter Six.

16 In addition to the discussion of *bandhu* later in this chapter, see *Rig Veda* 10.125.

17 Cassirer, *Language and Myth*, 46.

18 Mircea Eliade, *Myth and Reality*, trans. Willard Trask (New York: Harper and Row, 1968), 16.

19 Yelle, *Explaining Mantras*, 24–8.

20 In addition to the discussion of this issue in connection with John Bulwer below, see Maurice Olender, *The Languages of Paradise: Race, Religion, and Philology in the Nineteenth Century*, trans. Arthur Goldhammer (Cambridge, MA: Harvard University Press, 2009).

21 On *bandhu*, see Brian K. Smith, *Reflections on Resemblance, Ritual, and Religion* (New York: Oxford University Press, 1988); Patrick Olivelle, *The Early Upaniṣads* (New York: Oxford University Press, 1998), 25.

22 For example, *Bṛhadāraṇyaka Upaniṣad* 1.4.17, 4.1; in Olivelle, *Early Upaniṣads*.

23 *Chāndogya Upaniṣad* 6 provides a good example of this: everything is said to be composed of three different fundamental essences, which in later Hindu philosophy are called the three strands or qualities (*guṇa*).

24 *Bṛhadāraṇyaka Upaniṣad* 1.2.1–2. Trans. Olivelle.

25 Yelle, *Explaining Mantras*, 26.

26 Johanna Drucker, *The Alphabetic Labyrinth: The Letters in History and Imagination* (London: Thames and Hudson, 1995), 56.

27 Yelle, *Explaining Mantras*, 55.

28 *Padārthādarśa*, commentary on *Śāradātilaka Tantra*, 14.91. Arthur Avalon, ed., *Śāradātilaka Tantra* (Delhi: Motilal Banarsidass, 1996).

29 D. T. Suzuki, "Painting, Swordsmanship, Tea Ceremony," in William Barrett, ed., *Zen Buddhism: Selected Writings of D. T. Suzuki* (New York: Doubleday, 1996), 335–54.

30 Yelle, *Explaining Mantras*, 24.

31 Ibid. at 40.

32 Nancy Jay, *Throughout Your Generations Forever: Sacrifice, Religion, and Paternity* (Chicago: University of Chicago Press, 1994).

33 Seth Kunin, *The Logic of Incest: A Structuralist Analysis of Hebrew Mythology* (Sheffield, UK: Sheffield Academic Press, 1995), 96–7.

34 See Jill Robbins, "Sacrifice," in Mark C. Taylor, ed., *Critical Terms for Religious Studies* (Chicago: University of Chicago Press, 1998), 285–97 at 295.

35 Lévi-Strauss, *Structural Anthropology*, 216.

36 For a related discussion of these structures and their ideological function, see Yelle, *Explaining Mantras*, 90–9.

37 Nöth, *Handbook of Semiotics*, 123, 126; Bouissac, *Encyclopedia of Semiotics*, s.v. "icon."

38 *Chāndogya Upaniṣad* 6.2–4 is the apparent source of this idea, although the term *guṇa* is not actually used there.

39 Victor Turner, "Colour Classification in Ndembu Ritual: A Problem in Primitive Classification," in Michael Banton, ed., *Anthropological Approaches to the Study of Religion* (London: Tavistock, 1966), 47–84 at 80–3. Another example is the Hohman spell against worms noted in note 55 to Chapter Two of this volume, which enumerates the worms of these three colors.

40 For a review and critique of these theories, see Claude Lévi-Strauss, *Totemism*, trans. Rodney Needham (Boston: Beacon, 1971).

41 Émile Durkheim and Marcel Mauss, *Primitive Classification*, trans. Rodney Needham (Chicago: University of Chicago Press, 1963).

42 Or six, if one includes Empedocles's two forces of attraction (*philia*) and repulsion (*neikos*).

43 Pierre Bourdieu, *Outline of a Theory of Practice*, trans. Richard Nice (Cambridge: Cambridge University Press, 1977), 224, n.48; Bruce Lincoln, "The Tyranny of Taxonomies," in *Discourse and the Construction of Society*, 137–41.

44 Émile Durkheim, *The Elementary Forms of the Religious Life*, trans. Joseph Ward Swain (New York: Free Press, 1965), 144, 148–9.

45 See the criticisms of Durkheim on this point in Yelle, *Explaining Mantras*, 114–15 and Richard Parmentier, "The Pragmatic Semiotics of Cultures," *Semiotica* 116 (1997): 1–114 at 7.

46 On this concept, see Arthur O. Lovejoy, *The Great Chain of Being: A Study of the History of an Idea* (Cambridge, MA: Harvard University Press, 1976).

47 Francisco Sizzi, *Dianoia Astronomica, Optica, Physica* (Venice, 1611). Translation from William Thompson Sedgwick and Harry Walter Tyler, *A Short History of Science* (London: Macmillan, 1917), 222–3. Cf. Francis Bacon, *The New Organon and Related Writings*, ed. Fulton H. Anderson (Englewood Cliffs, NJ: Prentice Hall, 1960), Book 1, chap. 45, p. 50.

48 Müller, *Lectures on the Science of Language*, 2: 267.

49 Trans. Olivelle.

50 Olivelle, *Early Upaniṣads*, 25.

51 Johannes Bronkhorst, "Etymology and Magic: Yāska's *Nirukta*, Plato's *Cratylus*, and the Riddle of Semantic Etymologies," *Numen* 48 (2001): 147–203 at 148.

52 Ibid. at 183–91.

53 Ibid. at 155.

54 Ibid. at 191.

55 Bronkhorst (ibid. at 163) argues that there are major differences between the *nirvacana* tradition and the Tantric analysis of the meaning of sounds, which is largely concerned not with ordinary words but with *bījas*. By contrast, Eivind Kahrs, *Indian Semantic Analysis: The* Nirvacana *Tradition* (Cambridge: Cambridge University Press, 1998), 55–97, provides an extensive analysis of *nirvacana*-type analyses in the Tantric tradition of Kashmiri Śaivism, and emphasizes the continuities between the Vedic and Tantric traditions in this regard.

56 Arthur Avalon, ed., *Kulārṇava Tantra* (Madras: Ganesh and Co., 1965).

57 Ibid., 17.54: *mananāt tattvarūpasya devasyāmita tejasaḥ trāyate sarvabhayatas tasmān mantra itīritaḥ*; my trans.

58 *Lalitāsahasranāma*, 777–9 (my trans.), in R. A. Sastry, *Lalitā Sahasranāma* (Madras: Adyar Library, 1988).

59 Yelle, *Explaining Mantras*, 14, 42–4 refers to these as "acronymic *bījas*."

60 Sanjukta Gupta, trans., *Lakṣmī Tantra* (Delhi: Motilal Banarsidass, 2000).

61 Arthur Avalon, *The Garland of Letters* (Madras: Ganesh and Co., 1998), 70–81.

62 *Mīmāṃsāsūtra*, 1.5. In Ganganatha Jha, *Shabara-Bhāṣya*, 3 vols (Baroda: Oriental Institute, 1933).

63 *Deśopadeśa*, 8.3., in Kahrs, *Indian Semantic Analysis*, 95 (my trans.): *guṇarahito rutakārī śiṣyavadhūnāṃ sadā gurur gaditaḥ dīnārakṣayakaraṇād dīkṣety uktā kṛtā tena.*

64 Bronkhorst, "Etymology and Magic," 169.

65 Plato, *Cratylus*, 384c.

66 See Nietzsche, "On Truth and Lying," 248, and the discussion in Yelle, *Explaining Mantras*, 64–6, 146–7.

67 Bronkhorst, "Etymology and Magic," 182.

68 For an account of these aspects of the British linguistic tradition, see also Chapter Four and Yelle, *Language of Disenchantment*, 35–6, 42–50, 55–61.

69 Thomas Hobbes, *Leviathan*, ed. Edwin Curley (Indianapolis: Hackett, 1994), chap. 34, "Of the Signification of Spirit, Angel, and Inspiration in the Books of Holy Scripture."

70 Cf. Hans Aarsleff, *From Locke to Saussure: Essays on the Study of Language and Intellectual History* (Minneapolis: University of Minnesota Press, 1982), 249. There were also religious dimensions to such projects, which are examined in relation to John Bulwer later in this chapter and in relation to Jeremy Bentham in Chapter Four.

71 Yelle, *Language of Disenchantment*, 50–5, 62–70.

72 Aarsleff, *From Locke to Saussure*, 32, 36–7, 290.

73 See, for example, Friedrich Max Müller, *Introduction to the Science of Religion*, reprint edn (Varanasi: Bharata Manisha, 1972), 147; Müller, *Chips from a German Workshop*, 5 vols (New York: Charles Scribner's Sons, 1895), 4: 65–6; Müller, *Natural Religion*, 2nd edn (London: Longmans, Green and Co., 1892), 375.

74 Müller, *Lectures on the Science of Language*, 2: 93.

75 See Chapter Two.

76 *Divyatattva*, sec. 216. Trans. Lariviere.

77 Charles K. Ogden, *Bentham's Theory of Fictions* (Paterson, NJ: Littlefield, Adams and Co., 1959), cxxiii.

78 Theodor Gomperz, *Greek Thinkers: A History of Ancient Philosophy* (London: John Murray, 1949), 399.

79 Ibid. at 399–400.

80 Ibid. at 400.

81 Ibid. at 401.

82 Ibid. at 395. Bronkhorst, "Etymology and Magic," 149, notes the same example, but for him it is just another instance of semantic etymology.

83 Friedrich Max Müller, *Lectures on the Science of Language*, 2: 99–101; Müller, *The Science of Thought*, 2 vols (New York: Charles Scribner's Sons, 1887), 200–3; Müller, *Last Essays*, *First Series* (London: Longmans, Green and Co., 1901), 20–1.

84 Müller, *Science of Thought*, 202.

85 Müller, *Chips*, 4: 217.

86 Ibid. at 2: 254–6

87 Ibid. at 2: 157–8.

88 Friedrich Max Müller, *Three Introductory Lectures on the Science of Thought* (Chicago: Open Court, 1898), 87.

89 Yelle, *Language of Disenchantment*, 53–5, 62–5. See also the discussion in Chapter Four.

90 See esp. Adam Kendon, *Gesture: Visible Action as Utterance* (Cambridge: Cambridge University Press, 1994); Ray L. Birdwhistell, *Kinesics and Context: Essays on Body Motion Communication* (Philadelphia: University of Pennsylvania Press, 1970).

91 Two versions of this quote, with different minor variations, have circulated: (1) "No, I can't explain the dance to you. If I could say it, I wouldn't have to dance it." (2) "If I could tell you what it meant, there would be no point in dancing it."

92 Roland Barthes, *The Fashion System*, trans. Richard Howard and Matthew Ward (Berkeley and Los Angeles: University of California Press, 1990).

93 Quintilian [Marcus Fabius Quintilianus], *The Orator's Education* [*Institutio oratoria*], trans. H. E. Butler (London: William Heinemann, 1921), XI.iii.86–7.

94 John Bulwer, *Chirologia: or the Natural Language of the Hand* and *Chironomia: or the Art of Manual Rhetoric*, ed. James W. Cleary (Carbondale: Southern Illinois University Press, 1974 [1644]).

95 Gilbert Austin, *Chironomia: Or a Treatise on Rhetorical Delivery*, ed. Mary Margaret Robb and Lester Thonssen (Carbondale: Southern Illinois University Press, 1966 [1809]), 467–8.

96 Florence A. Fowle Adams, *Gesture and Pantomimic Action* (New York: Edgar S. Werner, 1891), 8, 10.

97 Quintilian, *The Orator's Education*, XI.iii.88.

98 Bulwer, *Chirologia*, 163.

99 Plato, *Sophist*, 267–8.

100 Aristotle, *Poetics*, 1447a.

101 Hermann Koller, *Die Mimesis in der Antike* (Bern: A. Francke, 1954), 37.

102 Bulwer, *Chirologia*, 57; cf. ibid. at 235 and Austin, *Chironomia*, 398, 402, defending the use of the left hand in contravention of the rhetorical tradition.

103 Henry Home [Lord Kames], *Elements of Criticism*, quoted in Austin, *Chironomia*, 470–1. Cf. Johann Jakob Engel, *Ideen zu einer Mimik*, trans. Henry Siddons as *Practical Illustrations of Rhetorical Gesture and Action*, 2nd edn (London: Sherwood, Neely, and Jones, 1822), 7–8: "I conclude, therefore, that this sign is *natural* and *essential*, because it is *general*, and holds place with all people . . . I do not know of any one country on the face of the earth, any one class of men who would strive to express esteem, respect, or veneration, by lifting up their heads, or seeming to give additional height to their stature; as, on the contrary, I am inclined to believe that there is no nation or body of men who do not express pride and contempt by a deportment exactly the reverse; that is to say, by an exaltation of the head, by a straightening of the back, and sometimes erecting themselves on their toes, to give an air more commanding and imposing to the general contour of the figure."

104 Robert Hertz, "The Pre-eminence of the Right Hand: A Study in Religious Polarity," in Rodney Needham, ed., *Right and Left: Essays on Dual Symbolic Classification* (Chicago: University of Chicago Press, 1973), 3–31.

105 Barry Schwartz, *Vertical Classification: A Study in Structuralism and the Sociology of Knowledge* (Chicago: University of Chicago Press, 1981).

106 See references in note 22 to Chapter One.

107 On the religious dimensions of these projects, see Yelle, *Language of Disenchantment*, 87–8, 89–92; and Robert Stillman, *The New Philosophy*

and Universal Languages in Seventeenth-Century England: Bacon, Hobbes, and Wilkins (Lewisburg, PA: Bucknell University Press, 1995), 15–16.

108 See discussion in Yelle, *Language of Disenchantment*, 90.

109 Francis Bacon, *New Atlantis* (1626), in *The Works of Francis Bacon*, ed. James Spedding, Robert Leslie Ellis, and Douglas Denon Heath (Cambridge: Riverside Press and New York: Hurd and Houghton, 1869), 5: 372–3. See Lewis, *Language, Mind and Nature*, 19 for a discussion of this passage.

110 John Wilkins, *An Essay towards a Real Character and a Philosophical Language* (London: printed for Samuel Gellibrand, 1668).

111 See esp. Robert Hunt, discussed in Yelle, *Language of Disenchantment*, 92, 219n109.

112 See Bulwer, *Chirologia*, xiii–xxxix; Jeffrey Wollock, "John Bulwer (1606–1656) and the Significance of Gesture in 17th-century Theories of Language and Cognition," *Gesture* 2 (2002): 227–58; Kendon, *Gesture*, 25–8.

113 Bulwer, *Chirologia*, 16.

114 Ibid. at 6.

115 Ibid. at 10.

116 Ibid. at 18–19.

117 Genesis 2:19 (Vulgate).

118 Eco, *Perfect Language*, 8.

119 Wollock, "John Bulwer," 5, xiii; Russell Fraser, *The Language of Adam: On the Limits and Systems of Discourse* (New York: Columbia University Press, 1977), 88; Mary M. Slaughter, *Universal Languages and Scientific Taxonomy in the Seventeenth Century* (Cambridge: Cambridge University Press, 1982), 85.

120 Bulwer, *Chirologia*, 16.

121 Macdonald Critchley, *Silent Language* (London: Butterworths, 1975), 56–7.

122 Bulwer, *Chirologia*, 114, 116.

123 Ibid. at 212.

124 Wilkins, "Dedicatory Epistle"; John Locke, *An Essay concerning Human Understanding*, 2 vols (New York: Dover, 1959 [1690]), 2: 130–1.

125 Bulwer, *Chirologia*, 149.

126 Mandakranta Bose, *Movement and Mimesis: The Idea of Dance in the Sanskritic Tradition* (Dordrecht: Kluwer Academic Publishers, 1991), 18; Phillip Zarrilli, *The Kathakali Complex* (New Delhi: Abhinav Publications, 1984), 126.

127 N. P. Unni, trans., *Nāṭyaśāstra* (Delhi: Nag Publishers, 1998), chap. 9.

128 Manomohan Ghosh, trans., *Abhinayadarpaṇa*, 2nd edn (Calcutta: K. L. Mukhopadhyay, 1957), v.186.

129 Unni, *Nāṭyaśāstra*, chap. 9, vv. 97–8.

130 Ghosh, *Abhinayadarpaṇa*, v. 37 (my trans.).

131 Unni, *Nāṭyaśāstra*, chap. 1, v. 112; Bose, *Movement and Mimesis*, 75.

132 Bose, *Movement and Mimesis*, 28–9.

133 Unni, *Nāṭyaśāstra*, chap. 4, v. 269.

134 Cf. Bose, *Movement and Mimesis*, 15.

135 Ananda Coomaraswamy and Gopala Kristnayya Duggirala, trans., *The Mirror of Gesture* (New Delhi: Munshiram Manoharlal, 1970), 4.

136 Zarrilli, *The Kathakali Complex*, 129.

137 Ibid. at 128–9.

138 Eliade, *Patterns*, 32, 410.

139 Unni, *Nāṭyaśāstra*, chap. 1, v. 15.

140 Ibid., chap. 1, v. 19.

141 Ibid., chap. 1, v. 66.

142 See, for example, Premakumar, *The Language of Kathakali: A Guide to Mudrās* (Allahabad and Karachi: Kitabistan, 1948), 18–19.

143 Bose, *Movement and Mimesis*, vii, 2, 33, 51.

144 André Padoux, "Contributions à l'étude du mantraśāstra 2: Le *Nyāsa*, l'imposition rituelle des *mantra*," *Bulletin de l'école française d'extrême orient* 67 (1980): 59–102 at 62, n.1. See also Padoux, "Nyāsa: The Ritual Placing of Mantras," in *Tantric Mantras: Studies on Mantrasastra* (Oxford and New York: Routledge, 2011), 54–80.

145 Yelle, *Explaining Mantras*, 38–41.

146 Ibid. at 41.

CHAPTER FOUR

1 Yelle, *Language of Disenchantment*, 11, 18–24, 30–1.

2 Max Weber, *The Protestant Ethic and the Spirit of Capitalism*, trans. Talcott Parsons (New York: Charles Scribner's Sons, 1958), 105. See Yelle, *Language of Disenchantment*, ix, 7–8, 11, 30–1.

3 Bacon, *New Organon*, Book 1, chap. 59–60, pp. 56–8.

4 W. P. Stephens, *The Theology of Huldrych Zwingli* (Oxford: Clarendon Press, 1986), 218–50.

5 Tertullian, *Adversus Marcionem*, trans. as "The Five Books against Marcion," in Alexander Roberts and James Donaldson, eds, *The Ante-Nicene Fathers* (Grand Rapids, MI: Wm. B. Eerdmans Publishing Company, 1951), 3: 269–474; Augustine, *Contra Faustum Manichaeum*, trans. as "Reply to Faustus the Manichaean," in Philip Schaff, ed., *A Select Library of the Nicene and Post-Nicene Fathers* (Grand Rapids, MI: Wm. B. Eerdmans Publishing Company, 1956), 4: 155–345.

6 For example, John Weemes, *An Explanation of the Ceremoniall Lawes of Moses, As They Are Annexed to the Tenne Commandements* (London: printed by T. Cotes for John Bellamie, 1632), 176; John Lightfoot, *The Works of the Reverend and Learned John Lightfoot* (London: printed by W. R. for Robert Scot, Thomas Basset, and Richard Chiswell, 1684), 1187.

7 John Toland, *Christianity Not Mysterious* (London: printed for Samuel Buckley, 1696), 115.

8 Ibid. at 73.

9 See discussion in Chapter Three.

10 Hobbes, *Leviathan*, chap. 4, sec. 21.

11 See Yelle, *Language of Disenchantment*, chapter 2.

12 Robert Merton, *Science, Technology & Society in Seventeenth-Century England* (New York: Harper Torchbooks, 1970).

13 Thomas Sprat, *History of the Royal Society* (London: printed by T. R. for J. Martyn and J. Allestry, 1667), 362–3.

14 Jones's contributions to the issue are contained mainly in three articles: "Science and English Prose Style in the Third Quarter of the Seventeenth Century," *PMLA* 45 (1930); "The Attack on Pulpit Eloquence in the Restoration: An Episode in the Development of the Neo-Classical Standard for Prose," *Journal of English and Germanic Philology* 30 (1931); and "Science and Language in England of the Mid-Seventeenth Century," *Journal of English and Germanic Philology* 31 (1932). These articles were republished in Jones, *The Seventeenth Century: Studies in the History of English Thought and Literature from Bacon to Pope* (Stanford: Stanford University Press, 1951).

15 See Jones, *The Seventeenth Century*, 114, n.8 and 124, respectively.

16 In addition to 2 Corinthians 3: 12–13 (KJV), cited in note 17 to Chapter One, see Alexander Nowell, *A True Report of the Disputation or Rather Private Conference Had in the Tower of London, with Ed. Campion Jesuite* (London: printed by Christopher Barker, 1583): ". . . and yet in this plaine style, the Apostle [Paul in Corinthians] was of al others most mightie & most eloquent"; Anthony Burgess, *Spiritual Refining: Or a Treatise of Grace and Assurance* (London: printed by A. Miller for Thomas Underhill, 1652), 497: "the simple and plain stile of the Scripture . . . this plain way of Gods Word preached. . . ."; Thomas Fuller, *Abel Redevivus or, The Dead Yet Speaking* (London: printed by Thomas Brudnell for John Stafford, 1652), 444: "the plaine stile of the Scripture . . ."; Joseph Glanvill, *A Seasonable Defence of Preaching and the Plain Way of It* (London: printed by M. Clarke for H. Brome, 1678). For a general discussion of these ideas, see Peter Auksi, *Christian Plain Style: The Evolution of a Spiritual Ideal* (Montréal: McGill-Queen's University Press, 1995).

17 C. John Sommerville, "The Secularization of Language," in *The Secularization of Early Modern England* (New York: Oxford University Press, 1992), 44–54 at 50.

18 Harrison, *The Bible*, 116.

19 Keane, *Christian Moderns*, 77–9, 179–81. This anthropological category was originally from a Portuguese word, and was developed most famously by the Frenchman Charles De Brosses, whose *Du culte des dieux fétiches* ([Paris],1760) purported to find the origins of primitive religion in the worship of rude objects as divine. Although not specific to Protestantism, the critique of primitive religion as a mistaken worship of the symbol in place of the reality is most closely associated with the iconoclasm inspired by the Reformation, and

Keane accordingly grants a privileged place to Protestants as the vanguard of the modern critique of the fetish.

20 Tertullian (*c*. 160–225 CE), *De praescriptione*, vii. Trans. as "The Prescription against Heretics," in Roberts and Donaldson, *The Ante-Nicene Fathers*, 3: 243–65 at 246.

21 Cf. Jan Assmann's concepts of the "Mosaic distinction" and of "counterreligions." Assmann, *The Price of Monotheism*, trans. Robert Savage (Stanford: Stanford University Press, 2010), 1–4.

22 See Bruce Lincoln, "Revolutionary Exhumations in Spain," in *Discourse and the Construction of Society*, 103–27.

23 Yelle, *Language of Disenchantment*, 113–15.

24 Ibid. at 29, 68, 87–8, 92, 95, 96–7.

25 Ibid. at 50–5, 61–70.

26 Müller, *Chips*, 1: 351.

27 Friedrich Max Müller, *Theosophy or Psychological Religion* (London: Longmans, Green and Co., 1903), ix.

28 Bentham, *Works*, 10: 570.

29 Ibid. at 3: 63; cf. 3: 209.

30 Ibid. at 3: 205, 211.

31 H. L. A. Hart, "Positivism and the Separation of Law and Morals," *Harvard Law Review* 71 (1958), 593, 596–7, 616 (quoting John Austin on the separation of law from religion).

32 William Graham, *Beyond the Written Word: Oral Aspects of Scripture in the History of Religion* (Cambridge: Cambridge University Press, 1987); Laurie Patton, ed., *Authority, Anxiety, and Canon: Essays in Vedic Interpretation* (Albany: SUNY Press, 1994); Miriam Levering, *Rethinking Scripture: Essays from a Comparative Perspective* (Albany: SUNY Press, 1989).

33 Smith, "Sacred Persistence," in *Imagining Religion*, 43.

34 Ibid.

35 See Costas Douzinas and Lynda Nead, ed., *Law and the Image: The Authority of Art and the Aesthetics of Law* (Chicago: University of Chicago Press, 1999).

36 Cf. Pierre Bourdieu, "The Force of Law: Toward a Sociology of the Juridical Field," *Hastings Law Journal* 38 (1987): 814, 820.

37 Barbara Shapiro, "Codification of the Laws in Seventeenth-Century England," *Wisconsin Law Review* 2 (1974): 428, 430, 449–50, 455.

38 Ibid. at 430.

39 Indeed, Bentham disapproved of the code developed in the Massachusetts Bay Colony in the 1630s and 1640s, which borrowed from Biblical law, most notably by using the Ten Commandments as a framework for defining capital crimes. Cf. Jeremy Bentham, *A Comment on the Commentaries and A Fragment on Government*, ed. J. H. Burns and H. L. A. Hart (London: Athlone Press, 1977), 25–7, 200. For the code in question, see *The Book of the General Lawes and Libertyes concerning the Inhabitants of the Massachusets*

(Cambridge, MA: printed by [Matthew Day] according to order of the General Court, 1648), facsimile ed., (San Marino, CA: The Huntington Library, 1975). See George Lee Haskins, *Law and Authority in Early Massachusetts: A Study in Tradition and Design* (New York: Macmillan, 1960) for a comprehensive account of this code and its context.

40 Gerald Postema, *Bentham and the Common Law Tradition* (Oxford: Oxford University Press, 1986), 425. The phrase "Luther of Jurisprudence" appears in Bentham, *Works*, 7: 270; 2: 477 extends the comparison between his movement for legal reform and the earlier religious Reformation. Postema's analogy between Bentham's codification proposal and that of the radical Levellers is apposite. *See also* H. L. A. Hart, *Essays on Bentham: Studies in Jurisprudence and Political Theory* (Oxford: Oxford University Press, 1982), 29.

41 Bentham, *Works*, 1: vii; Bentham also compared himself to the same Jewish patriarch (ibid. at 1: 172).

42 Jeremy Bentham, *University College Manuscript Collection*, xcvii.94–5, xxvii.124, quoted in David Lieberman, *The Province of Legislation Determined: Legal Theory in Eighteenth-Century Britain* (Cambridge: Cambridge University Press, 1989), 253.

43 Bentham, *Works*, 4: 332, 483; 5: 236; 7: 189; Bentham, *Auto-Icon; or, Farther Uses of the Dead to the Living* 2, in James Crimmins, ed., *Bentham's Auto-Icon and Related Writings* (Bristol: Thoemmes Press, 2002).

44 Bentham, *Works*, 4: 484.

45 Jeremy Bentham, *Church-of-Englandism and its Catechism Examined* (London: Effingham Wilson, 1818), Introduction, 9–10.

46 Assaf Likhovski, "Protestantism and the Rationalization of English Law: A Variation on a Theme by Weber," *Law and Society Review* 33 (1999): 365–91, has extended Weber's thesis of an intimate association between Protestantism and rationalization to the domain of law. Likhovski argues that the early codification proposals advanced by the Levellers and Diggers were deeply influenced by the Reformation. Various of these proposals for legal reform exhibited the influence of parallel theological movements: that to replace the unwritten common law with a written code echoed the doctrine of *sola scriptura* (374–5); that to simplify the language of the law reflected Protestant "plain style" (370); that to replace Law French with English as the medium of legal discourse resembled religious movements for vernacularization (376). Only the latter proposal was successful, albeit temporarily, under Cromwell's reign, from the early 1650s to 1658 (369). Likhovski suggests that "Demands for radical law reform similar to those made by the Radicals appeared in the legal thought of reformers like Jeremy Bentham," although he allows that these developments may have been unconnected (385 and n.7). Bentham (*Works*, 4: 501) does refer approvingly to Cromwell's ideas for legal reform. In fact, the two parallel reform movements were connected, if only through their mutual dependence on the very features of the Protestant tradition that Likhovski has pointed to.

47 Goodrich, *Oedipus Lex*, ix, 11, 44, 63, 65, 103, n.146.

48 Bentham, *Comment*, 411; Bentham, *Works*, 1: 235, note.

49 This was actually a process that began in 1362 with the Statute of Pleading, which required proceedings to be conducted in English but provided for records to be made in Latin. 36 Edward III c.15 (AD 1326). Cromwell's requirement to use English as the language of the records, reversed under Charles II, was again enforced by George II. 4 George II c.26 (AD 1731).

50 A number of scholars have provided illuminating interpretations of Bentham's concept of fictions, although none has previously noted the extent of its religious dimensions. See Charles K. Ogden, *Bentham's Theory of Fictions* (London: Kegan Paul, Trench, Trubner and Co., 1932); Lon Fuller, *Legal Fictions* (Stanford: Stanford University Press, 1967); Mary Mack, *Jeremy Bentham: An Odyssey of Ideas* (New York: Columbia University Press, 1963), 151–203; James Steintrager, *Bentham* (Ithaca: Cornell University Press, 1977), 20–43; Hart, *Essays*, 21–39; Gerald Postema, "Fact, Fictions, and Law: Bentham on the Foundations of Evidence," in William Twining, ed., *Facts in Law* (Wiesbaden: Steiner, 1983), 37–64; Bernard Jackson, "Truth and the Semiotics of Law," *Current Legal Problems* 51 (1998): 493–531; Nomi Maya Stolzenberg, "Bentham's Theory of Fictions: A 'Curious Double Language'," *Cardozo Journal of Law and Literature* 11 (1999): 223–61.

51 Bentham, *Works*, 1: 41 (Introduction).

52 Ibid., 8: 198.

53 Emmanuelle de Champs, "The Place of Jeremy Bentham's Theory of Fictions in Eighteenth-Century Linguistic Thought," *Journal of Bentham Studies* 2 (1999): 10, http://ucl.ac.uk/Bentham-Project/journal/nldechmp.htm, correctly locates Bentham within the nominalist tradition reinvigorated by Hobbes.

54 Bentham, *Works*, 2: 448–9; cf. 8: 249–50.

55 Ibid. at 8: 206.

56 Ibid. at 10: 77.

57 Ibid. at 8: 342.

58 Ibid. at 8: 238–9.

59 Ibid. at 10: 75.

60 Ibid. at 11: 73; cf. 1: 205: "By habit, whenever a man sees a name, he is led to figure to himself a corresponding object, of the reality of which the *name* is accepted by him, as it were of course, in the character of a *certificate*."

61 Ibid. at *Works*, 8: 199; cf. 9: 77. See also L. J. Hume, "The Political Functions of Bentham's Theory of Fictions," *The Bentham Newsletter* 3 (Dec. 1979), at 18, 19. Bentham acknowledged the utility, indeed the necessity, of some fictions in logic and language. Bentham, *Works*, 8: 119; see also ibid. at 8: 198. Fictions served as a kind of shorthand, and could enrich language through figuration. Ibid. at 8: 318–19. All language was figurative to some degree. However, the goal was to limit the use of fictions to only those that were absolutely necessary. Ibid. at 8: 331.

62 Bentham identified two related methods for dealing with fictions: paraphrasis and archetypation. Bentham, *Works*, 8: 126–7, note; 8: 246. An admirably clear description of what Bentham meant by these terms appears in Philip

Schofield, *Utility and Democracy: The Political Thought of Jeremy Bentham* (Oxford: Oxford University Press, 2006), 23–6. Paraphrasis consisted of replacing the fiction with the name of a corresponding real entity in a sentence: for example, "The Church requires support from its members" would become "The clergy beg money from parishioners." Archetypation consisted of reducing a fiction, so far as possible, to the underlying material image on which it was based: thus, for the abstract term "obligation," think of the concrete image of a cord or tie, on which the Latin root *ligo* and its English derivative "obligation" ultimately depended. This method was close to etymological analysis, which had been used by Bentham's predecessors, Locke and Horne Tooke, for a similar purpose. Bentham's nominalism also led him to adopt "the substantive-preferring principle," a preference for the use of nouns over verbs, which meant replacing many complex verbs with simpler verbs such as "have" or "take," combined with noun phrases. Bentham, *Works*, 8: 315, 1: 8, 3: 267, 10: 569.

63 Bentham frequently referred to Bacon and even referred to part of his own works as "nova organa." Bentham, *Works*, 3: 285. He depicted himself as the successor of Bacon, Locke, and Newton. Ibid. at 10: 588. Bacon was interested in legal codification, and may have served as another, indirect influence on Bentham's ideas for legal reform. Barbara Shapiro, "Codification," 445, states that "the ideas on law reform, codification, and simplification which are to be found in this book [Bacon's *De augmentis scientarum*] were one major source of the movement for codification which was so prominent during the interregnum years."

64 A late representative of this tradition, Charles K. Ogden (1889–1957), snatched Bentham's theory of fictions from the dustbin of history in order to give philosophical support to his proposal for a "Basic English" consisting only of the most common and useful terms, shorn of redundancy and ambiguity. See Ogden, *Bentham's Theory of Fictions*; Ogden, *Basic English: A General Introduction with Rules and Grammar* (London: Kegan Paul, Trench, Trubner and Co., 1930).

65 Bentham, *Works*, 10: 22. Bentham states that legal codification would have been impossible before Locke's epistemology. Ibid. at 10: 70; cf. 10: 142.

66 Ibid. at 3: 286.

67 Ibid. at 8: 120: "And in that work [*Diversions of Purley*], . . . by *Horne Tooke*, the distinction, between names of *real* and names of *fictitious* entities, will constitute a capital and altogether indispensable instrument." See James Crimmins, *Secular Utilitarianism: Social Science and the Critique of Religion in the Thought of Jeremy Bentham* (Oxford: Oxford University Press, 1990), 34–5, for Bentham's relation to Tooke. See de Champs, "The Place of Jeremy Bentham's Theory of Fictions," for a general discussion of the intellectual ancestry of Bentham's linguistics.

68 Bentham, *Works*, 8: 150; cf. 8: 126, note; 8: 327.

69 Bentham probably took the specific etymological analysis of "spirit" from either Locke or Horne Tooke. Bentham, *Works*, 8: 120. See de Champs, 11–12 and nn.72, 74. De Champs notes the occurrence of this formula in Locke, Horne Tooke, and Bentham. Hobbes, *Leviathan*, chap. 34, appears to be its original

source. Like Hobbes, Bentham blamed the Greeks; he claimed that Plato and Aristotle were most guilty of perpetuating such pneumatology. Bentham, *Works*, 8: 120. James Crimmins has argued that the references to Hobbes in Bentham's oeuvre are few and equivocal. James Crimmins, "Bentham and Hobbes: An Issue of Influence," *Journal of the History of Ideas* 63 (2002): 677–96 at 683–6.

70 Bentham, *Works*, 8: 84, note.

71 Ibid. at 8: 329. Cf. ibid. at 8: 120: "In speaking of any *pneumatic* (or say *immaterial* or *spiritual*) object, no name has ever been employed, that had not first been employed as the name of some *material* (or say *corporeal*) one."

72 Ibid. at 8: 121–6. See also Postema, *Bentham*, 433; Lieberman, *The Province of Legislation Determined*, 263.

73 Bentham's encyclopedic classification of language explicitly invoked the precedent of John Wilkins's real character and philosophical language. However, Bentham faulted Wilkins for his lack of empiricism, which had led him to begin his classification with incorporeal concepts. Bentham, *Works*, 8: 150–5. Wilkins's classification of concepts had begun by distinguishing between "Being" and "Nothing," "Thing" and "Apparence," "Notion" and "Fiction." In the last category he enumerated a set of examples including "Mythology, Fairy, Nymph, Centaur, Griffin, Bugbear, Goblin, Chymera, Atlantis, Utopia." Wilkins, *Essay*, 26. Although Bentham criticized Wilkins for beginning with such non-entities, rather than from empirical reality, Bentham's own classification of entities began with a very similar division into "real" and "fictitious" entities, and his category of "fabulous entities" closely paralleled Wilkins's "fictions." For both thinkers, the attack on the names of mythological beings played an important role in their respective projects of purifying language of its fictions.

74 Bentham, *Works*, 8: 196; cf. 8: 189, 208. Bentham distinguishes between God and the soul, however, in the following way: if not an inferential real entity, God is to be classified as a non-entity, whereas the soul, if taken as unreal, would instead be a fiction depending on the abstraction of the various faculties of the human intellect. See ibid. at 8: 196, note.

75 Ibid. at 8: 196. Although Bentham attributes this statement to St. Paul, who says something quite similar at 1 Timothy 6:16, the statement itself is actually found at John 1:18 (KJV).

76 Bentham, *Works*, 8: 196, note. Non-entities overlap with another category Bentham distinguished elsewhere, namely "fabulous entities," which included "*Heathen Gods, Genii*, and *Fairies*" (ibid. at 8: 126, note), as well as "Gods of different dynasties,—kings, such as Brute and Fergus,—animals, such as dragons and chimaeras,—countries, such as El Dorado . . ." (8: 262, note). Fabulous entities are those of which, although they do not exist, real existence can be predicated. Unlike fictitious entities, they raise up specific, though erroneous, mental images (8: 262–3).

77 Bentham, *Works*, 8: 129.

78 In addition to Bacon, Wilkins, and Hobbes, Bentham had read Bishop William Warburton's *Divine Legation of Moses*, 2 vols (London, 1737–41), which presented a linguistic interpretation of pagan polytheism and located the cause of idolatry especially in Egyptian "hieroglyphs," a term Bentham used

occasionally to refer to the Common Law. *Works*, 1: 235, 3: 206; cf. Bentham's reference to orthodox religion as a set of "hieroglyphical chimeras," in Crimmins, *Secular Utilitarianism*, 123. For Bentham's references to Warburton, see Bentham, *Works*, 2: 391, note; 2: 449; 10: 73, 143; letter to Samuel Parr dated January 27, 1804, in Jeremy Bentham, *The Correspondence of Jeremy Bentham*, ed. Timothy Sprigge, et. al., 12 vols (London: Athlone Press and Oxford: Oxford University Press, 1968–2006), 7: 259–62 at 261 and Bentham, *Works*, 10: 411–12 at 412; letter to Étienne Dumont dated May 14, 1802, in Bentham, *Correspondence*, 7: 24–9 at 25; UC, 69/140 (quoted in Crimmins, *Secular Utilitarianism*, 82). On Bentham's relation to Warburton, see Crimmins, *Secular Utilitarianism*, 94, 160.

79 Bentham, *Works*, 8: 77.

80 Ibid. at 8: 125; see also 2: 501.

81 Ibid. at 8: 77; cf. 9: 76; 1: 104 and 3: 170 refer to religion as an "allegorical personage."

82 Ibid. at 2: 448–9; see also 8: 249–50.

83 Ibid. at 2: 448.

84 Bentham, *Comment*, 399.

85 Bentham, *Comment*, 7; cf. 162. Bentham attacked the idea of natural law on similar grounds, arguing that the "Law of Nature" is "a *word* . . . ripened into a *tangible substance*" (Bentham, *Works*, 8: 21); and the common law, although granted priority by lawyers, is actually the "Shadow of the Statute Law," as it was only from the existence of statutes that the word "law" could have been abstracted in the first place (8: 119). Common Law, or the Law of Nature with which Blackstone paired it, described a fiction, a "set of imaginary objects" (8: 11), a "metaphorical personage" (8: 216), a "non-entity" (8: 20), a "mask . . . varnished" (8: 124), personified as Blackstone's "Divinity the Common Law" (8: 228), which made his discourse a "theological grimgribber" (8: 10).

86 William Blackstone, *Commentaries on the Laws of England* (Oxford: Clarendon Press, 1765–69), reprint edn (Chicago: University of Chicago Press, 1979), 1: 69.

87 Bentham, *Comment*, 195, expanded this analogy between the common law and idolatry: "The Common Law, in order to make it the fitter for adoration, was to be turned into an abstruse and invisible quiddity and which like certain Tyrants of the earth, was never to show itself in public: like them it was to make its existence perceivable only by means of its delegates: these judicial decisions, which whenever the Common Law was asked for were to be produced *corum populo* [in public], as the ostensible images of its person, not as themselves being that thing, but as evidences of there being such a thing somewhere. Thus, to use our Author's [Blackstone's] own apposite similitude, the Oracles were not the words of the Pythia that spake them, but her words were the evidence of an *Apollo* whose oracles they were." Bentham here shifts to a different meaning of "oracle": not the one who speaks the words of the deity, but the words themselves. Cf. Bentham, *Works*, 2: 502, where he attacks the "French oracle" that divines the fiction of "natural rights."

88 Bentham, *Works*, 10: 483.

89 Acts 19:28, 19:34, 17:23.

90 Bentham, *Works*, 10: 483–4.

91 Bentham, *Auto-Icon*, 2.

92 Ibid. at 3.

93 Ibid. at 2.

94 Ibid. at 5.

95 See, for example, Richard Hooker, *Of the Lawes of Ecclesiasticall Politie* (London: printed by Will. Stansby, 1617), Book 5, chap. 75, pp. 401–4 (addressing such Puritan objections).

96 Bentham, *Auto-Icon*, 16.

97 Bentham, *Works*, 2: 392–3, 399.

98 Bentham, *Auto-Icon*, 3.

99 Ibid. at 15.

100 Crimmins, *Secular Utilitarianism*, 287.

101 Ibid. at 205, 211, 271, 282.

102 During his lifetime, Bentham published several major writings on religion: *Church-of-Englandism*; *An Analysis of the Influence of Natural Religion*, with George Grote; and *Not Paul, But Jesus* (London: John Hunt, 1823), with Francis Place. The second and third were published under the pseudonyms Philip Beauchamp and Gamaliel Smith, respectively, presumably to avoid public criticism and a potential blasphemy charge. (Crimmins, *Secular Utilitarianism*, 207.) Bentham published *Church-of-Englandism* under his own name because his publisher refused to print the work otherwise; to have done so would have been to expose the publisher himself to greater risk for prosecution. (Crimmins, *Secular Utilitarianism*, 163; Delos B. McKown, *Behold the Antichrist: Bentham on Religion* (Amherst, NY: Prometheus Books, 2004), 306, n.1.) Bentham's concern over the reception of this work can be seen in his letter dated January 24, 1818, to William Smith, in Bentham, *Correspondence*, 9: 151–3.) Also noteworthy among Bentham's writings on religion is the satirical pamphlet "Auto-Icon" discussed above. None of these writings appeared in the collected edition of Bentham's works published in 1843 by his disciple and executor, John Bowring, a circumstance that has hindered the proper appreciation of Bentham's ideas on religion. Recently, especially through the efforts of James Crimmins, some of these writings have been republished and reinterpreted. For more recent interpretations of Bentham's works on religion, see McKown, *Behold the Antichrist*; Schofield, *Utility*, esp. chapter 7, "The Church," 171–98, and the discussion of the Auto-Icon at 337–42. McKown sympathizes with Bentham's atheism. Some of Schofield's other views on Bentham's religion are discussed below. Bentham's writings on religion are at least apparently either a continuation or an extension of a standard Protestant project to purify Christianity by removing illegitimate accretions to the words of Jesus. *Church-of-Englandism* argued for the removal of any additions to the Gospel made by the Church, including the 39 articles of faith sworn to by adherents. No interpretation, including the distillation represented by the catechism, should be allowed to take the place of a direct engagement with scripture. *Not Paul, But Jesus* argued for

the illegitimacy of any additions made to Jesus's own words by the apostle Paul. *The Analysis of Natural Religion* made a characteristically utilitarian argument against religion. However, its criticisms were limited to "natural religion," which, as opposed to "revealed religion," lacked the support of scripture (Bentham, *Analysis*, iv–v; cf. 3): "Revelation alone communicates a known and authoritative code, with which the actual conduct of believers may be compared and the points of conformity or separation ascertained." (Ibid. at 59; cf. *Works*, 6: 270: ". . . in the case of *book-religions*, the original and authentic repositories of the rule of action [should] be taken for the standard, not any glosses that in later ages may have been put upon them.") Of course, this distinction avoided a direct confrontation with Christianity, which was likely Bentham's real target. He came close in this work to advocating atheism, but stopped just short of doing so (Bentham, *Analysis*, 31). Schofield, *Utility*, 186, quotes and discusses a letter from Bentham to Jean Baptiste Say dated August 4, 1823, and reproduced in Bentham, *Correspondence*, 11: 277, in which he affirms that his goal in the *Analysis* is to temporarily conciliate the proponents of revealed religion. *Not Paul, But Jesus* commenced the second part of Bentham's strategy, in which he extended his criticisms to the Christian Bible. See Schofield, *Utility*, 193.

103 Crimmins, *Secular Utilitarianism*, 174, 205, 230.

104 Ibid. at 174.

105 Ibid. at 134.

106 Ibid. at 299.

107 McKown, *Behold the Antichrist*, 267.

108 Philip Schofield, "Political and Religious Radicalism in the Thought of Jeremy Bentham," *History of Political Thought* 20 (1999): 272, 276. For a response, see James Crimmins, "Bentham's Religious Radicalism Revisited: A Response to Schofield," *History of Political Thought* 22 (2001): 494.

109 Schofield, "Political and Religious Radicalism," 280–1, 291.

110 In addition to his critique of fictions, analyzed above, several additional considerations suggest Bentham's atheism: his arguments that the testimony of declared atheists was trustworthy and judicially admissible, as these had already proved their honesty by so declaring. Bentham, *Works*, 5: 457, 7: 420–3.

111 Exodus 33:20 (RSV).

112 See note 75 in this chapter.

113 Bentham, *Works*, 11: 73. Cf. 3: 209: "The same ideas, the same words. Never employ other than a single and the same word, for expressing a single and the same idea."

114 Ibid. at 8: 315. The same Latin formula appears at 3: 260, and at 10: 561, together with its corollary: "*Ideis diversis vocabula diversa.*"

115 Ibid. at 4: 554.

116 Müller, *Science of Language*, 2: 490.

117 Fuller, *Legal Fictions*, 15.

118 Ibid. at 118.

119 Peter Goodrich, *Oedipus Lex*.

120 Douzinas and Nead, *Law and the Image*, 8–9.

121 Ibid. at 9.

122 Ibid. at 3–4.

123 Goodrich, *Oedipus Lex*, 30.

124 Friedrich Nietzsche, "The Birth of Tragedy," sec. 11, in Kaufmann, *Basic Writings*, 15–144 at 76.

125 Yelle, *Language of Disenchantment*, 18–22.

126 See Yelle, "The Rebirth of Myth?"

127 Friedrich Nietzsche, "On the Genealogy of Morals," in Kaufmann, *Basic Writings*.

128 Friedrich Nietzsche, "Beyond Good and Evil," in Kaufmann, *Basic Writings*, 179–435, e.g. at 199–200.

129 Charles Taylor, *A Secular Age* (Cambridge, MA: Harvard University Press, 2007), 37–42, 134–42, 300–7.

CHAPTER FIVE

1 Bentham, *Works*, 1: 6, note.

2 See also Bentham, *Comment*, 419, where he describes Jurisprudence as a game of "crambo," or trading rhymes. Elsewhere, Bentham stated that "The end of poetic language and the end of legal language are precisely opposite. The end of the Poet is to throw the mind into a kind of pleasing delirium. . . . The purpose of the legislator requires that both the composer and the reader be as much as possible in their sober senses . . ." (Quoted in Steintrager, 27).

3 Bentham addressed similar complaints against Blackstone: "The merit to which, as much perhaps as to any, the work stands indebted for its reputation, is the enchanting harmony of its numbers: a kind of merit that of itself is sufficient to give a certain degree of celebrity to a work devoid of every other. So much is man governed by the ear" (Bentham, *Comment*, 413–14; cf. 11, 296). On the other hand, the fact that Blackstone's poetry was *disguised* as prose became additional grounds for complaint: "Why would not our author write in rhyme? The jingle of the words would then have been a warning bell to the young student to guard against deception. The reader not expecting the plain truth of things would neither be disappointed nor misled: the false colouring spread continually over every object touched upon would have had a continual apology: and the 'King's Majesty' and the like amplifications of College-Rhetoric would have stood excused by the necessities of metre" (ibid. at 121). In his proposals for the stylistic reform of the law, Bentham criticized tautology or "virtual repetition" as well as "literal repetition," a vice he attributed to the Koran but which was admittedly less common in contemporary legal discourse. (Bentham, *Works*, 8: 271; other references to legal tautology appear in ibid. at 1: 235, 3: 208, 7: 281.) Poetry was a source of fictions, and consequently there was "between poetry and truth . . . a natural opposition . . ." (ibid. at 2: 253).

4   Indeed, as described in Chapter Four, Bentham insisted on identifying the same
    thing by the same word, and different things by different words. In his *Book of
    Fallacies*, in *Works*, 2: 450, he defined the fallacy of "sweeping classification"
    as "that way of ascribing to an individual object . . . any properties of another,
    only because the object in question is ranked in the class with the other, by
    being designated with the same name."

5   Frederick Pollock, *The Genius of the Common Law* (New York: AMS Press,
    1967 [1911]), 14–16.

6   Bentham condemned also the use of quasi-magical judicial oaths. His most
    extended treatment of this subject appeared in the essay "Swear Not at All,"
    the title of which was taken from Christ's prohibition against oath-taking
    in Matthew 5:34. Bentham, *Works*, 5: 187–229; cf. 5: 457–8. A number of
    his complaints also echoed the Puritan theologians examined just below, as
    when he compared oaths to "magical incantations," which were supposed to
    coerce the deity "from the ceremony . . . alone," or *ex opere operato*. Ibid. at
    5: 192, 194; cf. 6: 309. This was based upon the error of anthropomorphism:
    "God made man after his own image, says the text: man has returned him the
    compliment . . ." Ibid. at 6: 310.

7   For a detailed account of this theological tradition and its influence on the
    British attitude toward Hindu mantras and other practices, see Yelle, *Language
    of Disenchantment*, chapter 4.

8   Ibid. at 128–30, 134–5.

9   Ibid. at 112.

10 See Yelle, "Hindu Moses," "Moses' Veil."

11 Peter Burke, "The Repudiation of Ritual in Early Modern Europe," in *The
    Historical Anthropology of Early Modern Italy: Essays on Perception and
    Communication* (Cambridge: Cambridge University Press, 1987), 223–38.
    Cf. Douglas, "Away from Ritual," in *Natural Symbols*, 19–39; Smith, *To
    Take Place*, 99–103; Bell, "Ritual Reification," in *Ritual: Perspectives and
    Dimensions* 253–67; Asad, "Toward a Genealogy of the Concept of Ritual," in
    Genealogies of Religion, 55–79.

12 Burke, "The Repudiation of Ritual," 224.

13 Bell, *Ritual: Perspectives and Dimensions*, 255.

14 Thomas, "An Anthropology of Religion and Magic, II."

15 Tambiah, *Culture*, 153.

16 Ibid. at 153.

17 Ibid. at 161–2.

18 Ibid. at 140.

19 Ibid. at 153.

20 Ibid. at 162.

21 Ibid. at 164–6.

22 For a more extended critique of this and other cognitive theories of religion,
    see Yelle, "To Perform or Not to Perform?"

23 Harvey Whitehouse, *Arguments and Icons: Divergent Modes of Religiosity* (Oxford: Oxford University Press, 2000); Whitehouse, *Modes of Religiosity: A Cognitive Theory of Religious Transmission* (Walnut Creek, CA: AltaMira Press, 2004).

24 McCauley and Lawson, *Bringing Ritual to Mind*, 100. Bernard Hibbitts, "'Coming to Our Senses': Communication and Legal Expression in Performance Cultures," *Emory Law Journal* 41 (1992): 883, 951–2, 960, also emphasizes the contribution of performance in multiple sensory modes to memorability.

25 Whitehouse, *Modes of Religiosity*, 99.

26 Harvey Whitehouse, "Modes of Religiosity and the Cognitive Science of Religion," *Method & Theory in the Study of Religion* 16 (2004): 321–35 at 324.

27 To give another example, in some tellings of the *Rāmāyaṇa* epic, the major episodes and dramatic culmination of which can already be presumed to be known by almost all of the hearers, there is persistent reference to episodes that will emerge later in the story; and even to how the rightful king Rāma will of course eventually kill the demon Rāvaṇa. Both the *Adhyātma Rāmāyaṇa* and Tulsi Das's better-known Hindi version, the *Ramcaritmanas*, contain such devices.

28 Tambiah, *Culture*, 24–5.

29 See Theodore Vial, "Modes of religiosity and popular religious practices at the time of the Reformation," in Harvey Whitehouse and Luther H. Martin, eds, *Theorizing Religions Past: Archaeology, History, and Cognition* (Walnut Creek, CA: AltaMira Press, 2004), 143–56.

30 Smith, "Sacred Persistence" and "The Bare Facts of Ritual," both in *Imagining Religion*.

31 John Aubrey, *Remaines of Gentilisme and Judaisme*, ed. James Britten (London: Folk-Lore Society, 1881 [1686–7]), 68.

32 For a discussion, see Yelle, *Language of Disenchantment*, 124–8.

33 Eric Havelock, *Preface to Plato* (Cambridge, MA: Harvard University Press, 1963); Jack Goody and Ian Watt, "The Consequences of Literacy," *Comparative Studies in Society and History* 5 (1963): 304–45. Goody's and Havelock's arguments have by no means been accepted universally by scholars of classical Greece. Many of these agree that something like a "Greek miracle" occurred, a moment of disenchantment or skepticism that contributed to the birth of science, philosophy, and literalism, or what we might generically term "rationality." However, to account for these historical developments, they have proffered other explanations. A major point of agreement among these accounts is that there did occur in ancient Greece in association with the rise of philosophy a series of polemics against certain, more or less closely related types of discourse, including myth, poetry, and magic. See esp. Lincoln, *Theorizing Myth*, chapters 1 and 2; G. E. R. Lloyd, *Demystifying Mentalities* (Cambridge: Cambridge University Press, 1990); Marcel Detienne, *The Masters of Truth in Archaic Greece*, trans. Janet Lloyd (New York: Zone Books, 1996).

34 Havelock, *Preface to Plato*, 100. Havelock's description (ibid. at 106–7) of the association of poetry with law and politics is both exemplary of his entire argument and, for our purposes, of particular relevance: "[S]uch a society also had constant need to frame short-term directives and legal formulas which, though designed to suit specific occasions, were nevertheless required to have a life of their own in the memories of the parties concerned for varying periods of time, or else the directive failed through lack of fixity in transmission, or the legal formula became unenforceable because the parties concerned had forgotten what it was or were in dispute because of variant versions. Such directives could therefore remain effective only as they were themselves framed in rhythmic speech of which the metrical shape and formulaic style gave some guarantee that the words would be both transmitted and remembered without distortion. The colloquial word-of-mouth which in our own culture is able to serve the uses of even important human transactions remains effective only because there exists in the background, often unacknowledged, some written frame of reference or court of appeal, a memorandum or document or book. The memoranda of a culture of wholly oral communication are inscribed in the rhythms and formulas imprinted on the living memory."

35 In his essay on the decline of oracular verse, Plutarch had already invoked the mnemonic function of poetry to account for its former prevalence: "Men in those days had to have a memory for many things." He didn't explain why the need for poetry, or memory, was greater in the past, nor connect the abandonment of verse with the advent of writing. *The Oracles at Delphi No Longer Given in Verse*, sec. 27, in Plutarch, *Moralia*, vol. 5, trans. Frank Cole Babbitt (Cambridge, MA: Harvard University Press, 1936).

36 Cf. Walter Ong, *Interfaces of the Word: Studies in the Evolution of Consciousness and Culture* (Ithaca: Cornell University Press, 1977), 284–5.

37 Plato, *Phaedrus*.

38 Goody and Watt, "The Consequences of Literacy"; Jack Goody, *The Domestication of the Savage Mind* (Cambridge: Cambridge University Press, 1977), 3, cf. 1, 50; Goody, *The Logic of Writing and the Organization of Society* (Cambridge: Cambridge University Press, 1986), 37; Goody, *The Interface between the Written and the Oral* (Cambridge: Cambridge University Press, 1987), 300; Goody, *Representations and Contradictions* (Oxford: Blackwell, 1997), 15, 155–6; Goody, *The Power of the Written Tradition* (Washington and London: Smithsonian Institution Press, 2000), 46.

39 Goody, *Representations*.

40 Goody, *Power*, 106.

41 Goody, *Interface*, 99: "The domination or *tyrannie de la formule* may resemble the tyranny of rhyme in later poetry, or of alliteration in early English verse. Might it be suggested that all these three, in their elaborated forms, were written developments of features found in oral works but not in the extent and consistency with which they are later used. . . . It might . . . be possible to explain all these features in terms of the early influence of writing in formalizing and elaborating poetic utterance . . ." Cf. Goody, *Power*, 26: "Many of the techniques we think of as oral, such as the assonance of Beowulf (or of Gerald [*sic*: Gerard] Manley Hopkins), the mnemonic structure of the

Rig Veda, the formulaic composition of the Greeks, and even the very pervasive use of rhyme, seem to be rare in cultures without writing."

42 Goody, *Power*, 43; Goody, *Interface*, 294.

43 Goody, *Power*, 61–2.

44 Bernard Jackson suggests that the simpler talionic formulas appearing in the Hebrew Bible may have developed originally in a culture in which law was transmitted orally and administered in a decentralized fashion by individuals or local bodies. Jackson, *Semiotics of Biblical Law*, 272–4, 283; Jackson, "Models in Legal History," *Journal of Law & Religion* 18 (2002): 1–30. The conditions of legal performance determined the appropriateness of such formulas, which served a narrative function: they suggested but did not mandate a perfect symmetry between crime and punishment; they established a flexible standard in the absence of a more fully elaborated code; and they provided an analogical model that could be adapted as necessary. The law of talion deployed evocative and exemplary images such as "an eye for an eye," which were intended to be taken as illustrations rather than as rigid and abstract rules. For the oral dimensions of Hindu law, see Ludo Rocher, "Orality and Textuality in the Indian Context," *Sino-Platonic Papers* 49 (1994).

45 Jackson, *Semiotics of Biblical Law*, 215–25; this is in contrast to John W. Welch, ed., *Chiasmus in Antiquity: Structures, Analyses, Exegesis* (Hildesheim: Gerstenberg, 1981), 12.

46 There is, of course, another basic, almost insurmountable difficulty with this association: all of the remains we have of an oral culture in ancient Greece are, after all, written. Absent anthropological data (which, being itself written down, reintroduces the possibility of bias), we simply cannot know what a purely oral culture looks like.

47 As Stuart Blackburn has argued, in the context of Tamil-speaking colonial South Asia, printing served a diversity of uses and, in some cases, perpetuated or enhanced the authority of oral traditions such as folklore. Blackburn, *Print, Folklore, and Nationalism in Colonial India* (Delhi: Permanent Black, 2003), 11–16.

48 Walter Ong, *The Presence of the Word* (Minneapolis: University of Minnesota Press, 1981), 274; Goody, *Domestication*, 51.

49 Ruth Finnegan, "Literacy versus Non-Literacy: The Great Divide?," in Robin Horton and Ruth Finnegan, eds, *Modes of Thought: Essays in Thinking in Western and Non-Western Societies* (London: Faber & Faber, 1973), 112–44 at 140.

50 See Lucien Febvre, *The Coming of the Book: The Impact of Printing 1450–1800* (London: Verso, 1976).

51 Ong, *Presence*, 280.

52 Ibid. Ong posited a relationship between the new print culture, an orientation toward (visual) space rather than time, and the Protestant logician Pierre Ramus' (1515–72) reduction of rhetoric in favor of logic, in which "the perfect rhetoric would be to have no rhetoric at all." Walter Ong, *Ramus: Method, and the Decay of Dialogue* (Cambridge, MA: Harvard University Press, 1958), 291, 307. Peter Goodrich has traced the influence

of Ramism on the failure of the law in sixteenth-century England to develop into a discipline with a consciousness of and theoretical engagement with rhetoric. Goodrich, *Languages of Law: From Logics of Memory to Nomadic Masks* (London: Weidenfeld and Nicolson, 1990). He has also argued that printing and Protestant iconoclasm colluded in stripping the common law tradition of its former dependence on images and emblems, thereby instituting a new language of legal literalism. See pages 125–6 and note 57 in this chapter.

53 Elizabeth Eisenstein, *The Printing Press as an Agent of Change: Communications and Cultural Transformations in Early-Modern Europe* (Cambridge: Cambridge University Press, 1980), at 378–9 (discussing Weber) and 436–7 (discussing Thomas). However, Weber did link print culture to iconoclasm: "The religious devaluation of art, which usually parallels the religious devaluation of magical, orgiastic, ecstatic, and ritualistic elements in favor of ascetic, spiritualistic, and mystical virtues, is intensified by the rational and literary character of both priestly and lay education in scriptural religions." Quoted in Noel Salmond, *Hindu Iconoclasts: Rammohun Roy, Dayananda Sarasvati, and Nineteenth-Century Polemics against Idolatry* (Waterloo, ON: Wilfred Laurier Press, 2004), 126.

54 Eisenstein, *The Printing Press*, 66–7.

55 Hildred Geertz, "An Anthropology of Religion and Magic, I," *Journal of Interdisciplinary History* 6 (1975): 71–89 at 87.

56 Burke, "The Repudiation of Ritual," 238.

57 Goodrich, *Oedipus Lex*, 11; cf. 44, 65, 103, n.146.

58 For one skeptical perspective, see Richard Ross, "Communications Revolutions and Legal Culture: An Elusive Relationship," *Law and Social Inquiry* 27 (2002): 637–84.

59 Richard Bauman and Charles L. Briggs, *Voices of Modernity: Language Ideologies and the Politics of Inequality* (Cambridge: Cambridge University Press, 2003), 12; cf. 106–7.

60 Ibid. at 13.

61 Ibid.

62 More evidence for these connections is given in Yelle, *Language of Disenchantment*, Chapter 3.

63 Cf. Tzvetan Todorov's account of the Spanish conquest of the native Americans, which also focused on the role played in this development by the Europeans' possession of writing. Todorov, *The Conquest of America: The Question of the Other* (New York: Harper & Row, 1984), 61, 79–81. I am grateful to Bruce Rosenstock for directing my attention to this work.

64 Shklovsky, *Theory of Prose*, 24, cf. 26.

65 Baumann and Briggs, *Voices of Modernity*, 237–8.

66 See Ramie Targoff, *Common Prayer: The Language of Public Devotion in Early Modern England* (Chicago: University of Chicago Press, 2001).

67 King Henry VIII had allowed the distribution of the Bible in English, though only in an approved translation, beginning in 1539.

68 Cranmer associated the decline of the vernacular in the primitive Church with "juggling" and "sorcery," and with the oral/aural fixation of "talkers" and "lip-gospellers," meaning those who only hear and do not obey God's word. Cranmer, "A Confutation of Unwritten Verities," in *The Works of Thomas Cranmer*, ed. John Edmund Cox, 2 vols (Cambridge: Cambridge University Press, 1846), 2: 1–67 at 9. In his catechism of the Ten Commandments, Cranmer also identified several forms of verbal idolatry. One was the use of "painted words," rather than painted images. His example of this was the Catholic distinction between *latria*, true worship, and *dulia*, reverence of a lesser sort. *Writings of the Rev. Dr. Thomas Cranmer* (London: The Religious Tract Society, 1860), 113. Catholics agreed that to direct the former to anything other than God would constitute idolatry (*idolo-latria*). However, they argued that the lesser degree of reverence might properly be directed to the image of a saint or of Jesus Christ. According to Cranmer, another form of idolatry was giving the name "God" to things which are not God, such as the sun, moon, and stars. Ibid. at 122, cf. 80. Yet another was abusing the literal meaning of scripture. Ibid. at 123.

69 Jacob Grimm, "Von der Poesie im Recht," *Zeitschrift für geschichtliche Rechtswissenschaft* (1816), vol. 2, pt. 1, pp. 25–99; reprint edn (Darmstadt: Hermann Gentner Verlag, 1957), 39, 41–2.

70 Kenneth Stevenson, *Nuptial Blessing: A Study of Christian Marriage Rites* (New York: Oxford University Press, 1983), 80, n.52; Stevenson, "Cranmer's Marriage Vow: Its Place in the Tradition," in Paul Ayris and David Selwyn, eds, *Thomas Cranmer: Churchman and Scholar* (New York: Boydell Press, 1993), 193.

71 Palgrave, *Rise*, pt. 2: 187.

72 Ibid., note b.

73 Charles Wheatly, *A Rational Illustration of the Book of Common Prayer of the Church of England* (London: printed for J. and J. Knapton and several others, 1728), 434, suggests that this phrase referred to the physical appearance of the spouse.

74 The phrase "bonour and buxom" originally meant "gentle and obedient." John Henry Blunt, ed., *The Annotated Book of Common Prayer*, 2nd edn (London, Oxford, and Cambridge: Rivingtons, 1876), 266–7; Francis Proctor and Walter Howard Frere, *A New History of the Book of Common Prayer* (London: Macmillan, 1961), 614; Mark Searle and Kenneth Stevenson, *Documents of the Marriage Liturgy* (Collegeville, MN: Liturgical Press, 1992).

75 Stevenson, *Nuptial Blessing*, 79; Stevenson, "Cranmer's Marriage Vow," 189–98 at 190.

76 For an analysis of the marriage vow, including this crucial declaration, in terms of contract law, see Wheatly, *A Rational Illustration*, 433.

77 Diarmaid MacCulloch, *Thomas Cranmer: A Life* (New Haven: Yale University Press, 1996), 420–1; Stevenson, "Cranmer's Marriage Vow," 193, 196; Stevenson, *Nuptial Blessing*, 136. Wheatly, *A Rational Illustration*, 434–5,

contradicts this: ". . . whatever meaning those words [bonair and buxum] have been perverted to since, they originally signified no more than to be *meek* and *obedient*."

78 The Puritans instead objected that the declaration "With my body I thee worship" was a form of idolatry. See Hooker, *Of the Lawes of Ecclesiasticall Politie*, Book 5, chap. 73, p. 399.

79 Cf. John Calvin, *A Harmonie upon the Three Evangelists* (London: George Bishop, 1584), 189: "For *Battologia* signifieth a superfluous and unsaverie repetition [*supervacua est et putida repetitio*]: but *Polulogia* is a vaine babling." Another early use of the phrase "vain repetitions" was in the 1561 English translation of Calvin's *Institutes*.

80 Thomas Wilson, *The Arte of Rhetorique* (London: printed for Richard Grafton, 1553), fol. 810.

81 Ibid., fol. 89.

82 Ibid., fol. 109.

83 Philip Zaleski and Carol Zaleski, *Prayer: A History* (Boston: Houghton Mifflin, 2005), 254, point out another example of Cranmer's poetry in the formula from the funeral rite: "ashes to ashes, dust to dust." Genesis 3:19 (KJV) includes a similar phrase as part of God's curse for eating the forbidden fruit: "for dust thou art, and unto dust shalt thou return."

84 Targoff, *Common Prayer*, 57. She does not explain what she means by such prejudice against rhyme, but numerous examples have of course already been given above.

85 Cf. Yelle, *Explaining Mantras*, 87–90; Yelle, "Poetic Justice." When making a similar argument earlier, I was not yet aware of the Protestant attack on vain repetitions, nor of the contribution that print culture made to the repression of such forms of language.

86 Grimm, "Von der Poesie im Recht," 17: "[It] is completely natural and necessary for poetry that it often is not content with expressing a phrase once, but must instead repeat it again. It cannot, so to speak, stand on one foot, but requires, in order to gain peace and comfort, a second support, another phrase similar to the first. It appears to me that the principles of alliteration and rhyme rest precisely and essentially on this basis" (my trans.). Cf. ibid. at 18, 20; Shklovsky, *Theory of Prose*, 24: "form creates for itself its own content. For that reason, whenever the corresponding twin of a word is absent, its place is taken by an arbitrary or derivative word. For example: helter-skelter, topsy-turvy, pell-mell, and so on."

87 Although there is no room to treat of the German examples here, the early thirteenth-century *Sachsenspiegel* and similar texts from which Grimm drew many of his examples may have represented a codification of oral tradition.

88 Rudolph Hübner, *A History of Germanic Private Law*, trans. Francis S. Philbrick (New York: Augustus M. Kelley, 1968), 10.

89 Ibid. at 12.

90 Cohen, *The Crossroads of Justice*, 64.

91 See Yelle, "Poetic Justice."

92 Peter M. Tiersma, *Legal Language* (Chicago: University of Chicago Press, 1999), 12–15. Such views are by no means new: see John Selden, *Titles of Honour* (London: printed by William Stansby for John Helme, 1614), 15–16; Thomas Hobbes, *Leviathan*, chap. 26: "And in ancient time, before letters were in common use, the laws were many times put into verse; that the rude people, taking pleasure in singing or reciting them, might the more easily retain them in memory." In the eighteenth century, Robert Wood argued that, in Homeric Greece "all was effected by memory; and the histories of ancient times were commemorated in verses. . . . Their law was entrusted to verse, and adapted to measure and music. From all which we learn, that all was consigned to memory; and that there was no written record." *An Essay on the Original Genius and Writings of Homer* (New York: Garland, 1971 [1775]), 253–4, quoted in Bauman and Briggs, *Voices of Modernity*, 104. Cf. Numa Denis Fustel de Coulanges (1830–89), "Religious Origins of Ancient Law,", in Albert Kocourek and John H. Wigmore, eds, *Primitive and Ancient Legal Institutions* (Boston: Little, Brown, and Co.; reprint edn. Littleton, CO: Fred B. Rothman & Co., 1979), 104–10 at 108: "During long generations the laws were not written. . . . Written or unwritten, these laws were always formulated into very brief sentences, which may be compared in form to the verses of Leviticus, or the slocas of the book of Manu. It is quite probable, even, that the laws were rhythmical. According to Aristotle, before the laws were written, they were sung. Traces of this custom have remained in language; the Romans called the laws *carmina* verses; the Greeks said *nomoi* songs."

93 Palgrave, *Rise*, pt. 1: 33–4. Cf. pt. 1: 120; pt. 2: 187; Arthur Engelmann, *A History of Continental Civil Procedure*, trans. Robert Wyness Millar (New York: Augustus M. Kelley, 1969), 173; Berman, *Faith and Order*, 48; *Law and Revolution*, 58–9; Hibbitts, 901–4 (on the oral character of such Anglo-Saxon laws), 951–2, 960 (on the mnemonic function of such modes of performance generally), 875–6, 880 (on the connection of print culture with iconoclasm and attacks against various modes of performance, including oral poetry). Whitehouse, *Arguments and Icons*, 184, although not a proponent of the literacy hypothesis, has similarly associated such formulas with the doctrinal mode of transmission, which depends on repetition for its memorability. David Rubin, *Memory in Oral Tradition*, 8, 11–12, building upon the work of Lord and Parry, has argued for the contribution of alliteration and rhyme to the memorability of verbal formulas; cf. McCauley and Lawson, *Bringing Ritual to Mind*, 52–4. That poetic repetition contributes to the memorability of formulas, especially in an oral culture, seems intuitively correct. Whitehouse, *Modes of Religiosity*, 167 notes that "We know relatively little about the psychological effects of high-frequency verbal reiteration on processes of analogical thinking." However, it seems likely, if not thoroughly established scientifically, that a range of forms of verbal repetition may contribute to memorability.

94 Grendon, "The Anglo-Saxon Charms," 181, 222, 229.

95 Palgrave, *Rise*, pt. 1: 120.

96 Ibid. at pt. 2: 188. Cf. Engelmann, *A History of Continental Civil Procedure*, 174: "[T]he procedure, as a whole, was dominated by a rigorous formalism . . ., in the necessity that the act itself should satisfy certain conditions definitely fixed in advance. And the coercive force of form, thus appearing, had an all-important significance."

97 Berman, *Faith and Order*, 48; Berman, *Law and Revolution*, 59.

98 Jakobson, "Closing Statement," 357.

99 The preceding discussion indicates some significant problems with Whitehouse's theory of modes of religious transmission as applied to the Reformation. In the first place, the crucial change in modes of transmission may have occurred, not with a shift from local imagistic rituals to doctrine, but rather with the replacement of oral tradition by writing. Whitehouse's association of repetitive ritual language with the doctrinal mode fails to account for this shift, and for the decline of such language. Rather than tedium, it was a combination of the partial obsolescence of poetic language in a print culture, and of polemics directed against the rhetorical function of such language, that led to its decline in certain genres, or for certain uses. Given his emphasis on the importance of transmission, it might be expected that Whitehouse would recognize the role of writing in these developments. However, he has specifically underestimated this role. He argues that during the Reformation transmission remained largely oral, rather than written. (Whitehouse, *Modes of Religiosity*, 152.) This claim may be granted, but it does not refute the fact of the growing importance of writing at that time, especially among the elite and influential sectors of society, who were largely responsible for the developments in question. Moreover, Whitehouse's contention (ibid. at 80) that the doctrinal mode precipitated the development of writing, rather than the other way around, seems especially dubious. McCauley and Lawson, *Bringing Ritual to Mind*, 46 (cf. 52), similarly downplay the significance of writing to these differences. Although they acknowledge that there is a greater need for repetition as a device for transmission in oral cultures, they conclude that, cognitive abilities being constant, "both Whitehouse and we hold that, finally, literacy is *not* the fundamental variable in this mix" (ibid. at 108).

100 Burke, "The Repudiation of Ritual," 238.

CHAPTER SIX

1 For a general discussion of the reasons for the commandments (*mitzvot*), see Isaac Heinemann, *The Reasons for the Commandments in Jewish Thought, From the Bible to the Renaissance*, trans. Leonard Levin (Boston: Academic Studies Press, 2008).

2 See discussion and references below in this chapter.

3 See Mary Douglas's summary of such interpretations in Douglas, *Purity and Danger*, 45–6. The *locus classicus* of this interpretation is Maimonides, who claimed that certain animals were prohibited because unhealthy: for example, pigs are dirty.

4 Milgrom, *Leviticus: A Book of Ritual and Ethics*, 103, 108.

5 Apart from Douglas, some early symbolic interpretations of the kosher laws include the second century BCE *Letter of Aristeas*'s claim that certain animals represent virtues or vices, Philo Judaeus's (1st century CE) claim that the dietary laws symbolize restraint and self-control, and later Christian allegorical or typological interpretations.

6 See note 57 to Chapter Two for general works on typology. For an application of typological interpretation to the Mosaic ceremonial laws, see, for example, Weemes, *An Explanation of the Ceremoniall Lawes*, 172; Isaac Watts, *A Short View of the Whole of Scripture History* (London: printed for C. Dilly and others, 1798), 60.

7 Weemes, *An Explanation*, 172; Watts, *A Short View*, 60; cf. Jacob Milgrom, *Leviticus 1–16: A New Translation with Introduction and Commentary*, Anchor Bible, vol. 3 (New York: Doubleday, 1991), 726.

8 Weemes, *An Explanation*, 76; Watts, *A Short View*, 60. See discussion and references in Yelle, "Moses' Veil," 29. For a discussion of the "accommodation theory," see Stephen D. Benin, "The 'Cunning of God' and Divine Accommodation," *Journal of the History of Ideas* 45 (1984): 179–91; Guy Stroumsa, "John Spencer and the Roots of Idolatry," *History of Religions* (2001): 1–23; Amos Funkenstein, "Accommodation and the Divine Law," in *Theology and the Scientific Imagination: From the Middle Ages to the Seventeenth Century* (Princeton: Princeton University Press, 1986), 222–43. This idea was expressed already by Maimonides: see Heinemann, *The Reasons for the Commandments*, 113–14, who says that Maimonides applied this only to the practice of sacrifice, and not to the other commandments. These views were echoed by some modern, "scientific" interpreters: see William Robertson Smith, *Lectures on the Religion of the Semites*, 3rd edn (London: A. & C. Black, 1927); reprint edn ([New York]: Ktav Publishing House, 1969), 4.

9 Maimonides was the classic source of this explanation, which was developed by John Spencer in his *De legibus hebraeorum ritualibus et earum rationibus libri tres* (Cambridge: Richard Chiswel, 1685). See Stroumsa, "John Spencer"; Heinemann, *The Reasons for the Commandments*, 112–13.

10 Douglas, *Purity and Danger*, 2.

11 Ibid. at 4.

12 Ibid. at 53.

13 Ibid. at 39.

14 Ibid. at 43.

15 Douglas, *Purity and Danger*, 30–2.

16 Mary Douglas, "The Forbidden Animals in Leviticus," *Journal for the Study of the Old Testament* 59 (1993): 3–23 at 16, states that "The dietary laws systematically pick up the order of creation in Genesis." The taxonomy of animals preserves and replicates the separation and orderly distribution associated with the cosmogony in Genesis 1. Cf. Jean Soler, "The Semiotics of Food in the Bible," in Robert Forster and Orest Ranum, ed., *Food and Drink in History: Selections from the Annales*, vol. 5, trans. Elborg Forster and Patricia Ranum (Baltimore: Johns Hopkins University Press, 1979), 126–38 at 131, 136. For a discussion, see Kunin, *We Think What We Eat*, 30.

17 Douglas, *Purity and Danger*, 40.

18 Ibid.

19 As the argument of this chapter should make clear, Durkheim's overemphasis on the role that religious symbols and ritual play in the construction of order

and social cohesion, which are supposedly necessary to ward off *anomie*, has caused some distortions in our understanding of religion.

20 Walter Houston, *Purity and Monotheism: Clean and Unclean Animals in Biblical Law* (Sheffield, UK: Sheffield Academic Press, 1993), 101.

21 Soler, "The Semiotics of Food in the Bible." For another approach to the Jewish dietary laws influenced by structuralism, see Michael P. Carroll, "One More Time: Leviticus Revisited," in Bernhard Lang, ed., *Anthropological Approaches to the Old Testament* (Philadelphia: Fortress Press, 1985), 117–26. I defer discussion of Carroll's account for another occasion.

22 Soler, "The Semiotics of Food in the Bible," 135.

23 Ibid. at 129.

24 Ibid.

25 Curiously, in a later article, Douglas reviews the earlier history of interpretation of the dietary laws, which included "psychological theories, fear of snakes, dread of creepy-crawlies and things that go bump in the night, discomfort in the face of anomaly." What is this last theory except a pithy restatement of Douglas's own? Mary Douglas, "Forbidden Animals," 5.

26 Robert Alter, "A New Theory of Kashrut," *Commentary* (August 1979): 46–52 at 47.

27 Ibid. at 51.

28 Milgrom, *Leviticus 1–16*, 719.

29 Milgrom, *Leviticus: A Book of Ritual and Ethics*, 109.

30 Ibid. at 114.

31 Ibid. at 115.

32 Milgrom, *Leviticus 1–16*, 718 (quoting *Sipra*, Qedoshim 11:22). Additional examples of this traditionalist view are given in Milgrom, *Leviticus: A Book of Ritual and Ethics*, 33–4 (quoting *Pesiq. Rab Kah.* 4:7), where Rabbi Yohanan ben Zakkai explains that the purifying power of the ashes of the red cow (Numbers 19) is simply by "decree"; Alter, "A New Theory of Kashrut," 46, glossing the third-century sage Rav's view (from *Midrash Tanhuma, Parashat Shemini*) that the dietary prohibitions are "arbitrary." For additional examples and discussion, see Jiří Moskala, *The Laws of Clean and Unclean Animals of Leviticus 11: Their Nature, Theology, and Rationale (An Intertextual Study)* (Berrien Springs, MI: Adventist Theological Society Publications, 2000), 112–15; Jeffrey H. Tigay, *Deuteronomy: The JPS Torah Commentary* (Philadelphia: Jewish Publication Society, 1996), 138, who summarizes that "The language of the dietary codes indicates that what is impure for Israel is so because God declares it to be so. . . . They [these laws] are understood as an expression of submission to God's authority" (Quoted in Moskala, 84–5); Gillian Feeley-Harnik, *The Lord's Table: The Meaning of Food in Early Judaism and Christianity* (Washington: Smithsonian Institution Press, 1981), 7: "Dietary laws are classified in the Pentateuch as *hukkim*, '"divine statutes," which by definition are not explained in the text,'" quoting "Dietary Laws," *Encyclopaedia Judaica* (Jerusalem: Keter Publishing House, 1971), 26–45 at 42; Houston, *Purity and Monotheism*, 15. For Kant's own attack on the Jewish

law as consisting merely of external commands, see Immanuel Kant, *Religion within the Limits of Reason Alone*, trans. Theodore M. Green and Hoyt H. Hudson, 2nd edn (La Salle, IL: Open Court, 1960), 90–1, 116, 166–7.

33 Moskala, *The Laws of Clean and Unclean Animals*, 114.

34 Heinemann, *The Reasons for the Commandments*, 16–17, 96–7.

35 See, for example, ibid. at xix, 16–17, 19–21, 160.

36 Ibid. at 17, 88.

37 Ibid. at 178.

38 Prior to structuralism, many definitions of the sign concentrated precisely on regularity and order as necessary to signification. According to this view, it is the constant or repeated conjunction of two events or occurrences that allows us to make the inference that one is the cause (or effect) of the other and therefore may serve as a sign of the other. The sign is an index of its referent, in the sense of enjoying an existential connection with its referent. Thomas Hobbes restated this opinion: "When a man hath *so often* observed like antecedents to be followed by like consequents, that *whensoever* he seeth the antecedent, he looketh for the consequent; or when he seeth the consequent, maketh account there hath been the like antecedent; then he calleth both the antecedent and the consequent, signs of one another, as clouds are signs of rain to come, and rain of clouds past." Hobbes proceeds to criticize such reasoning by experience as "conjectural." Hobbes, *The English Works of Thomas Hobbes of Malmesbury*, ed. William Molesworth, vol. 4 (London: John Bohn, 1840), 17. Also criticizing such reasoning, David Hume argued, famously, that we cannot validly infer causation from the empirical observation of the repeated conjunction of two events. Hume, *An Enquiry concerning Human Understanding* (1772), sec. 7, "Of the Idea of Necessary Connexion," pt. 2, in P. H. Nidditch, ed., *Enquiries concerning Human Understanding and concerning the Principles of Morals*, 3rd edn (Oxford: Clarendon Press, 1975), 73–9. Hume's characteristic skepticism in this case illuminated the arbitrariness of such signs. It is always possible that the next time two billiard balls collide, the first will not transmit its momentum to the second; that it will necessarily do so is merely an assumption we make out of habit and convenience. Although, for many, the failure of the second billiard ball to move would constitute a violation of the laws of nature, or even a miracle (like God blowing on a pair of dice), this would only prove that we had been mistaken about the laws of nature. Whatever is, is, and cannot be otherwise. Given that we cannot know what the laws of nature are to begin with, we have no "baseline" against which to declare any particular event as miraculous. Hume's skepticism cast doubt simultaneously upon (1) the ability of the observation of regularities in nature to discover signs that were such in anything more than a temporary, provisional, and defeasible sense; and (2) the capacity to recognize miracles, the sign-function of which depended on an utterly different basis, namely through deviation from a natural order that we could never know with certainty.

39 Paul Tillich, "Revelation and Miracle," in Richard Swinburne, ed., *Miracles* (New York: Macmillan, 1989), 71–4 at 71. On the religious dimensions of *semeion*, see also Patte and Gay, "Religious Studies," 797–8.

40 Tillich, "Revelation and Miracle," 71.

41 Numbers 16:28–31 (Holman).

42 Moses Lowman, *A Rational of the Ritual of the Hebrew Worship; in which the Wise Designs and Usefulness of that Ritual are Explain'd, and Vindicated from Objections* (London: printed for J. Noon, 1748), 218–19, 258.

43 Ibid. at 187.

44 Ibid. at 208.

45 Ibid. at 220. Cf. the discussion below in this chapter of Edwin Firmage and Walter Houston, both of whom make a similar argument.

46 Lowman, *A Rational of the Ritual of the Hebrew Worship*, 258.

47 Ibid. at 58.

48 Ibid. at 50.

49 Ibid. at 208.

50 Ibid. at 217.

51 Ibid. at 58.

52 See the quote from John Toland in Chapter One.

53 For references, see Yelle, "Moses' Veil," 28, n.23.

54 I have explored the connection between secularization and the Deist and, more broadly, Protestant critique of Judaism in the following essays: "Moses' Veil," "The Hindu Moses."

55 Matthew Tindal, *Christianity as Old as Creation: Or, the Gospel a Republication of the Religion of Nature* (London: printed for J. Peele, 1730).

56 Exemplary is Tindal, in ibid. at 118 ("merely positive and arbitrary precepts"). Even John Toland, who departed from the Deist norm in some respects by having a better opinion of Judaism—he advocated for the naturalization of the Jews and insisted that Jesus and Paul had never abrogated the Mosaic law (excepting that of sacrifice) for Jews, but had only held this to be unnecessary for Gentile converts—had a low opinion of the "externals" of religion, which he tolerated precisely because he regarded them as inessential. See Toland, *Nazarenus: Or, Jewish, Gentile, and Mahometan Christianity* (London: printed and sold by J. Brotherton, 1718), v–vi, 6.

57 Slaughter, *Universal Languages*, 205, argues that "the feature that distinguishes Locke's linguistic theory from his predecessors like Bacon and Wilkins" is his affirmation that "[t]here is no tie between language and the real nature of objects." Cf. Aarsleff, *From Locke to Saussure*, 24–6, 62.

58 Stroumsa, "John Spencer."

59 See Houston, *Purity and Monotheism*, 72–3 for a discussion of similar views on the part of scholars both contemporary and ancient. As Houston notes, Origen argued already in the third century CE that Moses declared unclean those animals used by the Egyptians in their rituals.

60 John Edwards, *A Compleat History or Survey of All the Dispensations and Methods of Religion* (London: printed for Daniel Brown, 1699), 244.

61 Indeed, Soler, "The Semiotics of Food in the Bible," 129, invoked in support of his argument the notion that the Hebrews' dietary practices were designed in some case specifically to oppose those of their neighbors.

62 Tindal, *Christianity as Old as Creation*, 54; cf. 207.

63 Ibid. at 262.

64 Ibid. at 388.

65 Ibid. at 92.

66 Ibid. at 99.

67 Ibid. at 246.

68 Ibid. at 152; cf. 261, 263.

69 Ibid. at 260, 263.

70 Ibid. at 263.

71 Ibid. at 152.

72 Toland, *Christianity Not Mysterious*, 73.

73 It is odd that Douglas ("Forbidden Animals," 5) characterizes Maimonides's view as having "insisted on the arbitrariness of the sign." Although Maimonides does introduce a principle of meaning-by-distinction that anticipates a structuralist approach to these laws, in his case as well, this was done in order to avoid the conclusion that the dietary laws were ultimately arbitrary or without reason. Neither was Maimonides a rationalist in the same sense as the Deists: as Heinemann, *The Reasons for the Commandments*, 96–7, 115, points out, Maimonides regarded all of the *mitzvot* as binding, whether or not one could identify a reason for each of them, while also upholding the right to inquire into their rationale.

74 See Rudolf Otto, *The Idea of the Holy*, trans. John W. Harvey, 2nd edn (Oxford: Oxford University Press, 1950 [1917]).

75 Carl Schmitt, *Political Theology: Four Chapters on the Theory of Sovereignty*, trans. George Schwab (Chicago: University of Chicago Press, 2005), 36–7.

76 Milgrom, *Leviticus: A Book of Ritual and Ethics*, 114.

77 Otto, *The Idea of the Holy*, esp. 12–30.

78 This is actually an interpretation of Tertullian, *De carne christi*, V.4: "certum est, quia impossibile."

79 See, for example, Houston, *Purity and Monotheism*, 103–7; Kunin, *We Think What We Eat*, 41.

80 Kunin, *We Think What We Eat*, 91.

81 Edwin Firmage, "The Biblical Dietary Laws and the Concept of Holiness," in J. A. Emerton, ed., *Studies in the Pentateuch* (Leiden: Brill, 1990), 177–208 at 185–6. Firmage is largely followed on these points by Houston, *Purity and Monotheism*, 155, who elaborates the argument. Firmage's further contention—that the dietary laws were designed to make the diet of the Israelites approximate that of Yahweh, as the consumer of sacrifices—is, as Milgrom has argued, less convincing. Cf. Jonathan Z. Smith's argument that sacrifice is founded upon the domestication of animals, and serves as a meditation on domesticity. Smith, "The Domestication of Sacrifice," in Robert G. Hamerton-Kelly, ed., *Violent Origins: Walter Burkert, René Girard, and Jonathan Z. Smith on Ritual Killing and Cultural Formation* (Stanford: Stanford University Press, 1988), 191–205.

82 See Hertz, "The Pre-eminence of the Right Hand."

83 Houston, *Purity and Monotheism*, 234.

84 Ibid. at 23.

85 Robertson Smith, *Lectures*, 16–17.

86 Heinemann, *The Reasons for the Commandments*, 2.

87 Eric Auerbach, *Mimesis: The Representation of Reality in Western Literature*, trans. Willard R. Trask (Princeton: Princeton University Press, 1953), 6–11. See Robbins, "Sacrifice," 292–3 for a discussion of Auerbach's interpretation of the Akedah.

88 Søren Kierkegaard, *Fear and Trembling*, ed. and trans. Howard V. Hong and Edna H. Hong, in *Kierkegaard's Writings*, vol. 6 (Princeton: Princeton University Press, 1983), 1–176.

89 Milgrom, *Leviticus: A Book of Ritual and Ethics*, 103.

90 Jonathan Z. Smith, "Sacred Persistence," in *Imagining Religion*.

91 Howard Eilberg-Schwartz, "Creation and Classification in Judaism: From Priestly to Rabbinic Conceptions," *History of Religions* 26 (1987): 357–81, argues that the Mishnah emphasized the flexibility of the purity classifications in Jewish law and their dependence on human intention and autonomy in a manner that diverged from earlier, biblical tradition.

92 It is surprising that Smith, in "Sacred Persistence," does not even cite Douglas's work despite the fact that they were both talking about such closely related topics. The following line from her *Purity and Danger* (94) might well have appeared in Smith's essay: "Order implies restriction; from all possible materials, a limited selection has been made and from all possible relations a limited set has been used."

93 Timothy Lubin, "Ritual Self-Discipline as a Response to the Human Condition: Toward a Semiotics of Ritual Indices," in Axel Michaels, Anand Mishra, L. Dolce, G. Raz, and K. Triplett, eds, *Ritual Dynamics and the Science of Ritual, Vol. 1: Grammars and Morphologies of Ritual Practices in Asia* (Wiesbaden: Harrassowitz, 2010), 263–74 at 276.

94 Cf. Keane, *Christian Moderns*, 49–58, which focuses on the agentive dimensions of Protestant semiotic ideology, especially the concept of sincerity in speech. This emphasis on autonomy contrasts with the emphasis on heteronomy in many ritual systems.

95 Louis Dumont, *Homo Hierarchicus: The Caste System and Its Implications* (Chicago: University of Chicago Press, 1980), 273–6.

96 Georges Bataille, *The Accursed Share: An Essay on General Economy*, trans. Robert Hurley, 3 vols (New York: Zone Books, 1988–91).

Conclusion

1 Colin Cherry, *On Human Communication*, 3rd edn (Cambridge: MIT Press, 1978), 14, 180.

2 See note 89 in Chapter Two.

BIBLIOGRAPHY

Aarsleff, Hans. *From Locke to Saussure: Essays on the Study of Language and Intellectual History*. Minneapolis: University of Minnesota Press, 1982.

Adams, Florence A. Fowle. *Gesture and Pantomimic Action*. New York: Edgar S. Werner, 1891.

Alter, Robert. "A New Theory of Kashrut." *Commentary* (August 1979): 46–52.

Aristotle. *The Basic Works of Aristotle*. Ed. Richard McKeon. New York: Random House, 1941.

Asad, Talal. *Formations of the Secular: Christianity, Islam, Modernity*. Stanford: Stanford University Press, 2003.

— *Genealogies of Religion*. Baltimore: Johns Hopkins University Press, 1993.

Assmann, Jan. *The Price of Monotheism*. Trans. Robert Savage. Stanford: Stanford University Press, 2010.

Attenborough, F. L. *The Laws of the Earliest English Kings*. Cambridge: Cambridge University Press, 1922.

Aubrey, John. *Remaines of Gentilisme and Judaisme*. Ed. James Britten. London: Folk-Lore Society, 1881.

Auerbach, Eric. "Figura." In *Scenes from the Drama of European Literature*, 11–78. Minneapolis: University of Minnesota Press, 1959.

— *Mimesis: The Representation of Reality in Western Literature*. Trans. Willard R. Trask. Princeton: Princeton University Press, 1953.

Augustine. *Contra Faustum Manichaeum*. Trans. as "Reply to Faustus the Manichaean." In Philip Schaff, ed., *A Select Library of the Nicene and Post-Nicene Fathers*, 4: 155–345. Grand Rapids, MI: Wm. B. Eerdmans Publishing Company, 1956.

Auksi, Peter. *Christian Plain Style: The Evolution of a Spiritual Ideal*. Montréal: McGill-Queen's University Press, 1995.

Austin, Gilbert. *Chironomia: Or a Treatise on Rhetorical Delivery*. Ed. Mary Margaret Robb and Lester Thonssen. Carbondale: Southern Illinois University Press, 1966.

Austin, J. L. *How to Do Things with Words*. Cambridge, MA: Harvard University Press, 1975.

Avalon, Arthur. *The Garland of Letters*. Madras: Ganesh and Co., 1998.

Avalon, Arthur, ed. *Kulārṇava Tantra*. Madras: Ganesh and Co., 1965.

— *Śāradātilaka Tantra*. Delhi: Motilal Banarsidass, 1996.

Bachofen, Johann Jakob. *Versuch über die Gräbersymbolik der Alten*. Ed. Karl Meuli. Vol. 4 of *Johann Jakob Bachofens Gesammelte Werke*. Basel: Benno Schwabe & Co., 1954.

Bacon, Francis. *The New Organon and Related Writings*. Ed. Fulton H. Anderson. Englewood Cliffs, NJ: Prentice-Hall, 1960.

— *The Works of Francis Bacon*. Ed. James Spedding, Robert Leslie Ellis, and Douglas Denon Heath. Cambridge: Riverside Press and New York: Hurd and Houghton, 1869.

Barthes, Roland. *The Fashion System*. Trans. Richard Howard and Matthew
    Ward. Berkeley and Los Angeles: University of California Press, 1990.
Bataille, Georges. *The Accursed Share: An Essay on General Economy*. Trans.
    Robert Hurley. 3 vols. New York: Zone Books, 1988–91.
Bauman, Richard and Charles L. Briggs. *Voices of Modernity: Language
    Ideologies and the Politics of Inequality*. Cambridge: Cambridge University
    Press, 2003.
Bell, Catherine. "Performance." In Mark C. Taylor, ed., *Critical Terms for
    Religious Studies*, 205–24. Chicago: University of Chicago Press, 1998.
— *Ritual: Perspectives and Dimensions*. New York: Oxford University Press, 1997.
— *Ritual Theory, Ritual Practice*. New York: Oxford University Press, 1992.
Bellah, Robert. *Religion in Human Evolution*. Cambridge, MA: Harvard
    University Press, 2011.
Benin, Stephen D. "The 'Cunning of God' and Divine Accommodation." *Journal
    of the History of Ideas* 45 (1984): 179–91.
Bentham, Jeremy. "Auto-Icon; or, Farther Uses of the Dead to the Living." In
    James Crimmins, ed., *Bentham's Auto-Icon and Related Writings*. Bristol,
    UK: Thoemmes Press, 2002.
— *Church-of-Englandism and its Catechism Examined*. London: Effingham
    Wilson, 1818.
— *A Comment on the Commentaries and A Fragment on Government*. Ed.
    J. H. Burns and H. L. A. Hart. London: Athlone Press, 1977.
— *The Correspondence of Jeremy Bentham*. Ed. Timothy Sprigge, et al. 12 vols.
    London: Athlone Press and Oxford: Oxford University Press, 1968–2006.
— *The Works of Jeremy Bentham*. Ed. John Bowring. 11 vols. Edinburgh:
    William Tait, 1843.
Bentham, Jeremy and Francis Place [Gamaliel Smith, pseud.]. *Not Paul, But Jesus*.
    London: John Hunt, 1823.
Bentham, Jeremy and George Grote [Philip Beauchamp, pseud.]. *An Analysis of
    the Influence of Natural Religion on the Temporal Happiness of Mankind*.
    London: R. Carlile, 1822.
Bercovitch, Sacvan. *Typology and Early American Literature*. Amherst:
    University of Massachusetts Press, 1972.
Berman, Harold. *Faith and Order: The Reconciliation of Law and Religion*.
    Atlanta: Scholars Press, 1993.
— *Law and Revolution: The Formation of the Western Legal Tradition*.
    Cambridge, MA: Harvard University Press, 1983.
Betz, Hans Dieter, ed. *The Greek Magical Papyri in Translation*. 2nd edn. Vol. 1.
    Chicago: University of Chicago Press, 1992.
Birdwhistell, Ray L. *Kinesics and Context: Essays on Body Motion
    Communication*. Philadelphia: University of Pennsylvania Press, 1970.
Blackburn, Stuart. *Print, Folklore, and Nationalism in Colonial India*. Delhi:
    Permanent Black, 2003.
Blackstone, William. *Commentaries on the Laws of England*. Oxford: Clarendon
    Press, 1765–69. Reprint edn. Chicago: University of Chicago Press, 1979.
Blunt, John Henry, ed. *The Annotated Book of Common Prayer*. 2nd edn.
    London, Oxford, and Cambridge: Rivingtons, 1876.
*The Book of the General Lawes and Libertyes concerning the Inhabitants of the
    Massachusets*. Cambridge, MA: printed by [Matthew Day] according to order

of the General Court, 1648. Facsimile edn. San Marino, CA: The Huntington Library, 1975.

Bose, Mandakranta. *Movement and Mimesis: The Idea of Dance in the Sanskritic Tradition*. Dordrecht: Kluwer Academic Publishers, 1991.

Bouissac, Paul, ed. *Encyclopedia of Semiotics*. New York: Oxford University Press, 1998.

Bourdieu, Pierre. "The Force of Law: Toward a Sociology of the Juridical Field." *Hastings Law Journal* 38 (1987): 805–53.

— *Outline of a Theory of Practice*. Trans. Richard Nice. Cambridge: Cambridge University Press, 1977.

Boys, Thomas. *Key to the Book of Psalms*. London: L. B. Seeley, 1825.

Brewer, G. and C. A. Hendrie. "Evidence to Suggest that Copulatory Vocalizations in Women Are Not a Reflexive Consequence of Orgasm." *Archives of Sexual Behavior* 40 (2011): 559–64.

Bronkhorst, Johannes. "Etymology and Magic: Yāska's *Nirukta*, Plato's *Cratylus*, and the Riddle of Semantic Etymologies." *Numen* 48 (2001): 147–203.

de Brosses, Charles. *Du culte des dieux fétiches*. [Paris], 1760.

Bulwer, John. *Chirologia: Or the Natural Language of the Hand and Chironomia: Or the Art of Manual Rhetoric*. Ed. James W. Cleary. Carbondale: Southern Illinois University Press, 1974.

Burgess, Anthony. *Spiritual Refining: Or a Treatise of Grace and Assurance*. London: printed by A. Miller for Thomas Underhill, 1652.

Burke, Peter. "The Repudiation of Ritual in Early Modern Europe." In *The Historical Anthropology of Early Modern Italy: Essays on Perception and Communication*, 223–38. Cambridge: Cambridge University Press, 1987.

Caesar, Michael, ed. *Dante: The Critical Heritage 1314(?)–1870*. London: Routledge, 1989.

Calvin, John. *A Harmonie upon the Three Evangelists*. London: George Bishop, 1584.

Carroll, Michael P. "One More Time: Leviticus Revisited." In Bernhard Lang, ed., *Anthropological Approaches to the Old Testament*, 117–26. Philadelphia: Fortress Press, 1985.

Cassirer, Ernst. *Language and Myth*. New York: Dover, 1953.

Caton, Steven. "*Salaam Tahiya*: Greetings from the Highlands of Yemen." *American Ethnologist* 13 (1986): 290–308.

de Champs, Emmanuelle. "The Place of Jeremy Bentham's Theory of Fictions in Eighteenth-Century Linguistic Thought." *Journal of Bentham Studies* 2 (1999): 1–28.

Cherry, Colin. *On Human Communication*. 3rd edn. Cambridge, MA: MIT Press, 1978.

Cohen, Esther. *The Crossroads of Justice: Law and Culture in Late Medieval France*. Leiden: Brill, 1993.

Colman, Rebecca. "Reason and Unreason in Early Medieval Law." *Journal of Interdisciplinary History* 4 (1974): 571–91.

Coomaraswamy, Ananda and Gopala Kristnayya Duggirala, trans. *The Mirror of Gesture*. New Delhi: Munshiram Manoharlal, 1970.

Coulanges, Numa Denis Fustel de. "Religious Origins of Ancient Law." In Albert Kocourek and John H. Wigmore, eds, *Primitive and Ancient Legal Institutions*, 104–10. Boston: Little, Brown, and Co. Reprint edn. Littleton, CO: Fred B. Rothman & Co., 1979.

Cranmer, Thomas. *The Works of Thomas Cranmer*. Ed. John Edmund Cox. 2 vols. Cambridge: Cambridge University Press, 1846.

— *Writings of the Rev. Dr. Thomas Cranmer*. London: The Religious Tract Society, 1860.

Creuzer, Friedrich. *Symbolik und Mythologie der alten Völker, besonders der Griechen*. 3rd edn. 4 vols. Leipzig and Darmstadt: Carl Wilhelm Leske, 1837–42.

Crimmins, James. "Bentham and Hobbes: An Issue of Influence." *Journal of the History of Ideas* 63 (2002): 677–96.

— "Bentham's Religious Radicalism Revisited: A Response to Schofield." *History of Political Thought* 22 (2001): 494.

— *Secular Utilitarianism: Social Science and the Critique of Religion in the Thought of Jeremy Bentham*. Oxford: Oxford University Press, 1990.

Critchley, Macdonald. *Silent Language*. London: Butterworths, 1975.

Dante Alighieri. *The Divine Comedy*. Trans. Mark Musa. 3 vols. New York: Penguin, 1986.

— "The Letter to Can Grande." In Robert Haller, trans., *Literary Criticism of Dante Alighieri*, 95–111. Lincoln: University of Nebraska Press, 1973.

Derrett, J. Duncan M. "Ancient Indian 'Nonsense' Vindicated." *Journal of the American Oriental Society* 98 (1978): 100–6.

Detienne, Marcel. *The Masters of Truth in Archaic Greece*. Trans. Janet Lloyd. New York: Zone Books, 1996.

Douglas, Mary. "The Forbidden Animals in Leviticus." *Journal for the Study of the Old Testament* 59 (1993): 3–23.

— *Leviticus as Literature*. Oxford: Oxford University Press, 1999.

— *Natural Symbols*. London: Barrie and Jenkins, 1973.

— *Purity and Danger: An Analysis of Concepts of Pollution and Taboo*. London: Routledge and Kegan Paul, 1966.

Douzinas, Costas and Lynda Nead, eds. *Law and the Image: The Authority of Art and the Aesthetics of Law*. Chicago: University of Chicago Press, 1999.

Driver, G. R. and John C. Miles. *The Babylonian Laws*. Vol. 2. Oxford: Clarendon Press, 1955.

Drucker, Johanna. *The Alphabetic Labyrinth: The Letters in History and Imagination*. London: Thames and Hudson, 1995.

Dumont, Louis. *Homo Hierarchicus: The Caste System and Its Implications*. Chicago: University of Chicago Press, 1980.

Durkheim, Émile. *The Elementary Forms of the Religious Life*. Trans. Joseph Ward Swain. New York: Free Press, 1965.

Durkheim, Émile and Marcel Mauss. *Primitive Classification*. Trans. Rodney Needham. Chicago: University of Chicago Press, 1963.

Eco, Umberto. *The Limits of Interpretation*. Bloomington: Indiana University Press, 1991.

— *The Search for the Perfect Language*. Trans. James Fentress. Oxford: Blackwell, 1995.

— *A Theory of Semiotics*. Bloomington: Indiana University Press, 1976.

Edwards, John. *A Compleat History or Survey of All the Dispensations and Methods of Religion*. London: printed for Daniel Brown, 1699.

Eilberg-Schwartz, Howard. "Creation and Classification in Judaism: From Priestly to Rabbinic Conceptions." *History of Religions* 26 (1987): 357–81.

Eisenstadt, S. N. *The Origins and Diversity of Axial Age Civilizations.* Albany: SUNY Press, 1986.

Eisenstein, Elizabeth. *The Printing Press as an Agent of Change: Communications and Cultural Transformations in Early-Modern Europe.* Cambridge: Cambridge University Press, 1980.

Eliade, Mircea. *Myth and Reality.* Trans. Willard Trask. New York: Harper and Row, 1968.

— *The Myth of the Eternal Return: Or, Cosmos and History.* Trans. Willard R. Trask. Princeton: Princeton University Press, 1974.

— *Patterns in Comparative Religion.* Trans. Rosemary Sheed. Lincoln: University of Nebraska Press, 1996.

— *The Sacred and the Profane: The Nature of Religion.* Trans. Willard R. Trask. New York: Harcourt Brace and Company, 1959.

Embree, Ainslie T., ed. *Sources of Indian Tradition.* Vol. 1. 2nd edn. New York: Columbia University Press, 1988.

Engel, Johann Jakob. *Ideen zu einer Mimik.* Trans. Henry Siddons as *Practical Illustrations of Rhetorical Gesture and Action.* 2nd edn. London: Sherwood, Neely, and Jones, 1822.

Engelmann, Arthur. *A History of Continental Civil Procedure.* Trans. Robert Wyness Millar. New York: Augustus M. Kelley, 1969.

Evans-Pritchard, E. E. *Witchcraft, Oracles, and Magic among the Azande.* New York: Oxford University Press, 1976.

Febvre, Lucien. *The Coming of the Book: The Impact of Printing 1450–1800.* London: Verso, 1976.

Feely-Harnik, Gillian. *The Lord's Table: The Meaning of Food in Early Judaism and Christianity.* Washington: Smithsonian Institution Press, 1981.

Finnegan, Ruth. "Literacy versus Non-Literacy: The Great Divide?" In Robin Horton and Ruth Finnegan, eds, *Modes of Thought: Essays in Thinking in Western and Non-Western Societies*, 112–44. London: Faber & Faber, 1973.

Firmage, Edwin. "The Biblical Dietary Laws and the Concept of Holiness." In J. A. Emerton, ed., *Studies in the Pentateuch*, 177–208. Leiden: Brill, 1990.

Fish, Stanley. *Is There a Text in This Class?: The Authority of Interpretive Communities.* Cambridge, MA: Harvard University Press, 1982.

Foucault, Michel. "The Order of Discourse." In Robert Young, ed., *Untying the Text: A Post-Structuralist Reader*, 48–78. London: Routledge & Kegan Paul, 1981.

Fraser, Russell. *The Language of Adam: On the Limits and Systems of Discourse.* New York: Columbia University Press, 1977.

Frazer, James George. *The Golden Bough: A Study in Magic and Religion.* Abridged edn. New York: Macmillan, 1951.

Freud, Sigmund. *The Interpretation of Dreams.* Trans. James Strachey. New York: Avon Books, 1965.

— "Obsessive Acts and Religious Practices." In James Strachey, ed., *The Standard Edition of the Complete Psychological Works of Sigmund Freud*, 9: 117–27. 24 vols. London: Hogarth Press, 1953–74.

Fuller, Lon. *Legal Fictions.* Stanford: Stanford University Press, 1967.

Fuller, Thomas. *Abel Redevivus or, The Dead Yet Speaking.* London: printed by Thomas Brudnell for John Stafford, 1652.

Funkenstein, Amos. *Theology and the Scientific Imagination: From the Middle Ages to the Seventeenth Century.* Princeton: Princeton University Press, 1986.

Gay, Volney P. and Daniel Patte. "Religious Studies." In Thomas Sebeok, ed., *Encyclopedic Dictionary of Semiotics*, 2: 797–807. 3 vols. Berlin: Mouton de Gruyter, 1986.

Geertz, Hildred. "An Anthropology of Religion and Magic, I." *Journal of Interdisciplinary History* 6 (1975): 71–89.

Genette, Gérard. *Mimologics.* Trans. Thaïs Morgan. Lincoln: University of Nebraska Press, 1995.

Ghosh, Manomohan, trans. *Abhinayadarpaṇa.* 2nd edn. Calcutta: K. L. Mukhopadhyay, 1957.

Glanvill, Joseph. *A Seasonable Defence of Preaching and the Plain Way of It.* London: printed by M. Clarke for H. Brome, 1678.

Gomperz, Theodor. *Greek Thinkers: A History of Ancient Philosophy.* London: John Murray, 1949.

Goodrich, Peter. *Languages of Law: From Logics of Memory to Nomadic Masks.* London: Weidenfeld and Nicolson, 1990.

— *Oedipus Lex: Psychoanalysis, History, Law.* Berkeley and Los Angeles: University of California Press, 1995.

Goody, Jack. *The Domestication of the Savage Mind.* Cambridge: Cambridge University Press, 1977.

— *The Interface between the Written and the Oral.* Cambridge: Cambridge University Press, 1987.

— *The Logic of Writing and the Organization of Society.* Cambridge: Cambridge University Press, 1986.

— *The Power of the Written Tradition.* Washington and London: Smithsonian Institution Press, 2000.

— *Representations and Contradictions.* Oxford: Blackwell, 1997.

Goody, Jack and Ian Watt. "The Consequences of Literacy." *Comparative Studies in Society and History* 5 (1963): 304–45.

Gorgias. "Helen." Trans. George Kennedy. In Patricia P. Matsen, Philip Rollinson, and Marion Sousa, eds, *Readings from Classical Rhetoric*, 34–6. Carbondale: Southern Illinois University Press, 1990.

Graf, Fritz. " Historiola." In Hubert Cancik and Helmuth Schneider, eds, *Brill's New Pauly.* Brill Online, 2012. http://referenceworks.brillonline.com/entries/brill-s-new-pauly/historiola-e515850

Graham, William. *Beyond the Written Word: Oral Aspects of Scripture in the History of Religion.* Cambridge: Cambridge University Press, 1987.

Grendon, Felix. "The Anglo-Saxon Charms." *Journal of American Folklore* 22 (1909): 105–237.

Grimm, Jacob. "Von der Poesie im Recht." *Zeitschrift für geschichtliche Rechtswissenschaft* (1816), vol. 2, pt. 1, 25–99. Reprint edn. Darmstadt: Hermann Gentner Verlag, 1957.

Gupta, Sanjukta, trans. *Lakṣmī Tantra.* Delhi: Motilal Banarsidass, 2000.

Gutting, Gary. "Michel Foucault." *The Stanford Encyclopedia of Philosophy.* Ed. Edward N. Zalta. http://plato.stanford.edu/archives/fall2011/entries/foucault

Harrison, Peter. *The Bible, Protestantism, and the Rise of Natural Science.* Cambridge: Cambridge University Press, 1998.

— *Religion and the Religions in the English Enlightenment.* Cambridge: Cambridge University Press, 1990.

Hart, H. L. A. *Essays on Bentham: Studies in Jurisprudence and Political Theory.* Oxford: Oxford University Press, 1982.

— "Positivism and the Separation of Law and Morals." *Harvard Law Review* 71 (1958), 593–629.

Haskins, George Lee. *Law and Authority in Early Massachusetts: A Study in Tradition and Design.* New York: Macmillan, 1960.

Havelock, Eric. *Preface to Plato.* Cambridge, MA: Harvard University Press, 1963.

Heinemann, Isaac. *The Reasons for the Commandments in Jewish Thought, From the Bible to the Renaissance.* Trans. Leonard Levin. Boston: Academic Studies Press, 2008.

Henninger, Joseph. "Sacrifice." In Lindsay Jones, ed., *Encyclopedia of Religion*, 7997–8008. 2nd edn. New York: Macmillan Reference USA, 2005.

Hertz, Robert. "The Pre-eminence of the Right Hand: A Study in Religious Polarity." In Rodney Needham, ed., *Right and Left: Essays on Dual Symbolic Classification*, 3–31. Chicago: University of Chicago Press, 1973.

Hibbitts, Bernard. "Coming to Our Senses: Communication and Legal Expression in Performance Cultures." *Emory Law Journal* 41 (1992): 873–960.

Hinton, Leanne, Johanna Nichols, and John J. Ohala, eds. *Sound Symbolism.* Cambridge: Cambridge University Press, 1994.

Hobbes, Thomas. *The English Works of Thomas Hobbes of Malmesbury.* Ed. William Molesworth. 11 vols. London: John Bohn, 1840.

— *Leviathan.* Ed. Edwin Curley. Indianapolis: Hackett, 1994.

Hohman, John George. *Pow-Wows; or Long-Lost Friend: A Collection of Mysterious and Invaluable Arts and Remedies for Man as Well as Animals.* Reprint edn. Pomeroy, WA: Health Research, 1971.

Hooker, Richard. *Of the Lawes of Ecclesiasticall Politie.* London: printed by Will. Stansby, 1617.

Houston, Walter. *Purity and Monotheism: Clean and Unclean Animals in Biblical Law.* Sheffield, UK: Sheffield Academic Press, 1993.

Hübner, Rudolph. *A History of Germanic Private Law.* Trans. Francis S. Philbrick. New York: Augustus M. Kelley, 1968.

Hume, David. *An Enquiry concerning Human Understanding.* In P. H. Nidditch, ed., *Enquiries concerning Human Understanding and concerning the Principles of Morals.* 3rd edn. Oxford: Clarendon Press, 1975.

Hume, L. J. "The Political Functions of Bentham's Theory of Fictions." *The Bentham Newsletter* 3 (1979): 18–27.

Jackson, Bernard. "An Eye for an I?: The Semiotics of Lex Talionis in the Bible." In William Pencak and J. Ralph Lindgren, eds, *New Approaches to Semiotics and the Human Sciences: Essays in Honor of Roberta Kevelson*, 127–49. New York: Peter Lang, 1997.

— "Models in Legal History." *Journal of Law & Religion* 18 (2002): 1–30.

— *Studies in the Semiotics of Biblical Law.* Sheffield, UK: Sheffield Academic Press, 2000.

— "Truth and the Semiotics of Law." *Current Legal Problems* 51 (1998): 493–531.

Jakobson, Roman. "Closing Statement: Linguistics and Poetics." In Thomas Sebeok, ed., *Style in Language*, 350–77. Cambridge, MA: MIT Press, 1960.

— "Two Aspects of Language and Two Types of Aphasic Disturbances." In Stephen Rudy, ed., *Roman Jakobson: Selected Writings*, 2: 239–59. 8 vols. Berlin: Mouton de Gruyter, 1962–88.

Jakobson, Roman and Linda R. Waugh. "The Spell of Speech Sounds." In Stephen Rudy, ed., *Roman Jakobson: Selected Writings*, 8: 181–234. 8 vols. Berlin: Mouton de Gruyter, 1962–88.

Jakobson, Roman and Morris Halle. *Fundamentals of Language*. Hague: Mouton and Co., 1956.

Jay, Nancy. *Throughout Your Generations Forever: Sacrifice, Religion, and Paternity*. Chicago: University of Chicago Press, 1994.

Jha, Ganganath. *Shabara-Bhāṣya*. 3 vols. Baroda: Oriental Institute, 1933.

Johnson, Jr, Alfred M. *A Bibliography of Semiological and Structural Studies of Religion*. In Dikran Y. Hadidian, *Bibliographia Tripotamopolitana*, Number XI. Pittsburgh: The Clifford E. Barbour Library, Pittsburgh Theological Seminary, 1979.

Jones, Lindsay, ed. *Encyclopedia of Religion*. 2nd edn. New York: Macmillan Reference USA, 2005.

Jones, Richard Foster. *The Seventeenth Century: Studies in the History of English Thought and Literature from Bacon to Pope*. Stanford: Stanford University Press, 1951.

Kahrs, Eivind. *Indian Semantic Analysis: The Nirvacana Tradition*. Cambridge: Cambridge University Press, 1998.

Kant, Immanuel. *Religion within the Limits of Reason Alone*. Trans. Theodore M. Green and Hoyt H. Hudson. 2nd edn. La Salle, IL: Open Court, 1960.

Keane, Webb. *Christian Moderns: Freedom and Fetish in the Mission Encounter*. Berkeley and Los Angeles: University of California Press, 2007.

— "From Fetishism to Sincerity: Agency, the Speaking Subject, and their Historicity in the Context of Religious Conversion." *Comparative Studies in Society and History* 39 (1997): 674–93.

— "Religious Language." *Annual Review of Anthropology* 26 (1997): 47–71.

— "Sincerity, Modernity, and the Protestants." *Cultural Anthropology* 17 (2002): 65–92.

Kendon, Adam. *Gesture: Visible Action as Utterance*. Cambridge: Cambridge University Press, 1994.

Kierkegaard, Søren. *Fear and Trembling*. In Howard V. Hong and Edna H. Hong, eds and trans., *Kierkegaard's Writings*, 6: 1–123. Princeton: Princeton University Press, 1983.

Koller, Hermann. *Die Mimesis in der Antike*. Bern: A. Francke, 1954.

Korshin, Paul. *Typologies in England 1650–1820*. Princeton: Princeton University Press, 1982.

Kreinath, Jens. "Semiotics." In Jens Kreinath, Jan Snoek, and Michael Stausberg, eds, *Theorizing Rituals: Issues, Topics, Approaches, Concepts*, 429–70. Leiden: Brill, 2006.

Kroskrity, Paul V. *Regimes of Language: Ideologies, Polities, and Identities*. Sante Fe, NM: School of American Research Press, 2000.

Kunin, Seth D. *The Logic of Incest: A Structuralist Analysis of Hebrew Mythology*. Sheffield, UK: Sheffield Academic Press, 1995.

— *We Think What We Eat: Neo-Structuralist Analysis of Israelite Food Rules and Other Cultural and Textual Practices*. London: T & T Clark, 2004.

Lariviere, Richard. *The Divyatattva of Raghunandana Bhaṭṭāchārya: Ordeals in Classical Hindu Law.* New Delhi: Manohar, 1981.

Leach, Edmund. *Culture and Communication: The Logic by which Symbols are Connected.* Cambridge: Cambridge University Press, 1976.

— "Ritualization in Man." *Philosophical Transactions of the Royal Society.* Series B, No. 772, 251 (1966): 403–08.

Leone, Massimo. *Religious Conversion and Identity: The Semiotic Analysis of Texts.* London and New York: Routledge, 2004.

— *Saints and Signs: A Semiotic Reading of Conversion in Early Modern Catholicism.* Berlin and New York: Walter de Gruyter, 2010.

Levering, Miriam. *Rethinking Scripture: Essays from a Comparative Perspective.* Albany: SUNY Press, 1989.

Lévi-Strauss, Claude. *The Elementary Structures of Kinship.* Boston: Beacon, 1969.

— *The Savage Mind.* Chicago: University of Chicago Press, 1966.

— *Structural Anthropology.* Trans. Claire Jacobson and Brooke Grundfest Schoepf. New York: Basic Books, 1963.

— *Totemism.* Trans. Rodney Needham. Boston: Beacon, 1971.

Lewis, Rhodri. *Language, Mind and Nature: Artificial Languages in England from Bacon to Locke.* Cambridge: Cambridge University Press, 2007.

Lieberman, David. *The Province of Legislation Determined: Legal Theory in Eighteenth-Century Britain.* Cambridge: Cambridge University Press, 1989.

Lienhardt, Godfrey. *Divinity and Experience: The Religion of the Dinka.* Oxford: Oxford University Press, 1961.

Lightfoot, John. *The Works of the Reverend and Learned John Lightfoot.* London: printed by W. R. for Robert Scot, Thomas Basset, and Richard Chiswell, 1684.

Likhovski, Assaf. "Protestantism and the Rationalization of English Law: A Variation on a Theme by Weber." *Law and Society Review* 33 (1999): 365–91.

Lincoln, Bruce. *Authority: Construction and Corrosion.* Chicago: University of Chicago Press, 1995.

— *Discourse and the Construction of Society.* New York: Oxford University Press, 1989.

— *Theorizing Myth: Narrative, Ideology, and Scholarship.* Chicago: University of Chicago Press, 1999.

Lloyd, G. E. R. *Demystifying Mentalities.* Cambridge: Cambridge University Press, 1990.

Locke, John. *An Essay concerning Human Understanding.* 2 vols. New York: Dover, 1959.

Lovejoy, Arthur O. *The Great Chain of Being: A Study of the History of an Idea.* Cambridge, MA: Harvard University Press, 1976.

Lowman, Moses. *A Rational of the Ritual of the Hebrew Worship; in which the Wise Designs and Usefulness of that Ritual are Explain'd, and Vindicated from Objections.* London: printed for J. Noon, 1748.

Lubin, Timothy. "Ritual Self-Discipline as a Response to the Human Condition: Toward a Semiotics of Ritual Indices." In Axel Michaels, Anand Mishra, L. Dolce, G. Raz, and K. Triplett, eds, *Grammars and Morphologies of Ritual Practices in Asia,* 263–74. Vol. 1 of *Ritual Dynamics and the Science of Ritual.* Wiesbaden: Harrassowitz, 2010.

MacCulloch, Diarmaid. *Thomas Cranmer: A Life*. New Haven: Yale University Press, 1996.

Mack, Mary. *Jeremy Bentham: An Odyssey of Ideas*. New York: Columbia University Press, 1963.

Maeder, Costantino, Olga Fischer, and William J. Herlofsky, eds. *Outside-in–Inside-out: Iconicity in Language and Literature 4*. Amsterdam and Philadelphia: John Benjamins, 2005.

Malinowski, Bronislaw. *Coral Gardens and Their Magic*. 2 vols. New York: American Book Company, 1935.

— *Magic, Science and Religion and Other Essays*. Boston: Beacon Press, 1948.

Masuzawa, Tomoko. *The Invention of World Religions, or, How European Universalism Was Preserved in the Language of Pluralism*. Chicago: University of Chicago Press, 2005.

Mauss, Marcel. *The Gift: The Form and Reason for Exchange in Archaic Societies*. Trans. W. D. Halls. New York: W. W. Norton and Co., 2000.

McCauley, Robert N. and E. Thomas Lawson. *Bringing Ritual to Mind: Psychological Foundations of Cultural Forms*. Cambridge: Cambridge University Press, 2002.

McKown, Delos B. *Behold the Antichrist: Bentham on Religion*. Amherst, NY: Prometheus Books, 2004.

Merton, Robert. *Science, Technology & Society in Seventeenth-Century England*. New York: Harper Torchbooks, 1970.

Milgrom, Jacob. *Leviticus 1–16: A New Translation with Introduction and Commentary*. Vol. 3 of *The Anchor Bible*. New York: Doubleday, 1991.

— *Leviticus: A Book of Ritual and Ethics*. Minneapolis: Fortress Press, 2004.

Mirecki, Paul Allan, Iain Gardner, and Anthony Alcock. "Magical Spell, Manichaean Letter." In Paul Allan Mirecki and Jason BeDuhn, eds, *Emerging from Darkness: Studies in the Recovery of Manichaean Sources*, 1–32. Leiden: Brill, 1997.

Moskala, Jiří. *The Laws of Clean and Unclean Animals of Leviticus 11: Their Nature, Theology, and Rationale (An Intertextual Study)*. Berrien Springs, MI: Adventist Theological Society Publications, 2000.

Müller, Friedrich Max. *Chips from a German Workshop*. 5 vols. New York: Charles Scribner's Sons, 1895.

— *Introduction to the Science of Religion*. Reprint edn. Varanasi: Bharata Manisha, 1972.

— *Last Essays. First Series*. London: Longmans, Green and Co., 1901.

— *Lectures on the Science of Language*. 2 vols. London: Longmans, Green and Co., 1877.

— *Natural Religion*. 2nd edn. London: Longmans, Green and Co., 1892.

— *The Science of Thought*. 2 vols. New York: Charles Scribner's Sons, 1887.

— *Theosophy or Psychological Religion*. London: Longmans, Green and Co., 1903.

— *Three Introductory Lectures on the Science of Thought*. Chicago: Open Court, 1898.

Murphy, Tim. *Representing Religion: Essays in History, Theory, and Crisis*. Sheffield, UK: Equinox, 2007.

Nietzsche, Friedrich. *Basic Writings of Nietzsche*. Ed. Walter Kaufmann. New York: Modern Library, 1968.

— "On Truth and Lying in an Extra-Moral Sense." In Sander Gilman, Carole Blair, and David Parent, eds, *Friedrich Nietzsche on Rhetoric and Language*, 246–57. New York: Oxford University Press, 1989.

Nöth, Winfried. *Handbook of Semiotics*. Bloomington: Indiana University Press, 1990.

Nowell, Alexander. *A True Report of the Disputation or Rather Private Conference Had in the Tower of London, with Ed. Campion Jesuite*. London: printed by Christopher Barker, 1583.

O'Flaherty, Wendy Doniger. *Śiva: The Erotic Ascetic*. New York: Oxford University Press, 1981.

Ogden, Charles K. *Basic English: A General Introduction with Rules and Grammar*. London: Kegan Paul, Trench, Trubner and Co., 1930.

— *Bentham's Theory of Fictions*. Paterson, NJ: Littlefield, Adams and Co., 1959.

Ohly, Friedrich. "Typology as Historical Thought." In *Sensus Spiritualis: Studies in Medieval Significs and the Philology of Culture*, 31–67. Chicago: University of Chicago Press, 2005.

Olender, Maurice. *The Languages of Paradise: Race, Religion, and Philology in the Nineteenth Century*. Trans. Arthur Goldhammer. Cambridge, MA: Harvard University Press, 2009.

Olivelle, Patrick, trans. *The Early Upaniṣads*. New York: Oxford University Press, 1998.

— *Manu's Code of Law*. New York: Oxford University Press, 1995.

Ong, Walter. *Interfaces of the Word: Studies in the Evolution of Consciousness and Culture*. Ithaca: Cornell University Press, 1977.

— *The Presence of the Word*. Minneapolis: University of Minnesota Press, 1981.

— *Ramus: Method, and the Decay of Dialogue*. Cambridge, MA: Harvard University Press, 1958.

Otto, Rudolf. *The Idea of the Holy*. Trans. John W. Harvey. 2nd edn. Oxford: Oxford University Press, 1950.

Padoux, André. "Contributions à l'étude du mantraśāstra 2: Le Nyāsa, l'imposition rituelle des mantra." *Bulletin de l'école française d'extrême orient* 67 (1980): 59–102.

— *Tantric Mantras: Studies on Mantrasastra*. Oxford and New York: Routledge, 2011.

Palgrave, Francis. *The Rise and Progress of the English Commonwealth: Anglo-Saxon Period*. London: J. Murray, 1832.

Parmentier, Richard. "The Pragmatic Semiotics of Cultures." *Semiotica* 116 (1997): 1–114.

Patton, Laurie, ed. *Authority, Anxiety, and Canon: Essays in Vedic Interpretation*. Albany: SUNY Press, 1994.

Payne, Joseph Frank. *English Medicine in the Anglo-Saxon Times*. Oxford: Clarendon, 1904.

Pendse, S. N. *Oaths and Ordeals in Dharmaśāstra*. Vadodara: University of Baroda Press, 1985.

Plato. *The Collected Dialogues of Plato*. Ed. Edith Hamilton and Huntington Cairns. Princeton: Princeton University Press, 1961.

Plutarch. *Moralia*. Vol. 5. Trans. Frank Cole Babbitt. Loeb Classical Library. Cambridge, MA: Harvard University Press, 1936.

Pollock, Frederick. *The Genius of the Common Law*. Reprint edn. New York: AMS Press, 1967.

Postema, Gerald. *Bentham and the Common Law Tradition*. Oxford: Oxford University Press, 1986.

— "Fact, Fictions, and Law: Bentham on the Foundations of Evidence." In William Twining, ed., *Facts in Law*, 37–64. Wiesbaden: Steiner, 1983.

Premakumar. *The Language of Kathakali: A Guide to Mudrās*. Allahabad and Karachi: Kitabistan, 1948.

Proctor, Francis and Walter Howard Frere. *A New History of the Book of Common Prayer*. London: Macmillan, 1961.

Quintilian [Marcus Fabius Quintilianus]. *Institutio oratoria*. Trans. H. E. Butler as *The Orator's Education*. Loeb Classical Library. London: William Heinemann, 1921.

Rai, Ram Kumar, ed. *Śāktānandataraṅginī*. Benares: Prachya Prakashan, 1993.

Rambelli, Fabio. "An Introduction to Buddhist Semiotics." Semiotics Institute Online. http://projects.chass.utoronto.ca/semiotics/cyber/ramout.html

— *Buddhist Theory of Semiotics*. London: Bloomsbury, forthcoming.

Robbins, Jill. "Sacrifice." In Mark C. Taylor, ed., *Critical Terms for Religious Studies*, 285–97. Chicago: University of Chicago Press, 1998.

Rocher, Ludo. "Orality and Textuality in the Indian Context." *Sino-Platonic Papers* 49 (1994).

Romilly, Jacqueline de. *Magic and Rhetoric in Ancient Greece*. Cambridge, MA: Harvard University Press, 1975.

Ross, Richard. "Communications Revolutions and Legal Culture: An Elusive Relationship." *Law and Social Inquiry* 27 (2002): 637–84.

Rothenberg, Jerome. *Technicians of the Sacred*. Berkeley and Los Angeles: University of California Press, 1985.

Rubin, David. *Memory in Oral Tradition: The Cognitive Psychology of Epic, Ballads, and Counting-Out Rhymes*. New York: Oxford University Press, 1995.

Salmon, Vivian. *The Study of Language in Seventeenth-Century England*. 2nd edn. Amsterdam: John Benjamins, 1988.

Salmond, Thomas Noel. *Hindu Iconoclasts: Rammohun Roy, Dayananda Sarasvati, and Nineteenth-Century Polemics against Idolatry*. Waterloo, ON: Wilfred Laurier Press, 2004.

Sastry, R. A. *Lalitā Sahasranāma*. Madras: Adyar Library, 1988.

Saussure, Ferdinand de. *Course in General Linguistics*. Trans. Wade Baskin. New York: McGraw-Hill, 1966.

Schechner, Richard. *Essays in Performance Theory, 1970–1976*. New York: Drama Book Specialists, 1977.

— *The Future of Ritual: Writings on Culture and Performance*. London: Routledge, 1993.

Schieffelin, Bambi B., Kathryn Ann Woolard, and Paul V. Kroskrity, eds. *Language Ideologies: Practice and Theory*. New York: Oxford University Press, 1998.

Schmitt, Carl. *Political Theology: Four Chapters on the Theory of Sovereignty*. Trans. George Schwab. Chicago: University of Chicago Press, 2005.

Schofield, Phillip. "Political and Religious Radicalism in the Thought of Jeremy Bentham." *History of Political Thought* 20 (1999): 272–91.

— *Utility and Democracy: The Political Thought of Jeremy Bentham*. Oxford: Oxford University Press, 2006.

Schwartz, Barry. *Vertical Classification: A Study in Structuralism and the Sociology of Knowledge*. Chicago: University of Chicago Press, 1981.

Schwartz, Benjamin I., ed. "Wisdom, Revelation, and Doubt: Perspectives on the First Millennium B.C." *Daedalus* 104, No. 2 (1975).

Searle, John. *Speech Acts: An Essay in the Philosophy of Language*. Cambridge: Cambridge University Press, 1969.

Searle, Mark and Kenneth Stevenson. *Documents of the Marriage Liturgy*. Collegeville, MN: Liturgical Press, 1992.

Sebeok, Thomas. *Contributions to the Doctrine of Signs*. Bloomington: Indiana University Press, 1976.

— *The Sign and Its Masters*. Austin: University of Texas Press, 1979.

— *Signs: An Introduction to Semiotics*. Toronto: University of Toronto Press, 1994.

— "The Structure and Content of Cheremis Charms." In Dell Hymes, ed., *Language in Culture and Society*, 356–71. New York: Harper and Row, 1964.

Sedgwick, William Thompson and Harry Walter Tyler. *A Short History of Science*. London: Macmillan, 1917.

Selden, John. *Titles of Honour*. London: printed by William Stansby for John Helme, 1614.

Senft, Gunter. "Trobriand Islanders' Forms of Ritual Communication." In Gunter Senft and Ellen B. Basso, eds, *Ritual Communication*, 81–102. Oxford: Berg, 2009.

Shapiro, Barbara. "Codification of the Laws in Seventeenth-Century England." *Wisconsin Law Review* 2 (1974): 428–65.

Shklovsky, Viktor. *Theory of Prose*. Trans. Benjamin Sher. Elmwood Park, IL: Dalkey Archive Press, 1990.

Silverstein, Michael. "The Improvisational Performance of Culture in Realtime Discursive Practice." In R. Keith Sawyer, ed., *Creativity in Performance*, 265–311. Greenwich, CT: Ablex Publishing Corp., 1998.

— "Metapragmatic Discourse and Metapragmatic Function." In John A. Lucy, ed., *Reflexive Language: Reported Speech and Metapragmatics*, 33–58. Cambridge: Cambridge University Press, 1993.

Silverstein, Michael and Greg Urban. *Natural Histories of Discourse*. Chicago: University of Chicago Press, 1996.

Slaughter, Mary M. *Universal Languages and Scientific Taxonomy in the Seventeenth Century*. Cambridge: Cambridge University Press, 1982.

Smith, Brian K. *Reflections on Resemblance, Ritual, and Religion*. New York: Oxford University Press, 1988.

Smith, Jonathan Z. "The Domestication of Sacrifice." In Robert G. Hamerton-Kelly, ed., *Violent Origins: Walter Burkert, René Girard, and Jonathan Z. Smith on Ritual Killing and Cultural Formation*, 191–205. Stanford: Stanford University Press, 1988.

— *Imagining Religion: From Babylon to Jonestown*. Chicago: University of Chicago Press, 1982.

— *Map Is Not Territory*. Chicago: University of Chicago Press, 1993.

— *To Take Place*. Chicago: University of Chicago Press, 1992.

Smith, William Robertson. *Lectures on the Religion of the Semites*. 3rd edn. London: A. & C. Black, 1927. Reprint edn. [New York]: Ktav Publishing House, 1969.

Soler, Jean. "The Semiotics of Food in the Bible." Trans. Elborg Forster and Patricia Ranum. In Robert Forster and Orest Ranum, eds, *Food and Drink in History*, 126–38. Vol. 5 of *Selections from the Annales*. Baltimore: Johns Hopkins University Press, 1979.

Sommerville, C. John. *The Secularization of Early Modern England*. New York: Oxford University Press, 1992.

Sørensen, Jesper. *A Cognitive Theory of Magic*. Lanham, MD: Rowman and Littlefield, 2006.

Spencer, John, *De legibus hebraeorum ritualibus et earum rationibus libri tres*. Cambridge: Richard Chiswel, 1685.

Sprat, Thomas. *History of the Royal Society*. London: printed by T. R. for J. Martyn and J. Allestry, 1667.

Staal, Frits. *Ritual and Mantras: Rules without Meaning*. Delhi: Motilal Banarsidass, 1996.

Starobinski, Jean. *Words upon Words: The Anagrams of Ferdinand de Saussure*. Trans. Olivia Emmet. New Haven: Yale University Press, 1979.

Steintrager, James. *Bentham*. Ithaca: Cornell University Press, 1977.

Stephens, W. P. *The Theology of Huldrych Zwingli*. Oxford: Clarendon Press, 1986.

Stevenson, Kenneth. "Cranmer's Marriage Vow: Its Place in the Tradition." In Paul Ayris and David Selwyn, eds, *Thomas Cranmer: Churchman and Scholar*, 189–98. New York: Boydell Press, 1993.

— *Nuptial Blessing: A Study of Christian Marriage Rites*. New York: Oxford University Press, 1983.

Stillman, Robert. *The New Philosophy and Universal Languages in Seventeenth-Century England: Bacon, Hobbes, and Wilkins*. Lewisburg, PA: Bucknell University Press, 1995.

Stolzenberg, Nomi Maya. "Bentham's Theory of Fictions: A 'Curious Double Language'." *Cardozo Journal of Law and Literature* 11 (1999): 223–61.

Stroumsa, Guy. "John Spencer and the Roots of Idolatry." *History of Religions* (2001): 1–23.

Styers, Randall. *Making Magic*. New York: Oxford University Press, 2004.

Suzuki, D. T. "Painting, Swordsmanship, Tea Ceremony." In William Barrett, ed., *Zen Buddhism: Selected Writings of D. T. Suzuki*, 335–54. New York: Doubleday, 1996.

Tambiah, Stanley. *Culture, Thought and Social Action*. Cambridge, MA: Harvard University Press, 1985.

Targoff, Ramie. *Common Prayer: The Language of Public Devotion in Early Modern England*. Chicago: University of Chicago Press, 2001.

Taylor, Charles. "The Future of the Religious Past." In Hent de Vries, ed., *Religion: Beyond a Concept*, 178–244. New York: Fordham University Press, 2008.

— *A Secular Age*. Cambridge, MA: Harvard University Press, 2007.

Tertullian. *Adversus Marcionem*. Trans. as "The Five Books against Marcion." In Alexander Roberts and James Donaldson, eds, *The Ante-Nicene Fathers*, 3: 269–474. Grand Rapids, MI: Wm. B. Eerdmans Publishing Company, 1951.

— *De praescriptione*. Trans. as "The Prescription against Heretics." In Alexander Roberts and James Donaldson, eds, *The Ante-Nicene Fathers*, 3: 243–65. Grand Rapids, MI: Wm. B. Eerdmans Publishing Company, 1951.

Thomas, Keith. "An Anthropology of Religion and Magic, II." *Journal of Interdisciplinary History* 6 (1975): 91–109.

— *Religion and the Decline of Magic*. New York: Charles Scribner's Sons, 1971.

Tiersma, Peter M. *Legal Language*. Chicago: University of Chicago Press, 1999.

Tigay, Jeffrey H. *Deuteronomy: The JPS Torah Commentary*. Philadelphia: Jewish Publication Society, 1996.

Tillich, Paul. "Revelation and Miracle." In Richard Swinburne, ed., *Miracles*, 71–4. New York: Macmillan, 1989.

Tindal, Matthew. *Christianity as Old as Creation: Or, the Gospel a Republication of the Religion of Nature*. London: printed for J. Peele, 1730.

Todorov, Tzvetan. *The Conquest of America: The Question of the Other*. New York: Harper & Row, 1984.

Toland, John. *Christianity Not Mysterious*. London: printed for Samuel Buckley, 1696.

— *Nazarenus: Or, Jewish, Gentile, and Mahometan Christianity*. London: printed and sold by J. Brotherton, 1718.

Turner, Victor. *The Anthropology of Performance*. New York: Performing Arts Journal Publications, 1987.

— "Colour Classification in Ndembu Ritual: A Problem in Primitive Classification." In Michael Banton, ed., *Anthropological Approaches to the Study of Religion*, 47–84. London: Tavistock, 1966.

— *Dramas, Fields, and Metaphors: Symbolic Action in Human Society*. Ithaca: Cornell University Press, 1974.

— *The Ritual Process: Structure and Anti-Structure*. Ithaca: Cornell University Press, 1977.

Tylor, E. B. *Primitive Culture*. 2 vols. Reprint edn. New York: Gordon Press, 1974.

Unni, N. P., trans. *Nāṭyaśāstra*. Delhi: Nag Publishers, 1998.

Vial, Theodore. "Modes of religiosity and popular religious practices at the time of the Reformation." In Harvey Whitehouse and Luther H. Martin, eds, *Theorizing Religions Past: Archaeology, History, and Cognition*, 143–56. Walnut Creek, CA: AltaMira Press, 2004.

Vickers, Brian. "Analogy Versus Identity: The Rejection of Occult Symbolism, 1580–1680." In *Occult and Scientific Mentalities in the Renaissance*, 95–163. Cambridge: Cambridge University Press, 1984.

Wallis, Mieczysław. *Arts and Signs*. Bloomington: Indiana University Press, 1975.

Wardy, Robert. *The Birth of Rhetoric: Plato, Gorgias, and Their Successors*. London: Routledge, 1996.

Watts, Isaac. *A Short View of the Whole of Scripture History*. London: printed for C. Dilly and others, 1798.

Weber, Max. *The Protestant Ethic and the Spirit of Capitalism*. Trans. Talcott Parsons. New York: Charles Scribner's Sons, 1958.

Weemes, John. *An Explanation of the Ceremoniall Lawes, as They Are Annexed to the Tenne Commandements*. London: printed by T. Cotes for John Bellamie, 1632.

Welch, John W., ed. *Chiasmus in Antiquity: Structures, Analyses, Exegesis*. Hildesheim: Gerstenberg, 1981.

— "Criteria for Identifying and Evaluating the Presence of Chiasmus." In John W. Welch and Daniel B. McKinlay, eds, *Chiasmus Bibliography*, 157–74. Provo, UT: Research Press, 1999.

Wheatly, Charles. *A Rational Illustration of the Book of Common Prayer of the Church of England*. London: printed for J. and J. Knapton and several others, 1728.

Whitehouse, Harvey. *Arguments and Icons: Divergent Modes of Religiosity*. Oxford: Oxford University Press, 2000.

— *Modes of Religiosity: A Cognitive Theory of Religious Transmission*. Walnut Creek, CA: AltaMira Press, 2004.

— "Modes of Religiosity and the Cognitive Science of Religion." *Method & Theory in the Study of Religion* 16 (2004): 321–35.

Wilkins, John. *An Essay towards a Real Character and a Philosophical Language*. London: printed for Samuel Gellibrand, 1668.

Wilson, Thomas. *The Arte of Rhetorique*. London: printed for Richard Grafton, 1553.

Wollock, Jeffrey. "John Bulwer (1606–1656) and the Significance of Gesture in 17th-century Theories of Language and Cognition." *Gesture* 2 (2002): 227–58.

Wood, Robert. *An Essay on the Original Genius and Writings of Homer*. New York: Garland, 1971.

Yelle, Robert A. "Bentham's Fictions: Canon and Idolatry in the Genealogy of Law." *Yale Journal of Law & the Humanities* 17 (2005): 151–79.

— *Explaining Mantras: Ritual, Rhetoric, and the Dream of a Natural Language in Hindu Tantra*. London and New York: Routledge, 2003.

— "Hindu Law as Performance: Ritual and Poetic Elements in *Dharmaśāstra*." In Timothy Lubin, Donald R. Davis, Jr, and Jayanth K. Krishnan, eds, *Hinduism and Law: An Introduction*, 183–92. Cambridge: Cambridge University Press, 2010.

— "The Hindu Moses: Christian Polemics against Jewish Ritual and the Secularization of Hindu Law under Colonialism." *History of Religions* 49 (2009): 141–71.

— *The Language of Disenchantment: Protestant Literalism and Colonial Discourse in British India*. New York: Oxford University Press, 2013.

— "Moses' Veil: Secularization as Christian Myth." In Winnifred F. Sullivan, Robert A. Yelle, and Mateo Taussig-Rubbo, eds, *After Secular Law*, 23–42. Stanford: Stanford University Press, 2011.

— "To Perform or Not to Perform?: A Theory of Ritual Performance versus Cognitive Theories of Religious Transmission." *Method & Theory in the Study of Religion* 18 (2006): 372–91.

— "The Rebirth of Myth?: Nietzsche's Eternal Recurrence and its Romantic Antecedents." *Numen* 47 (2000): 175–202.

— Review of *A Cognitive Theory of Magic*, by Jesper Sørensen. *Journal of the American Academy of Religion* 76 (2008): 527–31.

— "The Rhetoric of Gesture in Cross-Cultural Perspective." In Paul Bouissac, ed., "Gesture, Ritual and Memory," special issue of *Gesture* 6, no. 2 (2006): 223–40.

— "Rhetorics of Law and Ritual: A Semiotic Comparison of the Law of Talion and Sympathetic Magic." *Journal of the American Academy of Religion* 69 (2001): 627–47.

— "Semiotics." In Michael Stausberg and Steven Engler, eds, *Handbook of Research Methods in Religious Studies*, 355–65. London and New York: Routledge, 2011.

— "The Trouble with Transcendence: Carl Schmitt's 'Exception' as a Challenge for Religious Studies." *Method & Theory in the Study of Religion* 22 (2010): 189–206.

Zaleski, Phillip and Carol Zaleski. *Prayer: A History*. Boston: Houghton Mifflin, 2005.

Zarrilli, Phillip. *The Kathakali Complex*. New Delhi: Abhinav Publications, 1984.

INDEX

see also Baconianism; Bentham,
 Jeremy: critique of fictions;
 Protestantism: iconoclasm: and
 critique of language
norm, ideological reinforcement
 of 83, 153

Oedipus myth 62, 63, 68
Ogden, Charles K. 190n. 64
Olivelle, Patrick 72
Ong, Walter 125
onomatopoeia 29, 63, 66, 76, 78
 see also imitation: theory of language
  as; natural (iconic) language
oracles
 Bentham's critique of common law
  judges as 104, 110, 192n. 87
 and mnemonic function of
  poetry 198n. 35
 silencing of, and disenchantment 4,
  19, 92, 95, 110, 159
orality
 chiasmus, written versus oral 50
 in Hinduism 121–2, 123–4, 126,
  133, 135–6, 199n. 41, 199n. 44,
  203n. 92
 in symbolic punishments 123–4,
  199n. 44
 see also literacy hypothesis; printing
ordeals
 Anglo-Saxon 176n. 97
 Hindu 43–6, 77
 naturalistic explanations of 46
 parallels with formalism in
  modern law 45
 poetry in 44–5, 77
 repetition in 43–4, 176n. 97
 rhetorical function of 45–6, 77, 159
Otto, Rudolf 151

Padoux, André 90
Palgrave, Francis 129, 132, 133–4
palindromes *see* chiasmus
pantomime *see* gestures: imitation in
Parry, Milman 26
Pavlov's experiment 30, 43, 57–8
Payne, Joseph Frank 36
Peirce, Charles Sanders 5, 6, 8, 26,
 28–9, 30, 63, 155, 160

Pennsylvania Dutch spells 31, 38,
 172n. 24
performance *see* ritual: pragmatic
 (rhetorical) function of
performative utterances 25, 160–1
 contrasted with magic 56
 in early English and German
  law 128, 133–4
 in Hindu law 124
 poetic etymologies as 73, 77
 weaknesses of J. L. Austin's theory
  of 25–6, 130–1
 see also Christianity: *ex opere*
  operato
personification of words
 (prosopopoeia) 99, 103–4,
 108, 196n. 6 *see also* Bentham,
 Jeremy: critique of fictions;
 Protestantism: iconoclasm: and
 critique of language
Plato
 concept of *mimesis* 16, 63, 82
 Cratylus 61, 63, 74–5, 76, 77, 78,
  84
  poetic etymologies in 74–5
 critique of rhetoric 13, 15–17, 23,
  82, 97, 110, 111, 113, 162
  and human autonomy 16–17, 162
  and the literacy hypothesis 122,
  124, 126, 135–6
 Jeremy Bentham's
  criticism of 191n. 69
 Phaedrus 136
 talion in 174n. 62
Plutarch 110, 198n. 35
poetic function 4
 limitations of Roman Jakobson's
  concept of 67
 in ritual 12, 25, 27, 30, 31, 34, 49
 see also semiotic recognition
poetry
 in advertising 14, 15, 17, 23, 55,
  134, 136
 in ancient law 203n. 92
 in Dante's *Comedy* 51–3
 in English law 37, 113–14, 128–9,
  130–2, 133
 in etymologies 44–5, 47, 65–6,
  71–5, 77